# THE CULT OF ANTIQUITY

### AND THE

# FRENCH REVOLUTIONARIES

# THE CULT OF ANTIQUITY
## AND THE
# FRENCH REVOLUTIONARIES

### A STUDY IN THE DEVELOPMENT
### OF THE REVOLUTIONARY SPIRIT

By

HAROLD T. PARKER

1965
OCTAGON BOOKS, INC.
*New York*

*To*

CARL BECKER

AND

LOUIS GOTTSCHALK

*Reprinted 1965*
*by special arrangement with The University of Chicago Press*

OCTAGON BOOKS, INC.
175 FIFTH AVENUE
NEW YORK, N. Y. 10010

LIBRARY OF CONGRESS CATALOG CARD NUMBER: 65-25881

*Printed in U.S.A. by*
NOBLE OFFSET PRINTERS, INC.
NEW YORK 3, N. Y.

# PREFACE

THE general subject of this book was suggested by Professor Carl Becker. In reviewing Faÿ's *L'esprit révolutionnaire en France et aux Etats-Unis*, he wrote: "Will not someone write a book showing how the revolutionary state of mind of the eighteenth century was also nourished on an ideal conception of classical republicanism and Roman virtue? Just why did Madame Roland often weep to think that she was not born a Spartan? Just why did John Adams ask himself if Demosthenes, had he been a deputy to the first Continental Congress, would have been satisfied with non-importation and non-exportation agreements? To know the answers to these questions would help much to understand both the French and the American revolutions." To be sure, Mr. Becker also observed that problems like these constituted "a difficult and treacherous field of inquiry."[1] But this warning was (perhaps unwisely) ignored; and permission was asked of Mr. Becker to work upon the problem, a permission which was graciously, though somewhat dubiously, granted.

Before the work was finished, however, the study was limited in scope and modified in character. It was limited in space, as the American continent and the American Revolution were dropped from consideration. It was limited in time, as attention was focused not on the eighteenth century as a whole but only on that eighteenth-century generation which participated in the French Revolution. It was slightly modified in character when not only the revolutionaries but also the conservatives of that generation were taken (if only incidentally) for study. And the character

[1] *American Historical Review*, XXX (1924–25), 810, 811–12. (Quoted with permission of the author.)

of the conclusions was somewhat changed when it was discovered that before the Revolution, if the revolutionary spirit had depended for its nourishment on the vision of antiquity, it would have suffered from malnutrition, although, once the Revolution got well under way, it was a different story. As a result of these changes, the study came to be an attempt first to trace what members of the French revolutionary generation, and especially what revolutionaries, thought of antiquity from the high-school to the guillotine; and second, to show how what they thought sometimes affected their state of mind and their action. The emphasis, however, still rests on the relation between revolutionary spirit and the vision of antiquity.

In the course of time the investigation received the aid of a number of people. The officials of the Newberry Library and the librarians of the Universities of Chicago and of Cincinnati permitted the use of the libraries in their charge; Mr. E. R. B. Willis, at Cornell, kindly extended the courtesies of the Andrew White Library; while the officials of the Bibliothèque nationale and of the Archives nationales were helpful, as usual. To my mother, I am indebted for a clean copy made in long hand of a rough draft which was easily half-again as long as the final product. To Mr. Becker I owe not only the suggestion of the topic but also the detailed suggestion as to why in her twenties Mme Roland regretted that she had not been born a Spartan or a Roman. From Professor Jakob Larsen, of Chicago, the final draft received a careful reading and a correction of many errors of detail. Above all, I wish to thank Professor Louis Gottschalk for bibliographical leads and for a careful, helpful revision of the entire work. In addition, I am grateful to him for the policy of laissez faire which he has otherwise pursued in supervising my research and for the energetic self-restraint which in my case that policy must have cost him.

HAROLD T. PARKER

## TABLE OF CONTENTS

# CHAPTER I

## WHAT OTHERS HAVE SAID

AMONG the factors that have repeatedly given flavor and sometimes form to the history of western Europe, not the least significant has been the existence of a literary heritage from the classical past. A part of this heritage—the works of Aristotle—helped to give medieval scholasticism its method, while without this heritage there would have been no classical literature for Petrarch to revive, no Ancients for Moderns to battle, no battling books for Swift to immortalize, no Neo-Hellenism in Goethe's Germany, no cult of antiquity in revolutionary France.

Only less important than the heritage itself has been what men have seen in it, what images and ideas they have taken from it, what attitudes they have taken toward it, for these have directly influenced action and character. Yet, while influencing, these images and attitudes in turn have been influenced by the conduct and character of men; and perhaps because they have been so influenced, men's ideas about the classical past have varied from generation to generation and (within each generation) from individual to individual. Thus, to some individuals of the revolutionary generation in revolutionary France, the society of republican Greece and Rome, as they saw it pictured in this literary heritage, was raw, uncouth, and backward, too defective to be imitated by modern enlightened France. To others it was the ancient home of virtue, of liberty, and of men who have lived close to nature—a Garden of Eden from which man had fallen—a golden age too perfect to be imitated by modern civilized France. To yet a third group antiquity became an ideal neither too barbarous nor too perfect for France to imitate.

It was among the members of the last two groups that a veritable cult of republican antiquity grew up—a cult which first started as a thing of feeling among a few, then spread to the people and to the well-to-do, became a fashion and then a fad, was transformed from a thing of feeling to a thing of forms, declined and passed away. As it ran its course, furthermore, the cult became so prominent that, ever since the Revolution began, there have always been Frenchmen to believe that its influence explained certain features of the Revolution. Perhaps the first to hint at this explanation was a conservative journalist, Regnaud de Saint-Angély. In the summer of 1791 he attributed to a "thoughtless admiration" of Sparta and Rome the French republican movement for a referendum on all laws.[1] But it was Volney, another conservative, who, in his "Leçons d'histoire" first gave the theory extended philosophic development. In these Leçons, which were really history lectures given at the Ecole normale, Volney showed himself to be a curious creature—a professor of history who did not exalt the benefits that a study of his subject would bring, but who, on the contrary, dwelt on the harm such study had wrought. Like Gibbon he believed history to be little more than a register of the crimes, vices, and errors of mankind. Unlike Gibbon, he concluded, however, that since the picture of vice attacts rather than repels and since, in any case, men tend to imitate what they read, a reading of history had often fostered the growth of evil in men.[2] As an example of the pernicious influence history may have, he cited the revolutionary cult of antiquity. Briefly, he

---

[1] "Observations," *Postillon par Calais*, No. 519 (July 22, 1791), p. 2.

[2] Volney, "Leçons d'histoire" (1795), *Œuvres complètes* (Paris, 1860), p. 579.

sketched how revolutionaries in their youth had read Livy, Sallust, and Plutarch; how reading had led to enthusiasm for republican principles and sentiments; how enthusiasm had led to imitation, and imitation to the excesses of the Terror, to the attempt to model French laws on the half-savage institutions of Sparta.[3] He suggested that this revolutionary cult of antiquity had rivaled Christianity in its influence and resembled it in its manifestations. For its Bible, he said this cult turned to Livy; for its "Lives of Saints and Martyrs," to Plutarch;[4] and (he might have added) for its Garden of Eden, to the golden age of Greece and Rome.

Others came after Volney to support and to expand his thesis and to lend it the prestige associated with their names or their scholarship. Many of these observed that, as pupils in the *collèges* (the high schools) of the old régime, the revolutionaries-to-be had been taught by a reading of Cicero, Livy, and Plutarch to admire the republican heroes, the republican virtues, the republican principles, and the republican liberties of Greece and Rome.[5] Admiration of a republican past, these observers insisted, had led these youths to condemn the monarchical present and to desire more liberty for the future. Thus a revolution was accomplished in their heads before the Revolution itself had begun.

Even before Volney had lectured, Desmoulins, a liberal, had in this way and by this high-school instruction accounted, first, for the early kindling of the revolutionary spirit in revolutionaries-to-be, and second, for the rise of a republican movement during the Constituent Assembly

[3] *Ibid.*, pp. 577, 592.     [4] *Ibid.*, pp. 577, 592, 594.

[5] In addition to those mentioned below, the younger Bouillé, who attended the *collège* of Navarre from 1777 to 1785, also noted this tendency with disapproval. See Marquis de Bouillé, *Souvenirs et fragments* (Paris, 1906), I, 17.

(1789–91).[6] On the first point, he was echoed down
through the nineteenth century by others: by that keen
observer, the Comte de Ségur, who wondered that any
monarchy could be astonished to see ideas of liberty break-
ing out in a youth raised in admiration of Greek and Roman heroes;[7] by Beaulieu, who in part blamed the study of
the classics for Robespierre's and Desmoulins' fall from
dutiful loyalty to their king;[8] by Lanson, a historian of
French literature;[9] by Paris, who shared Beaulieu's opinion
concerning Robespierre;[10] and by De Benazé[11] and Rioux
de Maillou.[12]

The last of this group, Rioux de Maillou, did more, however, than echo Desmoulins. He traced the excesses of the
Terror back to the fact that the Jacobin committees falsely
visualized the antique past. They saw not the "true" antiquity of broadly human Athens but the artificial and
theatrical antiquity of Plutarch's Rome and Sparta. When
they felt urged to imitate the past, they attempted, therefore, to transform themselves and other Frenchmen into
theatrical, if austere, Romans and Spartans. Because of
this attempt, masses were executed (why, he does not explain). Because of the forced austerity associated with

---

[6] "L'histoire des brissotins" in *Archives parlementaires*, LXXV (October 3,
1793), 622, n. 1. (This latter collection will henceforth be referred to as the
"*A.P.*"). Saint-Simon, the founder of Saint-Simonism, also remarked that an
admiration for classical Greeks and Romans led the liberal members of the Constituent Assembly to dream of making France a republic. See Rioux de Maillou,
"La littérature et la Révolution," *Revue de la Révolution*, XIV (1889), 202–3.

[7] *Mémoires, souvenirs et anecdotes* (Paris, 1890), I, 52.

[8] See "Desmoulins" and "Robespierre" in *Biographie universelle* (Paris, 1814,
1824), XI, 214, and XXXVIII, 233.

[9] Quoted in H. Ferté, *Rollin* (Paris, 1902), p. 344.

[10] "La jeunesse de Robespierre," *Mémoires de l'Académie impériale des sciences, lettres et arts d'Arras* (Arras, 1869), 2d ser., II, 65, and 66, n. 3.

[11] "Révolutionnaires et classiques," *La Révolution française*, XL (1883),
91–92.

[12] *Op. cit.*, XV (1889), 119–21, 382.

this attempt, the reaction of Thermidorian licentiousness and immorality set in.[13]

Even more recent historians who have boasted—what historian has not?—of a historical method more sure than that of their predecessors have explained what the Jacobin said and did by what he thought of a distant past. This explanation does not bulk large in Taine's philosophy, it is true; yet he, too, viewed the Jacobin program in part as an attempt to revert to the institutions of Rome and of Sparta, "which the Jacobins take for their models."[14] To a certain extent, Aulard shared this point of view. In his treatment of the question, he supposed that in the *collèges* the Jacobins-to-be had gained their knowledge of classical eloquence and life from the *Conciones*, a collection of those orations which Livy and other Latin historians had invented for their historical characters. Some Jacobins, like Marat, lacked even this narrow Latin culture; others, like Danton and Desmoulins, had broadened their culture by a reading of celebrated Greek and French writers; while still other Jacobins (among these Aulard would seem to include Saint-Just, Robespierre, and Billaud-Varenne) had received and remembered this narrow Latin instruction but had not gone beyond it. During the Revolution, Aulard maintains, this narrow knowledge of the last group (when coupled with a fanatical desire to imitate antiquity) had unfortunate results. It led these Jacobins to model their eloquence on speeches that had never been made; and it led Saint-Just and Billaud-Varenne to try to model French life after a manner of Roman life that had never existed outside of Livy. "Many of their political errors," concludes Aulard, "came of the chimeras drawn from the deceptive and grandiose Latin declamations."[15]

[13] *Ibid.*, XIV, 205–6; XV, 123, 137, 401, 405, 406, 407–8.

[14] H. Taine, *The French Revolution* (New York, 1878–85), III, 90–91, 116.

[15] *Etudes et leçons: quatrième série* (Paris, 1904), p. 16; see also pp. 2, 12–17.

It accorded well with Aulard's pro-Dantonist bias that Danton and Desmoulins, then Robespierre and Saint-Just, and finally Marat should be arranged in descending degrees of culture. It accorded no less well with the bias of Mathiez, pupil and critic of Aulard, that he should disagree with his teacher and that he should grant to Marat a profound realism and an extensive knowledge of classical history. This realism, according to Mathiez, led Marat to perceive that, since reform could not be brought about by the people, for they were too incapable, it had to be accomplished by some other means. His knowledge of classical history, and not a reading of Rousseau, suggested this other means—the dictatorship—the expedient which occupied so large a place in his propaganda. It was not, however, to be dictatorship patterned after the Roman exemplar vaunted by Rousseau, but one modeled after the ancient Greek tyrannies of Dionysius of Syracuse, Polycrates of Samos, and others who had effected social and property reforms by means of mass proscriptions and executions.[16]

Besides those that have been mentioned, others—among them Flambert,[17] Condorcet,[18] Chateaubriand,[19] and the unknown author of Mirabeau's discourse on education[20]—approved in some one of its aspects the general thesis whose history has just been traced. They contributed, however, no novel element to this theory that the classical education which the revolutionary reformers had received had in-

[16] Reviewing Gottschalk, "Marat" in *Annales historiques de la Révolution française*, IV (1927), 601.

[17] Quoted in Rioux de Maillou, *op. cit.*, XV (1889), 408.

[18] "Rapport sur l'organisation de l'instruction publique" (1792), *Œuvres* (Paris, 1847), VII, 474, n. 1.

[19] *Essai sur les Révolutions*, quoted in M. Badolle, *L'Abbé Barthélemy* (Paris, n.d.), pp. 344, 365.

[20] *A.P.*, XXX (September 10, 1791), 546.

flamed some of them with an abiding idolatry for the heroes and institutions of republican Rome and Greece. This idolatry (so runs the theory) had then kindled in them a revolutionary spirit; had prompted a few, even during the Constituent Assembly, to propose a republic or republican institutions for France; and had led others, such as the Jacobins of the Terror, to attempt to mold France after a classical model. The theory held in brief that what these reformers said and did had in some important way been influenced by what they thought of a distant past.

A number of subsidiary explanations amplified and buttressed this theory. To explain why men's ideas about the past should have made them radical, as this theory stated, some, like Rioux de Maillou and Aulard, blamed the absolute historical untruth of these ideas. Others, like those who echoed Desmoulins, blamed the error of teaching these historical ideas (however true) in a conservative society. To explain why men came to have these ideas in the first place, all agreed in assuming that it was solely because the reformers had read certain histories like Livy and Plutarch (as if their view of the past had not been affected by what they saw in the present). Nearly all, except Taine and Mathiez, assumed, furthermore, that the reformers' thought concerning this past had been fixed in their youth and had remained unchanged unto maturity, as if their images and attitudes regarding the past had not at some time changed with the changing scenes and emotions of the present.

## CHAPTER II

## THE BOOKS THE REVOLUTIONARIES READ
## CONCERNING ANTIQUITY AND WHAT
## THESE BOOKS CONTAINED

### I

IN TRACING what the revolutionary generation thought of antiquity from the high school to the guillotine, it is well that we should first discover who attended high school and what they studied there. Ignoring those who said little about the classical past, we shall divide the remainder into two groups: those who admired and those who detested republican antiquity. Most of the first group, it may then be noted, had received a classical education at the *collèges* of France. Five of these studied at Parisian *collèges:* Desmoulins,[1] Robespierre,[2] and perhaps Louvet de Couvrai[3] at the *collège* of Louis-le-Grand; Billaud-Varenne at Harcourt;[4] Marie-Joseph Chénier at Navarre.[5] Six more were educated at the *collèges* main-

---

[1] J. Claretie, *Camille Desmoulins, Lucile Desmoulins* (Paris, 1875), p. 21.

[2] Robespierre first studied for a while at the *collège* of Arras, before, however, it was taken over by the religious order of the Oratoire. He was later admitted to the *cinquième* (second year of a six-year course) of Louis-le-Grand. See Paris, "La jeunesse de Robespierre," *Mémoires de l'Académie impériale des sciences, lettres et arts d'Arras*, 2d ser., III (1869), 57.

[3] Assuming that the Jean-Baptiste François Louvet registered at Louis-le-Grand (Archives nationales, H³ 2516, fol. 4) is the Jean-Baptiste Louvet of revolutionary fame. On Louvet's education, see C. Perroud, "Madame Louvet," *La Révolution française*, LX (1911), 220–21.

[4] Billaud-Varenne, "Mémoires de Billaud-Varenne," *La Révolution française*, XIV (1888), 751, 761, 929.

[5] A. Kuscinski, *Dictionnaire des conventionnels* (Paris, 1916), p. 135.

tained by the religious order of the Oratoire:   Danton[6] and
Courtois[7] at Troyes; Saint-Just at Soissons;[8] Barbaroux at
Marseilles;[9] Brevet de Beaujour at Angers;[10] Le Bon at
Arras.[11] The remainder attended local provincial *collèges*
independent of any far-flung religious order: Brissot[12] and
perhaps Pétion[13] attended Chartres; Gensonné[14] and
Guadet,[15] Guienne; Buzot, Evreux;[16] Vergniaud, Limo-
ges;[17] Chabot, Rodez;[18] Exchassériaux (aîné), Saintes;[19]
Viénot-Vaublanc, La Flèche.[20] Barère attended some *col-
lège*,[21] but which one I have been unable to discover; while

[6] Danton first was admitted to the Petit Seminaire at Troyes, then to a lay
*pension.* At both institutions he followed the courses given at the Oratoire
*collège* of Troyes. See H. Destainville, "La jeunesse de Danton," *Annales historiques*, nouvelle série, V (1928), 426.

[7] G. Carré, *L'enseignement secondaire à Troyes* (Paris, 1888), p. 202, n. 3.

[8] E. Hamel, *Histoire de Saint-Just* (Paris, 1859), p. 23.

[9] C. Perroud, "Enfance, première jeunesse et débuts politiques de Barbaroux,"
*La Révolution française*, LXXI (1918), 504–5.

[10] M. Bougler, *Mouvement provincial en 1789. Biographie des députés de
l'Anjou depuis l'Assemblée constituante jusqu'en 1815* (Paris 1865), I, 223.

[11] L. Misermont, "Le conventionnel Lebon avant son entrée dans la vie
publique," *Revue des études historiques*, LXXIX (1903), 277.

[12] J. P. Brissot de Warville, *Mémoires* (1754–93) (ed. C. Perroud; Paris, n.d.),
I, 33.

[13] C. Perroud, "Une lettre de Pétion à Brissot," *La Révolution française*, LXX
(1917), 74; C. A. Dauban, *Mémoires inédites de Pétion et mémoires de Buzot et de
Barbaroux* (Paris, 1866), p. 524; but also see C. Vatel, *Charlotte Corday et les
Girondins* (Paris, 1864–72), II, 266, where it is said that Pétion attended Ven-
dôme.

[14] Kuscinski, *op. cit.*, p. 289.

[15] J. Guadet, *Les Girondins* (Paris, 1861), I, 25.

[16] J. Herissay, *Un Girondin: François Buzot* (Paris, 1907), p. 20.

[17] C. Vatel, *Vergniaud* (Paris, 1873), I, 2–3, 178–80. Vergniaud later attended
Du Plessis, but only for his "philosophy," after he had completed his classical
studies at Limoges.

[18] Kuscinski, *op. cit.*, p. 121.

[19] F. Xambeu, *Histoire du Collège de Saintes* (Saintes, 1886), p. 140.

[20] M. le comte de Vaublanc, *Souvenirs* (Paris, 1838), I, 5.

[21] B. Barère, *Mémoires* (Paris, 1842), I, 204.

the education of Isnard and Français de Nantes rests in obscurity. Not all liberals, however, who admired antiquity attended *collèges;* but all of these—Barnave,[22] Manuel,[23] Mme Roland, Marat, and to a certain extent Babeuf—by reading some of the classics, had gained a knowledge of ancient life equal to that possessed by their contemporaries.[24]

From those who admired republican antiquity, we turn now to those who viewed it with open contempt or dislike, their attitudes varying from the disdain felt by a Condorcet and a Kersaint to the detestation expressed by a Montlosier. Yet most of these, like most of those who made a cult of the classical past, attended *collèges* in their youth. Cazalès, it is true, was an exception to this generalization;[25] and the early instruction of Kersaint, who was among the anticlassicists, rests in obscurity. But as for the rest, it is known that Condorcet was trained by the Jesuits of the *collège* of Reims,[26] that Montlosier was educated at Clermont-Ferrand,[27] Malouet at Juilly,[28] Mounier at Greno-

[22] Barnave was privately tutored in Latin and other subjects. See E. D. Bradby, *The Life of Barnave* (Oxford, 1915), I, 21.

[23] Manuel studied at the Grand-Séminaire of Sens. Later, at the *collège* of the Doctrinaires of Noyers he became teacher of the *humanités* (the fifth year of the six-year *collège* course). The fact that he occupied this position would suggest that he had at least a *collège* education; see M. l'Abbé Maillot, "Le conventionnel Manuel," *Les noms de l'Avallonnais* (Tours, 1894), p. 1.

[24] It is true that the last three of these five read the classics in translation; but this fact, I believe, is of no significance for the succeeding discussion.

[25] Cazalès, *Discours et opinions de Cazalès précédés d'une notice historique sur sa vie par M. Chare* (Paris, 1821), p. 5.

[26] Condorcet pursued his classical studies at Reims; for mathematics he went to the *collège* of Navarre. See Arago, "Condorcet," in Condorcet, *Œuvres*, I, ix.

[27] M. le Baron de Barante, "Notice sur la vie et les ouvrages de M. le Comte de Montlosier," *Annales scientifiques, littéraires et industrielles de l'Auvergne* (Clermont-Ferrand, n.d.), XV (1842), 130. Also, Bardoux, *Montlosier*, p. 9.

[28] Malouet, *Mémoires* (Paris, 1868), I, 2.

ble,[29] and Maury at Valréas.[30] Volney, like Brevet de
Beaujour, studied at Angers;[31] and presumably they read
there the same classical sources. Yet when the Revolution
came, how different were their attitudes. Brevet, to a society which enthroned both Enlightenment and Nature,
glorified the ancient republics as societies at once enlightened and close to nature.[32] But Volney, with unexampled
violence, condemned Greek and Roman institutions for
consecrating inequality and oppression, fell upon Spartan,
Athenian, and Roman generals for speaking like ambassadors from Attila, and belittled the Noble Spartan and the
Noble Savage, those two cherished eighteenth-century illusions, by suggesting that the Spartan was but a savage and
the Savage but a barbarian.[33] Differences in attitudes like
these, it may be noted, were not associated with, nor can
they be ascribed to, differences in youthful reading.
French secondary instruction was then so nearly uniform
in its choice of texts to study that when they attended their
collèges, those who came to censure antiquity read the same
classics as those who came to esteem it.

For that quarter of a century (1763–88) which saw the
reformers-to-be going to school, this uniformity of curriculum may be observed when the courses of study of the following collèges are compared: of Louis-le-Grand,[34] when

[29] L. de Lanzac de Laborie, *Jean-Joseph Mounier* (Paris, 1887), pp. 5–6.

[30] Maury, *Correspondance diplomatique et mémoires inédits du Cardinal Maury*
(ed. Mgr. Ricard) (Lille, 1891), I, vi–vii.

[31] Bougler, *op. cit.*, I, 150.       [32] *A.P.*, XVII (August 9, 1790), 665.

[33] Volney, "Leçons d'histoire," *Œuvres complètes*, p. 592.

[34] Louis-le-Grand, Harcourt, and Navarre, as *collèges* of the University of
Paris, were at this time governed, in the matter of textbooks, by a common regulation. For the regulation see Rolland d'Erceville, *Recueil de plusieurs des ouvrages
de Monsieur le président Rolland* (Paris, 1783), p. 102, n. 145; p. 109, n. 157. For
a list of the *collèges* governed by this regulation see Kilian, *Tableau historique de
l'instruction secondaire en France*, p. 40. That this regulation was not a dead
letter is in part proved by the following bits of evidence. Annually from 1766 to
1791, in the competitive fellowship examinations based on the preceding year's

Robespierre, Desmoulins, and Louvet de Couvrai studied
there; of Troyes, when Courtois and Danton pursued their
studies there;[35] of Harcourt, Navarre, La Flèche,[36]
Limoges,[37] Reims,[38] and Clermont-Ferrand,[39] when Bil-

work and held between the students of the various *collèges* of the University of
Paris, the students were asked to explain certain works of certain classical authors (L. Liard, *L'enseignement supérieur en France* [Paris, 1888], I, 55–56). The
fact that students from all these *collèges* participating in a common examination
based on the year's work were all asked to explain the same texts would suggest
that the *collèges* were under a common rule in regard to the choice of texts. The
fact that the works selected for the examination were always among those listed
in the regulation printed in Rolland d'Erceville would suggest that this latter
regulation was indeed the common rule. The fact that the texts selected for the
examinations were, from 1766 to 1791, drawn from the same circle of works by
the same circle of authors would suggest that this observance of this common rule
persisted throughout this period. Confirmation of the view that the regulation
quoted by Rolland d'Erceville was actually observed is found in the fact that the
textbooks purchased by students of the *sixième, cinquième,* and *quatrième* of
Louis-le-Grand during the years 1765–69 and 1772 (for the *cinquième* only) were
those specified by this regulation. Confirmation of the belief that the regulation
was observed without change year after year is found in the fact that the same
textbooks were purchased year after year. For the register of these textbook
purchases see: Archives nationales H³ 2460, fols. 3, 7, 12, 14, 16, 17, 42–51, 53,
55, 56, 70; H³ 2461, fols. 1, 12, 41, 46, 58, 63, 64, 66; H³ 2500, fols. 2, 5–8, 27, 28,
30–32, 41, 62–66, 78, 80–82; H³ 2502, fols. 2, 5, 12, 16–19, 40–44.

[35] Carré, *op. cit.,* pp. 345–48.

[36] From 1767 and at least until 1776, La Flèche was affiliated with the University of Paris and was ordered to conform to the usages of that University in all
matters pertaining to class instruction. See Rolland d'Erceville, *op. cit.,* p. 91,
n. 133, and p. 548.

[37] A. Leroux, *Inventaire-sommaire des Archives départementales antérieures à
1790. Haute-Vienne. Archives civiles.* Série D: *Fonds de l'ancien collège de
Limoges* (Limoges, 1882), pp. xviii, xxxiv.

[38] Condorcet's course of study at Reims, as it is of the 1750 decade, cannot be
used to demonstrate uniformity of French secondary instruction for the years
1763–88, but it is mentioned to indicate that the course he followed was similar
to that followed by others. His course was the one outlined in the Jesuit *Ratio
studiorum.* That this Jesuit *collège* of Reims did follow this *Ratio* is stated in
l'Abbé E. Cauly, *Histoire du collège des bons-enfants de l'Université de Reims*
(Reims, 1885), pp. 338–39. For the *Ratio studiorum,* see H. Ferté, *Ratio studiorum,*
pp. 95, 96, 99, 102, 104–5, 108, 110–12, 117, 121. The *Ratio studiorum* published
by Sicard in his *Etudes classiques,* pp. 557–59, is the revised one of 1832 and
hence should not be used, as he uses it, as evidence concerning Jesuit instruction
in the eighteenth century.

[39] E. Jaloustre, "Les anciennes écoles de l'Auvergne," *Mémoires de l'Académie
des sciences, belles-lettres et arts de Clermont-Ferrand,* XXIII (1881), 413–14.

laud-Varenne, Chénier, Viénot-Vaublanc, Vergniaud, Condorcet, and Montlosier were, respectively, among their
students; of Cambrai in 1765,[40] of Juilly in 1772,[41] Sorèze
in 1775,[42] Effiat in 1778,[43] Riom in 1788,[44] and of Aix for
the latter half of the eighteenth century.[45] Disregarding
Condorcet's and Viénot-Vaublanc's courses of study at
Reims and La Flèche, respectively, since the first is of the
1750 decade and the second is only imperfectly known,[46]
and counting Louis-le-Grand, Harcourt, and Navarre as
having the weight of only one *collège*, as they were under a
common regulation it may be said that all these ten[47] insti-

[40] L'Abbé A. Sicard, *Les études classiques avant la Révolution* (Paris, 1887),
p. 406, n. 1.

[41] *Exercices de Messieurs les pensionnaires de l'Académie royale de Juilly,
durant le mois d'Aoust 1772,* Archives nationales, M. 222, No. 10.

[42] Sicard, *op. cit.,* p. 451, n. 3.

[43] P. Lallemand, *Histoire de l'éducation dans l'ancien Oratoire de France*
(Paris, 1889), pp. 391–92.

[44] Jaloustre, *loc. cit.,* XXIII (1881), 415–16.

[45] E. Méchin, *Annales du Collège Royal Bourbon d'Aix* (Aix, 1892), III,
225–28.

[46] Viénot-Vaublanc, who attended La Flèche from 1765 to 1771, gives in his
*Souvenirs* only a partial list of the works he studied there: Vergil's *Aeneid,* Cice-
ro's *Catiline* and *Verrine Orations,* and Caesar's *Commentaries.* See Viénot-
Vaublanc, *op. cit.,* I, 6–7, 12–13, 25–26, 28, 37.

[47] The fact that the generalizations which follow are based on only ten examples would tend to diminish their value. Their value is enhanced, on the other
hand, by the fact that these ten examples are in all probability truly representative, since they are scattered widely over all France, since they are scattered over
a number of years, although concentrated within a quarter-century, and since
they include representatives of all the important types of *collèges:* local, independent, provincial *collèges* are represented by four examples, the *collèges* of the
Oratoire by three, military schools by two, one of them taught by the Oratoire,
and the University of Paris is represented by three *collèges* counted as one. The
value of the generalizations is enhanced, furthermore, by the fact that they are
confirmed by what is known about the texts studied in the *quatrième* and
*cinquième* of Arras in 1769 and in the *cinquième* of Mans in 1783; by imperfect
information concerning the courses of study of Mauriac, when Marmontel
studied there, of Doué when Besnard was there, of Montpellier in 1787, of
Quimper in 1768, 1777, 1780, and 1785; and by complete information concerning
the curriculums of Effiat in 1785 and Juilly in 1789. For Arras see: M. G. de

tutions in their courses of study included Vergil, Horace,
Livy, Cicero, and the *Fables* of Phaedrus; nine included
Sallust, the *De vita excellentium imperatorum* of Cornelius
Nepos, and the *De rebus gestis Alexandri magni* by Quintus
Curtius; eight, Ovid; seven, Tacitus; five, Heuzet's *Selectae
e profanis historiae.*

All ten institutions used Vergil's *Aeneid;* and of those
*collèges* that specified which sections, all mentioned the
first six books or four books chosen from the first six. Of
the eight *collèges* detailing what other works of Vergil they
employed, six indicated his *Bucolics* and six his *Georgics.*
Of the seven *collèges* indicating what work or works of
Horace they preferred, six specified his *Ars poetica,* five his
odes. Whenever a *collège* mentioned which work of Ovid it
used, it always named his *Metamorphoses.* Of the five *collèges* mentioning what works of Sallust they used in their
classes, all specified the *Conspiracy of Catiline,* while three
added the *Jugurthine War.* Of the four *collèges* indicating
what part of Livy they picked for study, two selected the
first three books and two the twenty-first book. Of the ten
institutions investigated, nine specified Cicero's orations,
six his philosophical works, and three his letters. Eight
detailed what orations they employed. Of these, seven
specified one or more of the three speeches in praise of
clemency that were addressed to Caesar, four mentioning
the *Pro Ligario,* two the *Pro Marcello,* and two the *Pro
rege Dejotaro.* Of the eight institutions, three named the

Hautelocque, "L'enseignement secondaire dans le Pas-de-Calais avant 1789,"
*Mémoires de l'Académie des sciences, lettres et arts d'Arras,* 2d ser., XIV (1883),
121, n. 4; for Mans: Archives nationales, M. 230, liasse No. 38; for Mauriac:
J. F. Marmontel, "Mémoires," *Œuvres complètes de Marmontel* (Paris, 1819), I,
9; for Doué: F. Y. Besnard, *Souvenirs* (Paris, 1880), I, 51; for Montpellier: A.
Germain, *La faculté des arts et l'ancien Collège de Montpellier* (Montpellier,
1882), p. 63; for Quimper: C. Fierville, *Histoire du Collège de Quimper* (Paris,
1864), p. 88, n. 3; for Effiat: Archives nationales, M. 222, liasse No. 7; for Juilly:
P. Lallemand, *Juilly en 1789* (Paris, 1889), pp. 18–31.

*Catilinarian Orations;* three the *Philippics* (always the *Second Philippic* whenever a particular one was named); three, the *Verrine Orations* (always the speeches *About the Statues* and *On the Punishments*); three, the *Pro Archia poeta;* two the *Pro Milone;* one the *Pro lege Manilia;* one the *Pro Murena;* and one the *Pro Sexto Roscio Amerino.* To these might be added the *Pro Plancio,* the *In Pisonem,* the *In Caecilium divinatio,* the *Pro domo sua;* they were included, along with the others above mentioned, in Wailly's famous "pony" for young *collège* instructors who found their knowledge insufficient when they came to face their classes.[48] Of all these authors, chief stress was placed on Cicero, for he was studied during four years; then on Horace and Vergil, for they were studied during three years of the six-year course. Other authors were construed but a single year.

Such in its general outlines was the course of study followed by Robespierre, Desmoulins, Danton, Courtois, Billaud-Varenne, Chénier, Louvet de Couvrai, Vergniaud, Viénot-Vaublanc, Condorcet, and Montlosier. Such in its general outlines was the course of study followed, it may be inferred, by all who attended French *collèges* during this quarter-century. Even though it is not exactly known what Saint-Just and other reformers-to-be studied when going to school, it is nearly certain that they read Livy, Vergil's *Aeneid,* the *Fables* of Phaedrus, and some of Cicero and of Horace; there are nine chances out of ten that they became acquainted with Cicero's orations, Sallust's *Conspiracy of Catiline,* Cornelius Nepos, and Quintus Curtius; about eight chances out of ten that they came to know Horace's *Ars poetica,* Ovid's *Metamorphoses,* Vergil's *Bucolics* and *Georgics,* and one of Cicero's orations ad-

[48] *Oraisons choisies de Cicéron, traduction revue par M. de Wailly, avec le Latin à côté* (Paris, 1772), I, 5.

dressed to Caesar; seven chances out of ten that they were asked to construe Horace's odes and Tacitus; an even chance that they read Sallust's *Jugurthine War*, Cicero's *Pro Ligario*, and Heuzet.[49] There was a slight chance, furthermore, that they read Rollin's *Histoire ancienne*, Vertot's *Histoire des révolutions arrivées dans le gouvernement de la République romaine*, Montesquieu's *Considérations sur les causes de la grandeur des Romains et de leur décadence*, and that they thus began, what many undertook in later life, a perusal of French secondary accounts of ancient history.[50]

The view that we have accurately inferred the character of the high-school curriculum and of the later course of reading is partly confirmed by the accompanying table. This table indicates the number of times classical authors were cited on any subject whatsoever,[51] and modern

[49] How these figures were calculated may be illustrated by this example: nine out of ten institutions chose Sallust for their classes; five of these nine told which works of Sallust they used, and of these five all named the *Conspiracy of Catiline*, three the *Jugurthine War*. Assuming that the proportion true of these five would also hold true in all nine who chose Sallust if we had complete information about them, then all nine used his *Conspiray of Catiline*, and three-fifths of the nine (about 5.4) used his *Jugurthine War*. Nine of the total ten therefore used the former work; about one-half, the latter.

[50] Vertot's *Histoire* and Montesquieu's *Considérations* were used at the Parisian *collèges* (Rolland d'Erceville, *op. cit.*, p. 102, n. 145); Vertot and Rollin at Juilly, when Arnault was there (A. V. Arnault, *Souvenirs d'un sexagénaire* [Paris, 1833], I, 59); Rollin at Aix (Méchin, *op. cit.*, III, 225–28). All three works were sometimes given as prizes or recommended for outside reading. Vertot and Montesquieu were given as prizes at Troyes and Louis-le-Grand (Carré, *op. cit.*, p. 230; Archives nationales, M. 155, liasse No. 7). Brissot at Chartres was encouraged to read outside in Vertot and Rollin (Brissot de Warville, *op. cit.*, I, 33). Viénot-Vaublanc at La Flèche read Montesquieu's *Considérations* (Viénot-Vaublanc, *op. cit.*, I, 52–53).

[51] This table does not include, however, citations of Tacitus' *Germania*, for participants in the Revolution turned to it for a picture not of the classical past but of the primitive Teutonic institutions to which French institutions might be traced. Furthermore, since epigraphs drawn from classical works do not indicate that participants in the Revolution continued to read these works or turned to them for a picture of the past, they have not been counted for this table.

authors cited on Greek and Roman history, in the debates of the National Assembly, of the Legislative Assembly, of the National Convention,[52] and in the following newspapers: Desmoulins' *Révolutions de France et de Brabant*, first and second series, and his *Tribune des patriotes;* Prudhomme's *Révolutions de Paris;* Gorsas' *Courrier* (for the National Assembly and the National Convention only); Brissot's *Le patriote français;* Robespierre's *Défenseur de la constitution* and *Lettres à ses commettans;* the first four volumes of *L'ami des patriotes*, edited first by Duquesnoy and then by Regnaud-de-Saint-Angély; Durosy's *Gazette de Paris;* Montjoie's *L'ami du roi;* and the paper entitled the *Actes des apôtres.*

From the table (pp. 18–19) it is evident that, as a group, participants in the Revolution tended to cite in their maturity only those classical works they had probably studied in their youth. In their youth, when attending school, they studied only the classics of Rome, not of Greece.[53] In their maturity and as a group, they cited, apart from Plutarch, who lived when Greece belonged to Rome, only the classics of Rome, not of Greece.[54] Apparently they were unac-

---

[52] Strictly speaking, this is a tabulation not of the citations occurring in the debates of the assemblies but of those citations that appear in those works and speeches of the deputies and their *suppléants* that are printed in the *Archives parlementaires* and in the reports of the debates that are given in the *Moniteur* (the latter for the period December, 1793—October, 1795, only). This means that, since the editors of the *Archives* included some printed speeches that were never given, and also a number of pamphlets, perhaps more citations appear in the table than actually occurred in the debates. But, as there is no reason to suppose that these speeches and pamphlets were not truly representative of the productions of members of all parties, there is no reason to suppose that the table would have shown a different result if it had been restricted only to those speeches actually given.

[53] Of the ten *collèges* studied, only one (the three *collèges* of the University of Paris) included a study of Greek in its curriculum during this period (Rolland d'Erceville, *op. cit.*, p. 102, n. 145).

[54] Plato is not an exception to this generalization since he was cited not by reformers as a group but only by Gorsas and Robespierre.

| | Total | National Assembly | Legislative Assembly | Convention | Desmoulins | Prudhomme | Gorsas | Brissot | Robespierre | Duquesnoy and Regnaud | Durosy | Montjoie | Actes des apôtres |
|---|---|---|---|---|---|---|---|---|---|---|---|---|---|
| Cicero | 83 | 6 | 1 | 5 | 43 | 1 | 7 | 5 | 3 | 1 | 3 | 4 | 4 |
|   Orations | 42 | 2 | .... | 3 | 29 | ... | 4 | 1 | .... | .... | 1 | ... | 2 |
|   Philosophical works | 10 | .... | 1 | ... | 4 | 1 | ... | .... | .... | .... | ... | 4 | .... |
|   Letters | 5 | .... | .... | 1 | 2 | ... | ... | 1 | .... | .... | 1 | ... | .... |
|   Rhetorical works | 2 | 2 | .... | ... | .. | ... | ... | .. | .... | .... | .. | ... | .... |
|   Unclassified | 24 | 2 | .... | 1 | 8 | ... | 3 | 3 | 3 | 1 | 1 | ... | 2 |
| | | | | | | | | | | | | | |
| Horace | 36 | 4 | .... | ... | 12 | 3 | 5 | 6 | ... | 1 | ... | 1 | 4 |
| | | | | | | | | | | | | | |
| Plutarch | 36 | 6 | 2 | ... | 10 | 1 | ... | 11 | 1 | .... | 1 | 3 | 1 |
|   Lives | 24 | 3 | 2 | ... | 5 | 1 | ... | 10 | .... | .... | 1 | 1 | 1 |
|   Morals | 2 | .... | .... | ... | .. | ... | ... | 1 | .... | .... | .. | 1 | .... |
|   Dits et faits | 1 | 1 | .... | ... | .. | ... | ... | .. | .... | .... | .. | ... | .... |
|   Unclassified | 9 | 2 | .... | ... | 5 | ... | ... | .. | 1 | .... | .. | 1 | .... |
| | | | | | | | | | | | | | |
| Tacitus | 25 | 1 | 3 | 2 | 2 | 3 | 1 | 7 | ... | 3 | ... | ... | 3 |
|   Histories | 6 | .... | .... | ... | .. | 1 | ... | 3 | .... | .... | .. | ... | 2 |
|   Annals | 4 | .... | .... | ... | .. | 1 | ... | 1 | .... | 1 | .. | ... | 1 |
|   Agricola | 3 | 1 | 2 | ... | .. | ... | ... | .. | .... | .... | .. | ... | .... |
|   Unclassified | 12 | .... | 1 | 2 | 2 | 1 | 1 | 3 | ... | 2 | ... | ... | .... |
| | | | | | | | | | | | | | |
| Vergil | 14 | 2 | .... | ... | 2 | 2 | 2 | .. | .... | 1 | 1 | 1 | 3 |
|   Aeneid (only first six books cited) | 9 | 2 | .... | ... | 1 | 2 | ... | .. | .... | .... | 1 | 1 | 2 |
|   Georgics | 1 | .... | .... | ... | .. | ... | ... | .. | .... | 1 | .. | ... | .... |
|   Unclassified | 4 | .... | .... | ... | 1 | ... | 2 | .. | .... | .... | .. | ... | 1 |
| | | | | | | | | | | | | | |
| Seneca | 13 | 1 | .... | ... | 1 | ... | ... | 9 | ... | 1 | ... | 1 | .... |
| | | | | | | | | | | | | | |
| Livy | 8 | .... | .... | 1 | 1 | 6 | ... | .. | .... | .... | .. | ... | .... |
|   First three books | 6 | .... | .... | 1 | 1 | 4 | ... | .. | .... | .... | .. | ... | .... |
|   Book VI | 1 | .... | .... | ... | .. | 1 | ... | .. | .... | .... | .. | ... | .... |
|   Unclassified | 1 | .... | .... | ... | .. | 1 | ... | .. | .... | .... | .. | ... | .... |
| | | | | | | | | | | | | | |
| Sallust | 8 | .... | .... | 6 | .. | ... | ... | 1 | ... | 1 | ... | ... | .... |
|   Catiline Conspiracy | 4 | .... | .... | 2 | .. | ... | ... | 1 | .... | 1 | .. | ... | .... |
|   Jugurthine War | 1 | .... | .... | 1 | .. | ... | ... | .. | .... | .... | .. | ... | .... |
|   Unclassified | 3 | .... | .... | 3 | .. | ... | ... | .. | .... | .... | .. | ... | .... |

The forty-two references to Cicero's orations were scattered among the following speeches: the *Philippics*, the *Verrines*, and *In Pisonem* were each cited six times; *Pro Plancio*, four times; *Pro Milone*, *Pro Cluentio*, and *Pro Sexto Roscio*

| | Total | National Assembly | Legislative Assembly | Convention | Desmoulins | Prudhomme | Gorsas | Brissot | Robespierre | Duquesnoy and Regnaud | Durosy | Montjoie | Actes des apôtres |
|---|---|---|---|---|---|---|---|---|---|---|---|---|---|
| Plato | 7 | .... | 1 | 1 | .... | .... | 3 | ... | 2 | .... | .... | .... | .... |
| Montesquieu | 16 | 5 | 3 | ... | 2 | 2 | 1 | 1 | .... | .... | .... | 1 | 1 |
| Esprit des lois | 7 | 1 | 2 | .... | .... | .... | 1 | 1 | .... | .... | .... | 1 | 1 |
| Considérations | 5 | 2 | 1 | .... | .... | 2 | .... | .... | .... | .... | .... | .... | .... |
| Unclassified | 4 | 2 | .... | .... | 2 | .... | .... | .... | .... | .... | .... | .... | .... |
| Rollin, Histoire | 14 | .... | .... | .... | 1 | .... | .... | .... | .... | .... | .... | 13 | .... |
| Rousseau | 9 | 2 | .... | 1 | 1 | 3 | .... | .... | .... | .... | .... | .... | 2 |
| Contrat social | 3 | .... | .... | .... | 1 | 1 | .... | .... | .... | .... | .... | .... | 1 |
| Considérations sur Pologne | 3 | 1 | .... | 1 | ... | 1 | .... | .... | .... | .... | .... | .... | .... |
| Emile | 1 | 1 | .... | .... | .... | .... | .... | .... | .... | .... | .... | .... | .... |
| Unclassified | 2 | .... | .... | .... | .... | 1 | .... | .... | .... | .... | .... | .... | 1 |
| Voltaire (his Brutus) | 7 | .... | .... | 2 | ... | 2 | ... | 2 | ... | 1 | ... | .... | .... |
| Mably | 4 | 1 | .... | .... | 3 | .... | .... | .... | .... | .... | .... | .... | .... |
| Entretiens de Phocion | 2 | .... | .... | .... | 2 | .... | .... | .... | .... | .... | .... | .... | .... |
| Principes de législation | 1 | 1 | .... | .... | .... | .... | .... | .... | .... | .... | .... | .... | .... |
| Unclassified | 1 | .... | .... | .... | 1 | .... | .... | .... | .... | .... | .... | .... | .... |

*Amerino*, each three times; *Pro domo sua*, twice; *Pro Ligario*, *Pro lege Manilia*, *Pro Archia poeta*, *Pro Rabirio*, *Pro Murena*, the *Catiline Orations*, and the speeches before Caesar were each cited once. Of the *Philippics*, the *Second* was cited four times, the *Fourth* and *Ninth* each once. Three of the six references to the *Verrines* can be traced to a particular pleading; of these three, two refer to the pleading *On Punishments*, one to the pleading *On Statues*.

Of the other classical authors, Pliny was cited six times; Juvenal and Suetonius, five; Homer, Caesar, Lucretius, Phaedrus, Aristotle, Lucan, Terence, Polybius, three times apiece; Demosthenes, Theophrastus, Pindar, Aristotle, each cited twice; Quintilian, Sertorius, Valerius Maximus, Heraclitus, Ovid, Epictetus, Euripides, Herodotus, Vopiscus, Varro, Pausanias, Ammianus Marcellinus, each mentioned once.

Of the other modern authors, Gordon (on Sallust) was cited three times; Vertot was cited twice; Barthélemy, Helvétius, Shakespeare, Gillies, Montaigne, Machiavelli, Folard, and Grotius were each cited once on Greek and Roman history.

quainted with the literary glories of ancient Greece—the tragedies of Aeschylus, Sophocles, and Euripides, the comedies of Aristophanes, the dialogues of Plato and the works of Aristotle, the orations of Demosthenes and Aeschines, and the histories of Herodotus, Thucydides, and Polybius. If only for this reason, their cult of antiquity could never resemble the Neo-Hellenism of their German contemporaries. It had to be a neo-Latin cult or a Neo-Hellenism inspired by Latin or Latinized sources.

In their youth, moreover, these Frenchmen studied only certain Latin classics. They had not been asked to construe Caesar's *Commentaries*, or Lucan's poetry, the comedies of Plautus and Terence, the philosophic poems of Lucretius, or the moral epistles of Seneca; and as a group they did not cite these works in later life.[55] Their classical education had stressed chiefly Cicero, then Horace and Vergil, and had introduced Tacitus, Livy, and Sallust, authors whom these Frenchmen constantly mentioned during the Revolution. Their classical education had emphasized, furthermore, only certain works of these authors: of Sallust, his *Conspiracy of Catiline*; of Livy, his first three books and his twenty-first book; of Vergil, the *Aeneid*, and of the *Aeneid*, the first six books; of Cicero, his orations, and of Cicero's orations, a certain few (listed on pp. 14–15 above), and of some of these few certain sections: of the *Philippics*, the *Second*; of his *Verrines*, the pleadings *About the Statues* and *On the Punishments*. And it is interesting that these Frenchmen should cite most frequently these very works: of Sallust, his *Catiline*; of Livy, his first three books; of Vergil, the *Aeneid*, and of the *Aeneid*, the first six books; of Cicero, his orations, and of his orations, some of those listed on pages 14–15; of his *Philippics*, the *Second*; of his *Ver-*

---

[55] Seneca is not an exception to this generalization since he was cited not by reformers as a group but only by Brissot.

*rines*, whenever the citation can be traced to a particular pleading, his pleadings *About the Statues* and *On the Punishments*. This correlation, visible wherever the evidence is forthcoming, between the list of authors and of works most frequently cited and the list of authors found on pages 14–15 of this chapter, suggests that, as a group, the participants in the Revolution tended to read or to remember in their maturity only those classics (always excepting Plutarch) they had studied in their youth.

They did not cite, however, all the authors they had studied when young. In the foregoing table, neither Phaedrus, Quintus Curtius, Cornelius Nepos, nor Ovid ranks high. Perhaps this was because these authors were no longer read during the Revolution (the works of the first three were primer readers, and who in maturity continues to read a primer?), or perhaps Frenchmen saw no relation between revolutionary circumstance and the content of their works. Whatever the reason, in the absence of evidence to prove that these authors continued to be read, they cannot be reckoned among the sources to which revolutionaries turned for a picture of the classical past. Nor can Horace and Vergil be reckoned among these sources. Revolutionaries turned to them not for a picture of the past but solely for telling quotable verse to clinch an argument or to embellish an oration. The sources to which they did turn were, therefore, reduced to certain of Cicero's orations, to Sallust's *Conspiracy of Catiline*, Livy's first three books, Tacitus' *Agricola*, *Histories*, and *Annals*, and to Plutarch's *Lives*.[56]

## II

Not only was the number of sources limited, but the view they presented of Roman history was a uniform

[56] In the succeeding paragraphs when Cicero, Sallust, Livy, Tacitus, and Plutarch are discussed, it is to be understood that we are discussing them only as authors of these particular works.

and hence a restricted one, perhaps because the period which saw their composition was circumscribed. All had been composed between 80 B.C., the date of Cicero's *Pro Sexto Roscio Amerino*, and 120 A.D., the year of Plutarch's death. All of these writers had lived, therefore, when the greatest days of the Roman *Republic* belonged to the past. All of them lived in a present which they all, except Cicero and possibly Plutarch, found unsatisfactory. All of them, except Cicero, tended to contrast their present with this republican past, to endow the latter with those virtues that were the converse of the vices they saw thriving about them, with the result that the more darkly they portrayed their present, the more brightly they painted their past.

Nowhere is this contrast between a past resplendent with virtue and a present disfigured with vice more sharply drawn than in Sallust. After the defeat of Carthage, he said, Roman morals decayed until:

Virtue began to lose its lustre, poverty to be considered a disgrace, blamelessness to be termed malevolence. Therefore as the result of riches, luxury and greed, united with insolence, took possession of our young manhood. They pillaged, squandered; set little value on their own, coveted the goods of others; they disregarded modesty, chastity, everything human and divine; in short they were utterly thoughtless and reckless.[57]

Before the fall of Carthage, however:

Good morals were cultivated at home and in the field; there was the greatest harmony and little or no avarice; justice and probity prevailed among them, thanks not so much to laws as to nature. Quarrels, discord, and strife were reserved for their enemies; citizen vied with citizen only for the prize of merit. They were lavish in their offerings to the gods, frugal in the home, loyal to their friends. By practising these two qualities, boldness in warfare and justice when peace came, they watched over themselves and their country.[58]

[57] *The Conspiracy of Catiline* xii. 1–2 (trans. J. C. Rolfe [London and New York, 1921], p. 21).

[58] *Ibid.* ix. 1–3 (Rolfe, p. 17).

The picture of existing society that Cicero incidentally gave in his orations was perhaps as dark as Sallust's sketch of latter-day depravity. The reason is simple: Cicero's orations were a lawyer's briefs,[59] which, since a lawyer always deals with the maladjustments of society, naturally gave prominence to the evil men did. In these orations, furthermore, the virtues of the good men that are mentioned were always praised as old-fashioned. The men themselves were taken as typical not of the present but of another age, when Romans themselves tilled their lands, did not covet what was not their own, protected the unhappy and hated the dishonest, lived lives of honor and of integrity, while displaying industry, temperance, and self-control.[60] For Tacitus too, the individual examples of virtue which appear in his histories savored of the "antique" and were typical not of the age of Tiberius and Nero, of "the most corrupt of centuries," but of an earlier and contrasting age, when remorse for crime was keenly felt and virtue was natural to Romans.[61]

To the virtues which Sallust and Cicero attributed to this earlier age—a simple life, frugality, industry, temperance, self-control, courage, integrity, and justice—Livy and Plutarch added only two, a love of country and of liberty. But by the magic of their prose all these abstract virtues were made flesh, as it were, in the persons of Rome's

[59] For the purposes of this remark even the *Philippics* and the *Catilinarian Orations* might be considered as a lawyer's briefs.

[60] Cicero *Pro lege Manilia* 14. 40–41 (trans. H. G. Hodge [London, 1927], p. 53); 22. 65–66 (p. 77); *Pro Cluentio* 35. 95 (trans. Hodge [London, 1927], p. 323); *Pro Sexto Roscio Amerino* 9. 26 (trans. J. H. Freese [London, 1930], p. 145); 10. 27 (p. 147); 18. 50–51 (p. 165); 25. 69–70 (pp. 181–83); *V in Verrem* 5 (trans. C. D. Yonge [London, 1921], I, 402–3); 37 (p. 436); *VI in Verrem* 18 (Yonge, p. 486).

[61] Tacitus *The Histories* i. 14 (trans. C. H. Moore [London and New York, 1925], p. 27); i. 18 (p. 37); ii. 5 (p. 167); ii. 37 (p. 223); ii. 69 (p. 271); iii. 51 (p. 413). Tacitus *Annals* ii. 33 (trans. A. J. Church and W. C. Brodribb [London and New York, 1895], p. 54); iii. 30 (p. 92); v. 1 (p. 150); xiv. 22 (p. 266).

early heroes: of the three Horatii; of Junius Brutus whose
love of country impelled him to set the preservation of the
state above the life of his two sons; of Horatius Cocles, the
intrepid defender of the Tiber bridge; of Mucius Scaevola;
and of Quinctius Cincinnatus, who, though oft dictator, yet
with praiseworthy simplicity and frugality tilled his small
farm.[62] Even Roman heroes, however, sometimes lapsed
from virtue—witness how the victorius Horatius of the
three Horatii ran his sister through with his sword for be-
wailing the death of her fiancé, one of the Curatii; scamps
and villains existed even in this golden age; while the Roman populace, at times heroic, at other times was fickle,
presumptuous, and unjust. But these glimpses of the hardness of humanity were but as alloy to these golden tales of
a golden age, aiding them, with the stamp of the author, to
pass current as history for centuries to come. Even this
golden age, however, came to an end, leaving Livy to la-
ment its passing and to contrast its poverty and simplicity
with the wealth, avarice, and self-indulgence of his own
day.[63] But in the study of this enchanted past he found, as
he once intimated, an escape from the calamities of his own
day,[64] and, I surmise, a satisfaction, if only in retrospective
reverie, of those wishes whose fulfilment had been thwarted
in actuality.

These republican heroes whose lives might excite any
eighteenth-century lover of virtue to imitation and to emulation moved in a society which, republican as it was even
down to Cicero's day, might seem an answer to many an

[62] Plutarch, "Parallel Lives" (trans. A. H. Clough [Boston, 1891]), I, 203–9,
218–20. Livy ii. 5 (trans. B. O. Foster [London and New York, 1919–22]), I,
233–35.

[63] Livy op. cit. i. (Preface, I, 7); iii. 20 (II, 71); iii. 26 (II, 89); iii. 57 (II, 193).
Plutarch makes the same comparison (Plutarch, "Parallel Lives," III, 49, 141,
158).

[64] Livy op. cit. i (Preface, I, 7).

eighteenth-century liberal's prayer. As depicted by Livy, Plutarch, Sallust, Cicero, and Tacitus (the latter by casual reference), it was a society where revolution, violent or peaceful, was a recurring thing, and generally worked increased liberty to the people; where a despotic king, like Tarquin the Magnificent, and usurpers, like the decemvirs and Julius Caesar, were got rid of by proudly independent men, who could not brook a tyrant;[65] where the chief officials, even the early kings, were elected by the people; where even the most obscure of citizens possessed personal liberty and was protected by law from arbitrary arrest and punishment; and where an official might be prosecuted if, like Verres, he violated one of these individual rights.[66] Finally, it was a society where self-made men, like Cicero— "new men," as the Romans called them—might, solely by virtue of their eloquence, rise to hold the highest positions in the state.[67]

> Never [said Cicero] has a state offered so much to the self-made man as does ours, wherein if a man of humble birth shows in his life a character such as to support the high standing which rank confers, his advancement is dependent only on hard work and a blameless record.[68]

In the phrase of a later day: "Les carrières étaient ouvertes aux talents."

This society, furthermore, had the sympathy of the Latin authors who described it: of Livy, who sometimes spoke of the "sweets of liberty";[69] of Sallust, who ascribed

[65] *Ibid.* i. 1 (I, 219); iii. 49 (II, 161). Sallust *op. cit.* vi. 7 (p. 13); Tacitus *Annals* i. 1, (p. 1). Plutarch, "Parallel Lives," I, 203–21; V, 311, 320. Cicero *Philippics (Second)* 11 (trans. C. D. Yonge [London, 1919], p. 30); 13 (p. 33); 44 (p. 66).

[66] Cicero *VI in Verrem* 65 (pp. 536–37).

[67] *Ibid.* 70–71 (pp. 541–42). Cicero *Pro Cluentio* 40. 110–12 (pp. 339–41). Plutarch, "Parallel Lives," III, 59–60. Sallust *op. cit.* xxiii. 5–6 (p. 43).

[68] *Pro Cluentio* 40. 110–12 (pp. 339–41).

[69] Livy *op. cit.* i. 17 (I, 61).

Rome's greatness to the love of glory animating Romans, and that love to the overthrow of kings and the conquest of liberty, since kings check, because they dread, the display of great ability by others;[70] of Cicero, who glorified the assassination of Caesar as "a godlike exploit" which had freed Rome from slavery, "the worst of all evils";[71] and of Tacitus who, though he might recognize that the empire was needed to end civil strife, yet contrasted the "slavery" of the Roman people under that empire with the liberty and equality of an earlier day.[72] There is something to be said for the view that the members of the revolutionary generation had in their youth, by the reading of Latin classics in French *collèges*, been invited to condemn the society of imperial Rome and to admire the virtues and republican liberties of republican Rome, to admire a society vastly different from the one in which they lived.

Let us not, however, exaggerate this difference. As in eighteenth-century France, inequalities of wealth, of social position, and of political power always existed in republican Rome. A division of citizens into classes each with a formal rank and some with privilege established by law or by custom always was to be found there.[73] And it is interesting to note that today contributors to the most conservative of French newspapers, the royalist *Action française*, can advocate the revival of Latin in French secondary schools on the ground that the Romans, at least, had a proper sense of formal rank and privilege. Yet in the eighteenth century, Frenchmen—conservatives and liber-

[70] Sallust *op. cit.* vii. 1–3 (pp. 13–14).

[71] *Philippics* (*Second*) 44 (p. 66).

[72] *Annals* i. 1 (p. 1); i. 4 (p. 3); i. 7 (p. 4); i. 8 (p. 6); iv. 33 (p. 128). Tacitus *Histories* I. 1 (p. 3); II. 37 (p. 221).

[73] Plutarch, "Parallel Lives," I, 53; V, 46. Livy *op. cit.* i. 42 (I, 149). Cicero *Pro Cluentio* 55. 150 (p. 385); 56. 154 (p. 391). Cicero *Pro Sexto Roscio Amerino* 47. 136 (p. 245).

als alike—regarded republican Rome as a liberal's dream, and with reason, not because their vision of Roman society differed from our own but because French society then was different from what it is now, because French society then was less democratic than it is now. In the twentieth century the society of republican Rome can appeal to conservative Frenchmen because it was less democratic than the one in which they live; in the eighteenth century the same society could appeal to liberal Frenchmen because it was more democratic than the one in which they lived.

What the Latin authors and Plutarch did for Rome, the latter alone did for Greece. He gave it a golden age of virtue, ending for Athens before the death of Pericles and for Sparta before that of Lysander;[74] peopled that age with heroes whose virtues invited imitation; added as alloy glimpses of the fickle Athenian multitude, often cruelly unjust to its wisest fellow-citizens;[75] pictured an Athens where more liberty (for citizens) and a Sparta where more equality (among citizens) existed than the reader could discover in eighteenth-century France;[76] and traced the fall of both cities to the increase of wealth and the decline of virtue.[77] It is not, however, primarily as a historian of cities that Plutarch writes, but as a biographer and a moralist. To see in his characters "duty performed and rewarded; arrogance chastised; hasty anger corrected,"[78] and, above all, virtue triumphant—such are his interests. But aside from this stand on virtue, the answer to the question "What does Plutarch teach?" presents the same ambiguity that is found when that question is put to history

[74] *Plutarch*, "*Parallel Lives*," I, 119, 123; III, 299.

[75] *Ibid.*, I, 33, 36; IV, 367.

[76] *Ibid.*, I, 93, 94, 95.

[77] *Ibid.*, IV, 447, 468.     [78] *Ibid.*, I, xxviii (Introduction by editor).

itself. Believing, as he did, that a biographer should dilate on a hero's virtues and be rather reticent about his faults,[79] Plutarch gives a sympathetic, fair treatment of Caesar and of his assassin Brutus, of the moderate Solon and of the radical Lycurgus, and of the attempts by Caesar to set up a monarchy, by Lycurgus to establish a system of balances, and by Dion to form a democracy.[80] Indeed, so sympathetic is Plutarch's treatment of what his heroes did, and so varied are the actions he portrays, that a reading of his *Parallel Lives*, like a reading of history itself, could help any man believe nearly anything he wanted to believe.

Readers of Plutarch might disagree as to what he taught, but no one could deny that he himself believed that the mission of his *Lives* and of history was to teach. To him, as to Livy and Cicero, and probably to Sallust and Tacitus, Clio was not only an agreeable storyteller but a schoolmistress as well, teaching wisdom and virtue by the examples she described and offered for imitation.[81] As Livy said:

> What chiefly makes the study of history wholesome and profitable is this, that you behold the lessons of every kind of experience set forth as on a conspicuous monument; from these you may choose for yourself and for your own state what to imitate, from these mark for avoidance what is shameful in the conception and shameful in the result.[82]

Livy's exhortation to study history in this spirit was repeated in eighteenth-century France by the translator Dacier and by *collège* textbook writers and instructors.

[79] *Ibid.*, III, 201.

[80] *Ibid.*, I, 90, 93, 161–63; V, 255–56, 363.

[81] *Ibid.*, I, 319–20; II, 107–8. Livy *op. cit.* i (Preface, I, 7). Cicero *Pro Archia poeta* 6. 14 (trans. N. H. Watts [London, 1923], p. 23). Tacitus *Histories* iii. 51 (p. 413); Tacitus *Annals* iii. 55 (p. 128); iv. 33 (p. 128). Sallust nowhere explicitly states his philosophy of history, but that his creed was similar to that of the others may be guessed from the character of his works and from a passage in his *Jugurthine War* (iv. 1–2 [trans. J. C. Rolfe (London and New York, 1921)], p. 137).

[82] Livy *op. cit.* i (Preface, I, 7).

This passage from Livy was itself quoted with approval in the third volume of Rollin's *Traité des études*,[83] which students at Louis-le-Grand read;[84] in Heuzet's *Selectae e profanis*,[85] which was used in half the *collèges* we have investigated; and in Dacier's notes to his translation of Plutarch,[86] a translation which Mme Roland read and whose editions, in this century, outnumbered those of Amyot's translation by more than two to one.[87]  The philosophy of history set forth by Livy was again stated not only in these three works but to a varying extent in Dotteville's notes to his translation of Sallust;[88] in Beauzée's Preface to his translation of Quintus Curtius;[89] in the Preface to Vaugelas' translation to Quintus Curtius,[90] a translation advertised for the *collège* trade by Barbou, a leading Parisian textbook publisher;[91] in the Preface to one of the textbook editions of Cornelius Nepos published by

[83] C. Rollin, *De la manière d'enseigner et d'étudier les belles lettres* (Paris, 1823), III, 23.

[84] See registers of book purchases by students: Archives nationales, H³ 2500, fols. 78, 80–82; H³ 2502, fols. 2, 5, 12, 16–19, 41–44.

[85] *Selectae e profanis* (Paris, 1764), I, x, n. *a*; *see also* I, iii, iv, ix.

[86] *Les vies des hommes illustres de Plutarque traduites par M. Dacier* (nouvelle édition; Paris, 1762), IV, 69, n. *a*. See also I, i–ii (Dacier's Preface) and III, 70, n. *c*.

[87] *British Museum Catalogue*, "Plutarch," p. 69. *Le catalogue de la Bibliothèque nationale*, II, 1097, 1101; XXXV, 39. J. M. Quérard, *La France littéraire* (Paris, 1835), VII, 224–30.

[88] Sallust, *Œuvres: Traduction avec des notes critiques par J.-H. Dotteville* (2d ed.; Paris, 1763), p. 131, n. 5. Dotteville was an instructor at Juilly when Malouet was there; see C. Hamel, *Juilly*, p. 290.

[89] Quintus Curtius, *Histoire d'Alexandre le Grand traduite par M. Beauzée* (Paris, 1781), Vol. I, Dedicatory epistle. The translation was intended for use in the *collèges:* see I, viii. Beauzée was one of Viénot-Vaublanc's instructors at La Flèche; see Viénot-Vaublanc, *op. cit.*, I, 55.

[90] Quintus Curtius, *Histoire d'Alexandre le Grand traduite par M. Vaugelas* (Paris, 1764), I, xix.

[91] See advertisements at the end of Jouvency's *Appendix de diis* (Paris, 1769), and Cicero's *Orationes* (Paris, 1768), Vol. II.

Barbou;[92] and in the "commencement exercises" of the pupils of Boulogne in 1783[93] and of Effiat in 1785.[94] All these pedagogues, furthermore, pressed their readers and pupils to imitate what was good and avoid what was evil in the *classical* past, thus bringing home to this particular French generation Livy's exhortation to all generations.

But the pedagogues parted company from Livy and other classical authors when they came to recommend what in this past should be imitated and what avoided. Had the advice given the reader by Livy, Plutarch, and (to a certain extent) by Cicero and Tacitus, to imitate and have his country imitate what was good and successful and avoid what was evil and a failure in past examples—had this advice been applied by the eighteenth-century reader to the examples portrayed by these historians—he himself would have imitated the virtues of the heroes of republican antiquity and avoided the vices of imperial Rome, while he would have had his country imitate the republican institutions of virtuous, successful republican Rome, Athens, and Sparta to the subversion of existing French institutions. As if aware of this danger to the existing order, schoolmasters of that day sometimes sought to discredit by censure the republican features of republican antiquity. Thus, if Cornelius Nepos lauds as glorious Miltiades' attempt to preserve Greek liberty by betraying his employer Darius, the textbook editor is quick to note that Nepos here speaks as a republican and that Miltiades should not have plotted unfaithfulness to the king.[95] If Sallust asserts that kings check because they dread the display of great

---

[92] Cornelius Nepos, *De vita excellentium imperatorum* (Paris, 1771), p. vi.

[93] Archives nationales, M. 230, liasse No. 38.

[94] Archives nationales, M. 222, liasse No. 7.

[95] Cornelius Nepos, *op. cit.*, p. 38, n. *u*. For another note of a conservative tenor, see p. 56, n. *x*. (Notes are by the editor.)

ability by others, the translator Dotteville observes that he speaks here as a republican. If Sallust boasts that perfect union existed among Roman citizens before the fall of Carthage, Dotteville asks: When, in times of peace and for two-years' running, did domestic concord exist in Rome? He adds that Sallust's picture of the good old days is too flattering.[96] The renowned Jesuit instructor Porée, like other Jesuit instructors and like Dacier[97] and an editor of Nepos.[98] elaborated with malicious pleasure on the jealous spirit of equality which, in the ancient republics, caused the populace to be cruelly unjust to the wisest citizens.[99] In 1778 Adry, instructor at Troyes,[100] as author of the commencement exercise *plaidoyers* "Sur la meilleure forme du gouvernement," had the student-judge prefer a monarchy to a republic and to an aristocracy partly on the ground that Athens and other Greek cities were no happier under a republic than under a king, while their wisest citizens always regretted the days when kings had ruled.[101]

[96] Sallust *op. cit.* (Dotteville trans.), p. 15, n. 14, and p. 17, n. 16.

[97] *Plutarch, "Lives"* (Dacier trans.), III, 200, n. *u*; III, 210, n. *m*; III, 280, n. *l*. For other conservative notes by Dacier, see II, 31, n. *p*; I, 193, n. *x*; II, 132, n. *i*; II, 149, n. *h*; II, 78, n. *b*; III, 159, n. *a*; III, 205, n. *d*.

[98] Cornelius Nepos, *op. cit.*, p. 84, Nn. *l* and *m* (notes are by the editor).

[99] A. Schimberg, *L'éducation morale dans les collèges de la Compagnie de Jésus* (Paris, 1913), pp. 154–55. Proyart also remarks that Jesuit comments on ancient history were of this character. See l'Abbé Proyart, "Louis XVI," *Œuvres complètes* (Paris, 1819), I, 179.

[100] Carré, *op. cit.*, p. 468, n. 1. A. M. P. Ingold, *Essai de bibliographie oratorienne* (Paris, 1880–82), p. 5.

[101] J.-F. Adry, *Le meilleur gouvernement, plaidoyers composés en 1778* (Paris, 1816), p. 65. The title of these *plaidoyers* has sometimes been cited to prove that even in the 1770's instruction in the *collèges* of the Oratoire displayed "the most ardent liberalism" (Carré, *op. cit.*, p. 121; A. Babeau, *Le théâtre de l'ancien collège de Troyes* [Troyes, 1881], p. 30). Yet a single group of *plaidoyers* given at a single *collège* is scarcely sufficient evidence to prove liberalism in that *collège*, let alone in the Oratorian order as a whole at this time. Furthermore, the *plaidoyers* themselves do not display "the most ardent liberalism": the arguments for a republic and an aristocracy are straw arguments, easily and victoriously refuted

Desmoulins recounts how his instructor of the *troisième*, seeing his class, while reading the *Catilinarian Orations*, fall to admiring their author, disparaged Cicero by ascribing his action against Catiline to a desire to dominate. The instructor added that two months later Cicero will flatter some of those he had just denounced and will then slander the people whose father he claimed to be.[102] If, furthermore, l'Abbé Royou (another of Desmoulins' instructors) is believed, *collège* pupils were asked to admire the first Brutus, not because he gave liberty to Romans but for his stoicism in sacrificing his relatives (his two sons and Tarquin) to his love of country.[103] Heuzet's account of this episode confirms this statement.[104] For these instructors did not wish their pupils to think that France should be a republic and themselves republicans. They did not, therefore, request their pupils to love liberty as republicans did.

by the advocate for the monarchy. In the 1780's, it is true, Oratorian instructors may have become more liberal, and it could be argued that they then discussed republican antiquity more sympathetically; but even if true, this argument has no bearing on this thesis since no leading participant in the Revolution except Saint-Just attended an Oratorian college during the eighties.

[102] C. Desmoulins and Merlin de Thionville, *Révolutions de France*, deuxième partie, No. 46, pp. 1–2. Since it is not indicated in this newspaper whether Desmoulins or Merlin wrote this passage, and since both these men attended a *collège* there is no certain evidence that this passage is by Desmoulins. There are, however, three fairly good indications that Desmoulins was the author: the *Catilinarian Orations* were indeed studied in the *troisième* at the *collège* Desmoulins attended; the style of the passage has the distinctive Desmoulins touch; and Desmoulins habitually engaged in reminiscence about his *collège* days. Complementing this censure of the republican features of republican antiquity was the praise by teachers of the royalist traditions of royalist France. *See* Desmoulins, *Révolutions de France*, No. 79, p. 14; Rollin, *op. cit.*, I, 404; Schimberg, *op. cit.*, pp. 153, 154–55; G. Dupont-Ferrier, *Du Collège de Clermont au Lycée Louis-le-Grand* (Paris, 1921), I, 487; L.-P. Herivaux, *Consolation à Madame la Dauphine* (Paris, 1766); *Ode latine à Monseigneur le Cardinal de la Roche—Aymon* (Paris, 1772); *Ode latine à son altesse Monseigneur le Prince Louis de Rohan* (Paris, 1777). Herivaux was Robespierre's favorite instructor.

[103] Royou, *L'ami du roi*, November 2, 1791, p. 2.

[104] Heuzet, *op. cit.*, Vol. I, Book III, chap. xxx.

The pupils, however, were asked to admire and imitate the private virtues of republican heroes, their simplicity, frugality, industry, honesty, self-control, courage, integrity and justice, and even their love of country.[105] In addition the pupils were asked to dress not only their lives but their rhetoric after a classical model, to imitate the Cicero of the orations—the cadence of his periods; the division of his speeches into exordium, narration, confirmation, refutation, and peroration; his introduction of thoughts that are true, novel, sublime, agreeable, ingenious, or beautiful; his insertion of metaphor, trope, exclamation, and interrogation; and his manner of using, in brief, proper words in their proper places. The instruction was, on the whole, an earnest attempt to make of the pupils upright men who would be eloquent, true orators after the famous ancient definition which revolutionary orators sometimes quoted: "Orator vir bonus dicendi peritus."

After this generation of Frenchmen left school, some of them read, as the table on page 19 would seem to show, those contemporary French comments on ancient history found in Montesquieu's *Considérations* and *L'esprit des lois*, Rousseau's *Du contrat social*, *Considérations sur le gouvernement de Pologne*, and his *Emile*, and Mably's *Entretiens de Phocion*.[106] There they found, as in the classical

---

[105] See the entire work of Heuzet; and in particular, I, iii, vii–ix, xii–xiii; also, Cornelius Nepos, *op. cit.*, pp. vi and 422, n. *b* (Preface and note by editor); *Plutarch "Lives"* (Dacier trans.), V, 69, n. *g*; Rollin, *op. cit.*, I, 32, 42–43; III, 98, 204–5. The methods of instruction described in Rollin's *Traité* were used in the Parisian *collèges* when he wrote (first half of eighteenth century) in 1762–63, and probably subsequently. See Rollin, *op. cit.*, I, 4–7, 81; Rolland d'Erceville, *op. cit.*, p. 102; Rolland d'Erceville, *Mémoire sur l'administration du collège de Louis-le-Grand* (Paris, 1778), p. 42; Dubarle, *Histoire de l'université* (Paris, 1829), II, 272.

[106] Although Rollin's *Histoire ancienne* ranks high in the table, it is not included among the above-mentioned works since its citation was peculiar to Montjoie. Badolle, as biographer of l'Abbé Barthélemy, believes that the latter's *Anacharsis* exercised an extensive influence over the revolutionaries, but, beyond a quota-

historians, a flattering picture of the heroes and institutions of republican antiquity.[107] There they found in addition a nuance typically *philosophe:* a nuance which appeared when Mably and Rousseau flatteringly asserted
that ancient republicans were "natural" folk, living more
in accord with nature's harmonies than did modern
Frenchmen;[108] a nuance which appeared when all three
writers, unlike the conservative pedagogues, lauded not
only the private virtues of ancient republicans but also
their public ones—their love of liberty, of equality, and of
country—and praised not only the virtues of republican
men but also the excellence of republican institutions.
There, in addition, the reader found that, while all three
authors admired the institutions of republican Rome, yet
in the case of Greece they differed. The more conservative
Montesquieu seemed to favor the institutions of Solon and
Athens; the more radical Rousseau and Mably preferred

---

tion from Taine, offers no proof for his assertion (Badolle, *op. cit.*, p. 366). It is
true that revolutionaries occasionally mention *Anacharsis.* Babeuf quoted it in
1790 (V. Advielle, *Histoire de Babeuf* [Paris, 1884], I, 80); it is quoted in *Le patriote français*, No. 738 (August 17, 1791), p. 198; Gorsas' library contained a copy
(Archives nationales, F⁷ 4729); Barère speaks of rereading *Anacharsis* after 18th
Fructidor (Barère, *op. cit.*, III, 67); Baudot mentions it in his *Notes historiques*,
which were written, it is true, after the Revolution (M.-A. Baudot, *Notes historiques* [Paris, 1893], pp. 121–22). Nevertheless, despite these bits of evidence,
it does not seem to me that Barthélemy's *Anacharsis* can be reckoned among
those sources to which revolutionaries turned for a picture of the classical past,
since it was cited only once in the table found on page 19 of this paper.

[107] See, for example, l'Abbé de Mably, "Les entretiens de Phocion," *Œuvres*
(Paris, l'an III), X, 46, 68–69, 73 n. 1, 108–10; J-J. Rousseau, "Du contrat social," *Œuvres* (Geneva, 1782), I, 198 n., 294–95, 320, 322, 326, 341–42; Rousseau,
"Considérations sur le gouvernement de Pologne," *Œuvres*, I, 421, 423–24, 451;
Rousseau, "Emile," *Œuvres*, IV, 44, 172, 185, 438; Montesquieu, *Considérations
sur les causes de la grandeur des Romains et de leur décadence* (Lausanne, 1750), pp.
3, 4, 7, 8, 9, 10, 13, 25–26, 29, 33, 96, 99; Montesquieu, *Esprit des lois* (Paris,
1893), pp. 10, 20, 38.

[108] Mably made the assertion for Sparta only: Mably, *op. cit.*, p. 46; Rousseau, *Emile*, V, 182–83.

those of Lycurgus and Sparta.[109]  This difference, however, was only a detail; and Rousseau and Mably could have said, as well as Montesquieu: "J'avoue mon goût pour les anciens; cette antiquité m'enchante."[110]

Yet, though all three were enchanted by this distant past, and though Rousseau, for example, praised the classical garb for its healthfulness, not one counseled a radical imitation of republican customs and institutions; not even Rousseau abandoned his eighteenth-century breeches for a classical toga. France was too large a country to be a republic, intimated all three, who were persuaded that only small countries could be republics.[111]  True, Rousseau and Mably allowed that a few classical institutions might be transplanted to the present. Even here, however, they were somewhat pessimistic as to the possible success of such reform. For them republican antiquity was not a Heavenly City toward which French society was tending or should tend, but a Garden of Eden, to regret and to set up as a standard of excellence which might reveal the shortcomings of the present.

Thus, the ideas that a Frenchman was likely to find in Montesquieu, Mably, and Rousseau would in part confirm and in part contradict what he had been taught in the *collège*. At the *collège* he had been told by the Latin historians and by the pedagogues to observe past examples and to imitate and have his country imitate those that were good and to avoid those that were evil. And since all the

[109] Mably, *op. cit.*, pp. 46, 68–69, 73 n. 1, 108–10, 117, 161, 217 n. 1; Rousseau, *Emile*, IV, 172.  See also for praise of Sparta, Rousseau, *Du contrat social*, pp. 234, 302, 336, 341–42, 352, and *Considérations sur Pologne*, pp. 423–24, 493; Montesquieu, *Esprit des lois*, pp. 32–34, 261, 481.

[110] Quoted in C.-A. Sainte-Beuve, "Montesquieu," *Causeries du lundi* (3d ed.; Paris, n.d.), VII, 43–44.

[111] See on these points, Mably, *op. cit.*, p. 206; Rousseau, *Du contrat social*, pp. 237–38, 264, 266–67, 294–95, 302; Montesquieu, *op. cit.*, p. 103.

*collèges* stressed only ancient history, our typical French-man, if he took this philosophy of history seriously, would naturally observe only those examples offered by the classical past and by that part of this past portrayed by Sallust, Livy, Tacitus, Cicero, and Plutarch and commented upon by Montesquieu, Rousseau, and Mably. But what examples in this restricted past would he imitate? What form, if any, would his cult for antiquity take? Would his cult be for the heroes, as his pedagogues desired, or for its institutions? And if it became a cult for the heroes, would he strive to emulate, as his instructors wished, their private virtues, their simplicity, frugality, austerity, and temperance; or would he, like the three *philosophes*, also admire their public virtues, their love of liberty, of equality, and of country? Or would it be their rhetorical skill that he would strive to duplicate? And how would he regard the institutions of antiquity: would he follow the implied counsel of the Latin historians, assume the attitude of the three *philosophes*, or obey his pedagogues? Would he have his country admire and imitate, admire without imitating, or condemn and avoid the republican institutions of republican antiquity?

# CHAPTER III

## THE JUVENILE CULT

WHEN the eighteenth-century adolescent reached to his table or to his bookcase, took a Sallust, a Cicero, a Livy, or a Plutarch, opened its pages, and began to read, in what spirit did he continue? Did he read with an eye to the clock, with restless shift of position and of attention, perhaps shutting the book before the end was reached? Or did he sit with the still quiet of absorbed fascination, deaf to noise, resentful of interruption, reading until called to dinner or to bed? If the latter were the case, what was going on behind that mask of fascination? What did he feel? What did he think? And what permanent effect, if any, did this reading leave upon him?

For answers to these questions in regard to the revolutionaries-to-be we must rely chiefly on the reminiscences of four of them—reminiscences, however, which may be critically examined in the light of other evidence. These four revolutionaries were Desmoulins, the first active, agitating republican of the Revolution; Mercier, celebrated (before 1789) for popular, light essays on Parisian fashions and foibles; Brissot, a leader of the Gironde, the prominent anti-Jacobin revolutionary party; and Mme Roland, who in childhood passed the time obscurely over her father's engraving shop near the Pont Neuf, but who in maturity for an evanescent moment lived brilliantly—friend to the Gironde, wife of the minister of the interior, victim of the guillotine.

All four revolutionaries agree in describing with what high delight, with what passionate absorption, they had

(while reading the classics) entered into the classical characters and had become one with the classical heroes. Brissot tells us how, devoured by a desire for fame, not contented by his petty *collège* successes, and desiring to escape
from an unsatisfying environment, he turned in his last
*collège* year to his imagination and to books (among them
to Plutarch) for self-flattering, satisfying daydreams. He
burned, he says, to resemble Phocion.[1] Mme Roland recounts how, when she was eight or nine, the *Parallel Lives*
transported her into the classical past, where she identified
herself with leading Plutarchian heroes and shared their
passions.[2] From Mercier we learn how, in reading the typical *collège* classics, he made war with the Senate against
the redoubtable Hannibal, razed Carthage the superb, followed in the triumphant march of the Roman generals in
Gaul, and without horror saw them conquer the country
of his birth.[3] While Desmoulins resorts to verse to describe
how at *collège:*

> Je vis avec ces Grecs et ces Romains fameux,
> J'étudie une langue immortelle comme eux ...
> Combien de fois, avec Plancius et Milon,
> Les yeux mouillés de pleurs, j'embrasai Cicéron.[4]

From the past, all but Brissot turned with regret to the
present. Mme Roland in early childhood wept, and Desmoulins in *collège* was in despair, for not having been born

---

[1] Brissot, *Mémoires*, I, 42.

[2] Mme Roland, *Mémoires* (ed. Cl. Perroud; Paris, 1905), I, 37; II, 22;
*Lettres d'amour* (ed. Cl. Perroud; Paris, 1909), p. 84; "Extrait de mon âme" in
*Lettres 1767–1780*, I, lii; and the letter to Sophie, December 12, 1778, *ibid.*, II,
341. Most of the letters of Mme Roland were published by Claude Perroud in
two two-volume series: *Lettres de Madame Roland 1767–1780* (Paris, 1913) and
*Lettres de Madame Roland 1780–1793* (Paris, 1909). Unless it is stated otherwise, if the letter bears the date of any of the years 1767–79, inclusive, the
reference is to the volume and page of the first series mentioned above; if the letter bears a later date, the reference is to the second of the above-mentioned series.

[3] Mercier, *Tableau de Paris* (1782), pp. 254–56.

[4] Claretie, *Camille Desmoulins, Lucile Desmoulins*, p. 25.

a Greek or Roman.[5] Mercier shrewdly remarked, probably from personal experience, that after reading of the superb Senate, of the victories and majesty of the Roman people, of the assassination of Caesar, and of the glorious suicide of Cato, "it is painful to leave Rome, and to find one's self still a commoner of the Rue des Noyers."[6]

Regret implied, of course, enthusiasm for the past, comparison of the past with the present, and a resulting discontent with the present. As adults, all three individuals—Mme Roland, Mercier, and Desmoulins—came to believe that their discontent had included dissatisfaction with French monarchical institutions. All three came to believe that their classical reading had made, or had tended to make, them republicans. In her *Mémoires* (written in 1793) and in letters written during the Revolution, Mme Roland gives the impression that her childhood weeping for not having been born a Spartan or a Roman arose out of regret for the liberty and for the republican institutions of antiquity, which did not exist in France.[7] In addition, she writes in her *Mémoires:*

> I shall never forget the Lent of 1763 (I was then nine years old) when I carried it [Plutarch] to church in place of my prayer book. It is from that moment that I date the impressions and ideas that were to make me a republican without my dreaming of becoming one.[8]

Amplifying this brief statement in a subsequent passage in her *Mémoires*, she wrote:

> Plutarch had disposed me to become a republican; he had aroused in me that force and pride which give republicanism its character, and he had inspired in me a veritable enthusiasm for the public virtues and for liberty.[9]

[5] Mme Roland, "Extrait de mon ame," *Lettres 1767-1780*, I, lii; *Lettres d'amour*, p. 84; *Mémoires*, I, 41; to Bancal, July 18, 1790, *Lettres*, II, 107–8; Desmoulins, "La France libre," *Œuvres* (Paris, 1906), I, 127.

[6] Mercier, *op. cit.*, p. 256.

[7] Mme Roland, *Mémoires*, I, 41; to Bancal, July 18, 1790, *Lettres*, II, 107–8.

[8] *Mémoires*, II, 22.  [9] *Ibid.*, p. 185.

One may suspect that here, as elsewhere in her *Mémoires*, she was manifesting the distorting tendency to
endow the child she used to be with the replican emotions
she was feeling in 1793.[10] But this suspicion cannot be confirmed because, to prove or to disprove her assertion, no
contemporary evidence exists. Her available letters do not
really begin until 1770, the year which saw her sixteenth
birthday. And since in her sentiments Mme Roland was
ever in her youth a chameleon, her views taking the color
of the last book she had read, and since even in emotion she
then tended to be, as we shall see, something of a change-
ling, these letters can scarcely be used as good evidence
concerning the attitudes of the little girl of nine.

Nevertheless, it is likely that those letters which were
written before the Revolution, being closer in time to her
childhood, are therefore more reliable than the *Mémoires*.
And these letters do give a different impression. In them,
in describing her early childhood reading, she tells how the
nobly virtuous actions of Plutarchian heroes, after kindling her enthusiasm, heightened her self-esteem, for they
awoke her confidence that had she been there or in similar
circumstances she would have acted as her heroes had acted. Even at the ages of nine or twelve, she regretted that
she had not been, or was not, in such similar circumstances,
and wept because she had not been born a Spartan or a
Roman. Regret for the past and discontent with the present, it may be noted, is here attributed to personal causes,
to the frustration of a desire for a career of active, heroic
virtue. Regret for the liberty and the republican institutions of antiquity is not mentioned.[11]

[10] C. L. Becker, "The Memoirs and Letters of Madame Roland," *American
Historical Review*, XXXIII (1927–28), 791–92, 793, 794.

[11] Mme Roland, "Extrait de mon âme," *Lettres 1767–1780*, I, lii; *Lettres
d'amour*, p. 84.

Even furthermore, if Plutarch, as her *Mémoires* and letters suggest, did indeed awaken in her a republican character, an enthusiasm for liberty and for public virtue, and
a discontent with the present, it is evident that he did not
maintain either the character, the enthusiasm, or the discontent. By 1770, by the time she was sixteen, all three no
longer existed. It is true that after 1770 she admired the
virtues of the republican heroes and heroines of antiquity.
But before 1776—before, in other words, she read Rousseau—she never manifested admiration for their public
virtues—their public integrity and their love of country,
and of liberty—but only for their private ones: their austerity, simplicity, poverty, and devotion to domestic duties. Nor before 1776 did she, in her letters, display an
enthusiasm for liberty. Finally, though during her later
adolescence her existence gave no opportunity to exercise
the heroic, Plutarchian virtues, yet during this period she
manifested no profound discontent with her way of life.
For from the ages of sixteen to twenty, in reading and enjoying the literary classics of France, she found a tranquil
happiness in the unheroic life of a student of books.[12]

At this time, furthermore, she was not discontented
with, but was cheerfully resigned to, the government under
which she lived. If she were so resigned, it was not because
she did not know that a more ideal order had once existed
in the past. Nor did her resignation spring from a failure to
compare this past with the present. For she did contrast
the virtue of early Sparta and Rome with the depravation
of libertine France; and, while a trip to Versailles was yet
fresh in her memory, she evidently did compare, if only
casually, the French monarchy with the ancient repub-

[12] On contentment see: To Sophie, June 7, 1771 *Lettres*, I, 33; March 28,
1772, I, 95; May 18, 1772, I, 105; February 20, 1773, I, 130; November 11, 1773,
I, 162; November 25, 1773, I, 170; *Mémoires*, II, 9.

lics.[13] But the comparison only leads her coolly to intimate that though she would have liked, it is true, to have been born in a classical republic, yet she finds "a beneficent king" "a being almost adorable."[14] It is apparent from the tone of this letter and of others that even the vision of a more ideal order in the past, even a comparison of this past with a less ideal present, did not now evoke a lively regret for that past or a spirited discontent with that present.

Though the evidence is perhaps insufficient to warrant any conclusion whatsoever, it might be inferred that the second quotation from her *Mémoires* is an exaggeration; that a reading of Plutarch did not inspire a veritable enthusiasm for the public virtues or for liberty; that perhaps, after all, in her early childhood Plutarch had only awakened that theoretic, academic, sentimental preference for republics which she always manifested until the Revolution—a preference which she translated seldom, if ever, into spirited condemnation of the existing monarchy, and never into agitation for its change.[15] Certainly that was the only permanent effect of her juvenile reading.[16]

Mercier, writing in 1782, reached a similar conclusion. After relating how as a *collège* youth he had identified himself with the republican heroes of antiquity, until he was a

[13] Inference from her letter describing her trip to Versailles. She said in this letter that, had choice been free, she would have chosen a republic for her home; but it would have been a republic unlike any that then existed in Europe, and hence, it would be necessary to change the time of her birth. Obviously, she is referring to the republics of antiquity (what else unless the Italian Renaissance republics, which is unlikely). Hence, probably compared French monarchy with antiquity.

[14] To Sophie, October 4, 1774, *Lettres*, I, 228; see the following letters to Sophie: May 9, 1774, I, 195; November 16, 1774, I, 237; December 13, 1774, I, 242.

[15] Becker, *op. cit.*, pp. 792, 794, 795, 796–97.

[16] Even this conclusion, though, would but tend to confirm the first quotation of the *Mémoires* that with a reading of Plutarch she first received impressions and ideas that were eventually to make her a republican.

"republican with all the defenders of the republic," he concludes from his own experience that "it is certain that one derives from the study of the Latin language a certain taste for republics, and that one would wish to be able to resurrect the particular republic . . . . whose great history one is reading."[17]

Mercier's evidence is, it is, true, a reminiscence (he was forty-two when he wrote, but had taught in a *collège* in his twenties). It is, however, a reminiscence written before the Revolution. It is not distorted, therefore, by that wish which warped the *Mémoires* of Mme Roland—the wish to believe and to have others believe that the writer had been a republican from childhood. Mercier, of course, could have no such wish. In 1782 he could not foresee that some day it might be to his advantage to have others believe he had always been a republican. In 1782 he had no presentiment of the Revolution and no fear that the classical education would subvert the monarchy. Even if he had been afraid that the throne was endangered by the teaching of the professors it paid, his own example would have reassured him. In time he became a loyal subject of the monarchy, his enthusiasm for republican Rome waned, and his admiration for the past changed to contempt as he became a modern of the moderns, and a citizen not of Rome but of Paris.

Writing in June, 1789, and again in the winter of 1790, Desmoulins intimated what he also asserted more clearly in 1793 that in *collège* the vision of republican antiquity kindled his first enthusiasm for liberty and his first hatred of the monarchy.[18] In view of the constant literary tendency in Desmoulins toward overstatement his affirmation is

[17] Mercier, *op. cit.*, p. 256.

[18] Desmoulins, *op. cit.*, I, 120–21, 127; *Révolutions de France*, No. 15, pp. 65-66; *A.P.*, LXXV (October 3, 1793), 622, n. 1.

to be taken with moderation. Nevertheless, the plausibility of what he said (in view of the evidence of Mercier), the appearance of his retrospective view early in the Revolution before certain factors could warp his memory, and the fact that he calls on a witness (Robespierre) who could contradict, all would suggest that the 1789 print of Desmoulins' memory was, in substance, correct.

Nevertheless, though his *collège* education, for the moment, may have inspired an enthusiasm for liberty and the classical republics, it did not teach him to anticipate in France either the approach of liberty or the downfall of the monarchy. In 1790 he exclaims, to Robespierre: "When [in *collège*] we regretted the tribune of Rome and of Athens, I was far from thinking that a constitution a thousand times more fine was so near at hand."[19] Nor did his education incite him to agitate for reform or for revolution. For after his graduation from *collège* and until the Revolution, he was no reformer but a struggling, stammering lawyer and lover, now distrusting his ability, then hopeful of success; but always ambitious to attain either by legal work or by a good marriage a better place in the existing order.[20] During these years, as he intimated in July, 1789, his love of liberty apparently existed, if it existed at all, hidden in the depths of his being, emerging into the open only with the events of 1788 and 1789.[21] While one of his phrases—"a few years ago [in *collège*] I sought everywhere for republican souls, I despaired at not having been born a Greek or a Roman"[22]—would perhaps suggest that between these *collège* years of regret and the Revolu-

[19] *Révolutions de France*, No. 15, pp. 65–66.

[20] *Ibid.*, No. 62, p. 438, n. 1; C. Vellay, "Desmoulins et Madame Duplessis, *Revue historique de la Révolution française*, I (1910), 238–39; Michel, "Camille et Lucile Desmoulins," *Revue des bibliothèques*, XVIII (1908), 185–87, 189.

[21] Desmoulins, "La France libre," *Œuvres*, I, 119–20.      [22] *Ibid.*, p. 127.

tion, there intervened a period when he too, like Mercier and Mme Roland, ceased to despair at not having been born a Greek or Roman.

There is evidence to indicate that, among the juveniles of France, experiences like those of Mme Roland, Mercier, and Desmoulins were not rare. Mercier assumed that his experience was typical, not peculiar. Desmoulins implied that his experience had been that of others, including Robespierre. Barère, in speaking of how Saint-Just in the Convention was ever consulting classical history and ever invoking in admiration the Plutarchian heroes, concluded by saying that in this Saint-Just was something of a schoolboy.[23] The newspaper known as the *Révolutions de Paris* remarked that the bourgeois think Roman examples should be proposed only to *collège* youths, whose imagination is, in this respect, still exalted.[24] Finally Mallet du Pan, in reviewing Chénier's play *Caius Gracchus*, wrote:

> One suspects that all the bombastic commonplaces directed against the great, the tirades about the people, the invectives directed to the Senate, and all the rubbish of a *collège* republican are to be found in the play.[25]

But this phenomenon appeared not only among members of the revolutionary generation and among *collège* students but also in others—in the young Rousseau, for example. And, of course, in its general features this experience was not peculiar to the youths of the eighteenth century but is common to many juveniles in all centuries. Tom Sawyer, for example, had not, it is true, read the classics; but he had read the *Tales* of Robin Hood and, with his friend, Joe Harper, had acted out the adventures

[23] Aulard, "Une interview de Bertrand Barère en 1840," *La Révolution française*, LXI (1911), 55.

[24] *Révolutions de Paris*, No. 87 (March 5–12, 1791), p. 456.

[25] *Mercure historique et politique*, March 3, 1792, p. 61.

of that medieval outlaw. Turning to the past, a reading of the *Tales* had transported Tom back into medieval England; and he dreamed of what a life would have been his in Sherwood Forest. Then, turning to the present, he grieved that no outlaws existed any more, and wondered what modern civilization could claim to have done to compensate for their loss.

Of course, in applying this nineteenth-century analogy to the eighteenth century, an objection could be made. It could be argued that since Mercier and Desmoulins were probably interested in the institutions of antiquity, as well as in its heroes, their interest may have been more adult in character than Tom's interest in Robin Hood. But not even this can be proved, since all we know concerning their juvenile interest is what they tell us as adults. In any case, their early interest was scarcely more significant than Tom's. It may have led them to feel that they did not live in the best of worlds, but it did not set them to doing anything about it; while with them, as with Rousseau, Brissot, Mme Roland, Tom Sawyer, and probably others, their childhood and early adolescent reveries faded away with the coming of the other preoccupations of later adolescence or of maturity. Any more formal conclusion concerning the relation between this juvenile interest and a revolutionary spirit must await the study of the more mature interest in antiquity which appeared in Brissot, Mme Roland, and Robespierre in their twenties, and in Marat in his thirties.

# CHAPTER IV

## CAREERS OPEN TO TALENT

### I

WHEN Robespierre had completed his *collège* course, he informed a friend that he planned to devote himself to the bar. "Of all the qualities necessary to gain distinction in that profession," he wrote, "I bring to it at least a lively spirit of emulation and an extreme desire to succeed."[1] Among his contemporaries, Robespierre, of course, was not alone in his desire for success. Brissot, for example, opens his *Mémoires* with the phrase: "J'ai prodigieusement aimé la gloire."[2] Marat, who, in describing another, often revealed more of himself than he did of the other, was constantly perceiving and praising in the distant great that absorbing "l'amour de la gloire" he himself possessed;[3] while the young Manon Phlipon (the maiden name of Mme Roland) used to weep because she could find no way to attain success. All four bourgeois, in brief, ardently desired a career. Yet all four lived in a society where to the *bourgeoisie* many careers were closed. At that time appointments to the higher, worth-while offices in the church, in the army and navy, in the judiciary, in the administration, and at the court were almost uniformly reserved to the nobility of the sword or of the robe. To the non-noble who had received the literary education of the *collège* and who was disinclined to de-

[1] M. Robespierre, *Œuvres complètes* (ed. E. Lesueur; Paris, 1913), II, 17.

[2] *Mémoires*, I, 1–2.

[3] J. P. Marat, *De l'homme* (Amsterdam, 1775), I, 296–97; *Eloge de Montesquieu* (Libourne, 1883), p. 69; *Les chaînes de l'esclavage* (Paris, 1792), p. 29.

grade himself by entering business, only two roads to success were open—the pen and the bar; and even here the
aspirant might find his way made difficult, in the one case
by censorship restrictions, in the other by the regulations
of the lawyer guilds.

Contemporaries were aware of this state of things.
Robespierre, for one, at least by 1784, realized that in
France many careers were closed to talent.[4] He believed,
furthermore, that such had not been the case in republican
antiquity, "where the careers leading to glory and to office
were always open to talent."[5] Marat went farther and
gave more than passing mention to how the love of glory
was recompensed in the Greek republics. There, he said,

Glory, that fruitful source of whatever men have done that is great
or beautiful, was the object of every reward.

It was at the Olympic games, before assembled Greece, that literary
merit was crowned. . . . .

Great men were supported by the state, statues were erected to
them, trophies were raised in their honor, crowns were bestowed upon
them.

He tells what honors Miltiades received and relates how,
for restoring liberty to Athens, Thrasybulus, was given a
crown of laurel. Marat concludes this passage by contrasting antiquity with his own times, where achievement is rewarded by mere gold, the pay of "the flat-
terer, the buffon, the mountebank, the mercenary, the
valet, and the slave."[6] In his own way, Marat was saying
what some of his contemporaries were saying, that for
those who loved glory and had talent, greater rewards and
wider careers were open in antiquity than in modern times.
One wonders whether he, in a moment of disappointment,
ever regretted that he had not been born a Spartan, ever

[4] Robespierre, *op. cit.*, I, 26, 28–29.

[5] *Ibid.*, p. 24.

[6] *Chaînes de l'esclavage*, pp. 29–30; see also p. 79, n. 1, and p. 87, n. 2.

dreamed how in antiquity his wish for glory would have been more fully gratified, or ever found, like Brissot and Manon Phlipon in their twenties, that his vision of the careers open in antiquity had intensified his revolutionary discontent.

With Brissot, this intensification of discontent occurred after he had left his native Chartres for Paris, a youth of twenty in quest (as he later said) "of a stage worthy of my efforts." A few years in Paris, and then he suddenly aspired, in 1781–82, to shine as a lawyer, to emulate a legal luminary of the day, Linguet.[7] The bar then seemed to Brissot the career open to talent: "the bar appeared to me to be . . . . that career where talent could develop itself freely."[8] Cicero became his ideal:

> Cicero [he said] completely realized the portrait of this encyclopedic orator. Philosopher, politician, poet, orator, lover of all the beaux arts, Cicero was everything, shone in everything. Young orator, if this brilliant model does not inflame you, if you do not burn with the noble desire to follow him, all is up with you; you will never be anything more than a mediocre lawyer.[9]

And Brissot to himself appeared cut out to be a French Cicero—he, too, would attain eminence in all branches of intellectual endeavor, and, as a special recommendation to lawyers of the Parisian Parlement, would bring to the bar, like Cicero, "a knowledge of literature and a taste for the sciences."[10]

He soon discovered, however, that the guild of full-fledged lawyers of Paris required an apprenticeship so long and a compliance with regulations so shackling that he gave up the attempt to be a French Cicero.[11] But since he

---

[7] Brissot, *Un indépendant à l'ordre des avocats* (1782), pp. 344–45.

[8] *Ibid.*, p. 345.                    [9] *Le sang innocent vengé*, p. 193.

[10] *Un indépendant à l'ordre des avocats* (1782), p. 345.

[11] *Ibid.*, p. 347; see also 1781 edition, pp. 38–39.

retained his ambition, he naturally became discontented
with the Parisian bar. With the bringing-on of this discontent, his admiration of Cicero, however, had little to do.
It had little to do with his craving for fame; with the attempt to satisfy that craving by turning to the law; or with
the check and abandonment of this attempt. For Cicero's
example did not determine him to enter the legal profession, but rather his own approaching marriage, Linguet's
example, and the realization that to educated bourgeois
talent the law was the lucrative career then open. Though,
furthermore, the Parisian bar (so he says) had checked
Brissot's attempt to imitate Cicero's cultivation of all the
sciences, this check did not cause his grumbling, but rather
the long apprenticeship and the minute regulations.

His bid for glory thwarted,[12] he reread Cicero's *De Ora-
tore* and perhaps his orations. By selecting passages from
them, he built up a vision of a Roman society where his
wish for a career would have been gratified. In a work entitled *Un indépendant à l'ordre des avocats, sur la décadence
du barreau en France*, he set up this vision of the ancient
Roman bar and society as a lost Garden of Eden which
revealed the defects of its French counterpart. In Cicero's
days, Brissot wrote, a young man who planned to be, and
later became, a lawyer was free from the restraints binding
French aspirants: free to cultivate the arts and sciences
without incurring the ill will of his elders of the bar;[13] free,
if talented, rapidly to become a lawyer of note, since no
guild regulations retarded the advance of aspirants;[14] free,
when speaking, to move about on a large tribune, instead
of being cooped up in a narrow inclosure;[15] and free to ex-

---

[12] *Un indépendant à l'ordre des avocats* (1781), p. 30.

[13] *Ibid.*, p. 34.

[14] *Ibid.*, pp. 34–35.                    [15] *Ibid.*, p. 19.

press his opinion on any subject, since freedom of speech was not curbed. And if the young man continued to show talent, what a career was his! From the tribune, he pleaded, not only before the court, but also before the people;[16] and he not only defended or prosecuted individuals, but he spoke on affairs of moment—the complaints against proconsuls, the bequests of sovereigns, and the passage of new laws.[17] Above all, the way was open to become, like Cicero, a consul, a first man in the state.[18] Is it any wonder that Brissot, who believed that he, too, would have been a personage had the way been open, should sigh for the days that had vanished, never to return except in a republic,[19] and should conclude: "The political constitution of Rome was very different from ours, and it was much better" for it was a state where, "in order to be first, it was necessary only to be first in merit."[20]

But for Brissot, the Rome of Cicero was not only a Garden of Eden to regret because Liberty and Opportunity and Careers-Open-to-Talent had once dwelt there; it was also in part a Heavenly City toward which French society should tend. He proposed that in France, as in Rome, large tribunes, from which lawyers could declaim freely to a vast audience, should be built; while the French state should offer honors, offices, and judgeships—a career, in brief—to lawyers of distinction.[21]

Brissot's encounter with the Parisian bar had thus transformed him from a conventional liberal with a conventional desire for fame into a more radical reformer violently desiring to change a sector of the existing order. With the promoting of this transformation his respect for the classical past played a part, perhaps, but unfortunately an inde-

[16] *Ibid.*, pp. 20–21.    [18] *Ibid.*, p. 47.    [20] *Ibid.*, pp. 47, 48.

[17] *Ibid.*    [19] *Ibid.*, p. 21.    [21] *Ibid.*, pp. 20, 48.

terminate one. We know, it is true, that his admiration of Cicero and of Rome had little to do with his initial dissatisfaction with the Parisian bar. But what about the spread of his discontent to French society in general? Was that provoked by admiration of the past? Here, on the one hand, it could be urged that it was his vision of Rome which first led him to perceive, to condemn, and to propose a remedy for, the failure of France to provide worth-while careers for topnotch lawyers; but evidence to establish this view is lacking. It could, on the other hand, be argued that it was the condemnation of French society that led him to perceive, to admire, and to set up as a model, its Roman counterpart. In any case, whichever was prior, Brissot's admiration of past society or condemnation of the present one, it may be presumed that in time vision of the past, discontent with the present, and hope for the future fed each other. Dislike of the present led him to perceive new things to admire in the past and to hope for in the future; admiration of the past led him to perceive new things to dislike in the present and to hope for in the future; while regret for the past and discontent with the present went on increasing. If it did not create, at least Brissot's cult of antiquity probably helped to maintain, a revolutionary spirit.

It was only for a moment, however, that his admiration of antiquity played this part. Within a year, as old ambitions gave way to new, old idols gave place to others. Cicero was toppled from his pedestal; Rousseau and Montesquieu were put in his place.[22] Soon, in 1784, Brissot was to condemn as childish the imitation of classical personages and was thus to signalize the end of one phase of his interest in antiquity.[23]

[22] Brissot, *De la vérité* (Neuchâtel, 1782), pp. 123, 195, 211.

[23] *Licée de Londres*, I (April, 1784), 227–28.

## II

In his conception of the life of Cicero, Brissot had found a career he desired to emulate. In her conception of the life of the matrons of early Rome and Sparta, Manon Phlipon found a career which aroused a similar desire. As with Brissot, furthermore, this classical conception intensified first complacency and then discontent, before being finally overtaken by indifference.

In her letters this conception is first described in 1773, when she was nineteen; it is hinted at again in 1776; it reappears in 1777 and in 1778. In November, 1773, to her confidant, Sophie, Manon praised the women of antiquity,

who found their glory in the happiness of their husbands, the care of their house and of their children. . . . . Retiring and sedentary, they brought the reign of peace and order to the interior of their homes; they were really respected, why? Because, as a Spartan woman answered, they knew how to form men [in virtue].[24]

Before three months were out, she dreamed of becoming such a wife—one who would bring happiness to a worthy husband, while she reared her children in virtue.[25] A few more months and, for no apparent reason, she became, in addition, animated by a desire to be useful to others and to promote the general good. She now regretted that she had not been born a man, since a man's opportunity to do good on a large scale was, she said, so extensive. But since she could not change her sex, she dreamed (this time more seriously) of marrying, of having male children, whom she would form into men of outstanding virtue, who would be useful to society—men of extraordinary merit—"for," as she remarked, "it is not worth while to marry merely to increase the number of ordinary men."[26] Henceforth, for

[24] To Sophie, November, 1773, *Lettres*, I, 166.

[25] To Sophie, February, 1774, *ibid.*, pp. 183–84.

[26] To Sophie, July 24, 1774, *ibid.*, pp. 211–12.

nearly two years this dream will be her new ideal design for living.[27] All that remained was to find a husband who could rear her children worthily. In the meantime, since she cannot be useful to others, since in her situation she can do more thinking than acting, she continues to study, not to attain eminence and glory in matters of intellect, for only men, she believes, have the ability to do that, but to perfect her own being that she may heighten her self-esteem and thus acquire happiness.[28]

Meanwhile, why should she regret the century of her birth: the past had nothing to offer that the present does not also afford. The present not only allows her to discover tranquil felicity in the perfecting of her being, but it also affords, or will afford, the opportunity to emulate the matrons of Sparta, to lead, as a wife, a life of active virtue and to find in the lives of extraordinary sons a vicarious career of heroic virtue. It may be presumed, indeed, that her admiration of classical heroines (accompanied, as it was, by a belief that she could in the future emulate them) would tend to increase her content with her opportunities and perhaps with the society which offered them. Certainly it cannot be maintained that at this time her particular classical vision tended to make her discontented with the existing order or kindled in her a revolutionary spirit.

In 1775 Manon's way of life changed, as the death of her mother in June brought grief, household cares, estrangement from her father, and less time for study. To top these chagrins, the man she loved was practically forbidden the house; and it seemed that her dream of a career

[27] To Sophie, September 19, 1774, *ibid.*, I, 225; and to Sophie, October 14, 1775, I, 327.

[28] To Sophie, March 15, 1775, *ibid.*, I, 274; to Sophie, October 14, 1775, I, 326–27. On her belief that no career in matters of intellect was open to women, see also: To Sophie, June 3, 1775, I, 304; to Sophie, January 11, 1775, I, 256; to Sophie, August 31, 1775, I, 315.

of active and vicarious virtue as a wife and a mother was frustrated. As a consequence, she considered returning to her studies, not as before to perfect her being, but to carve out a career and perhaps to achieve renown.[29] She quickly sensed, however, that a life of study would lead her no-where (she already believed, it may be remembered, that in matters of intellect women did not have the ability to succeed), and a spasm of discontent seized her. As she realized that no career was open to her, she looked upon herself and cursed her fate, for at this time she was not one to suffer insignificance willingly. Tortured by a "might-have-been" and conscious of her abilities, she cursed those circumstances—her sex and her century— which prevented her from using them. She now wrote:

In truth, I am vexed at being a woman: I should have had a different soul, a different sex, or another century. I was meant to be born a Spartan or a Roman woman, or at least a French man. As such, I should have chosen as my country the republic of letters, or one of those republics where one can be a man and obey only the laws.[30]

Like Brissot, I surmise, Manon ardently visioned antiquity as a Garden of Eden to regret, for there her desire for a career would have been gratified. But unlike Brissot, who thought that in antiquity a career would have been open to his talent, Manon imagined, I presume, that as a classi-cal wife and mother a career (both active and vicarious) would have been open to her virtue. Like Brissot, further-more, for the frustration of her desire for self-importance, Manon (in the next few sentences of her letter) blamed not only the particular circumstances in her case (including her position in society) but also the society in which she lived.

[29] To Sophie, February 5 and 29, 1776, *ibid.*, I, 374, 385.

[30] To Sophie, February 5, 1776, *ibid.*, I, 374. I am indebted to Mr. Becker for the suggestion that it was because Manon thought she would have had a career in Sparta or Rome that she regretted the time and place of her birth. I, alone, am responsible, of course, for the adoption of this suggestion and for the attempt to define more exactly just what sort of a career she thought she would have had.

Unlike Brissot, she did not attack specific institutions but general habits of thinking, "the fetters of opinion and the chains of prejudice."

Though a present chagrin precipitated her discontent, yet in preparing the ground, perhaps antiquity played a part. It could be argued, for example, that her vision of antiquity inspired the wish to lead the life of the classical matrons, and that the frustration of this wish by the temporary check of her marriage hopes explains her discontent. But evidence to establish the first point is insufficient; and for all we know, her wish to lead such a life may have preceded her focusing on the classical matrons. It is likely, however, that once her dissatisfaction was aroused, her glamorous vision of what she might have been in Greece and Rome made her feel how confining was life as a *petite bourgeoise* living near the Pont Neuf. At least this vision added the torturing quality of a might-have-been.

In any case, the spasm of dissatisfaction with the existing order, as distinguished from her discontent with her position in it, was momentary. She soon gave up the pursuit of glory and, temporarily, the hope of marriage. She ceased to champ at the bit which curbed her, and resigned herself to perfecting her being. Apparently, the only result of this episode was to increase her desire to escape reality by indulging in self-flattering reverie, and study, which had hitherto been Manon's life, now became an escape from life.[31] And though she found this escape chiefly in books by Frenchmen, yet occasionally she did, during these years, peruse a classic of antiquity and perhaps fly from

[31] To Sophie, October 8, 1775, *ibid.*, I, 325; January 13, 1776, I, 363; March 27, 1776, I, 396; September 1, 1776, I, 468; October 2, 1776, I, 490 and 491; October 8, 1776, I, 497; October 12, 1776, I, 502–3; December 24, 1776, I, 539–40; January 2, 1777, II, 3; January 5, 1777, II, 13; March 29, 1777, II, 54; April 12, 1777, II, 62; June 21, 1777, II, 86; August 19, 1777, II, 113; to Henriette, November 29, 1777, II, 162.

reality by reading in translation Homer, Vergil, Horace, Plato, and Cicero's letters.[32]

Perhaps because none of these classics were histories, a reading of them did not alter her view of the place of woman in antiquity. In her essay on "How the Education of Women Could Help To Make Men Better," written during the early months of the year 1777,[33] and in her *précis* of Xenophon's works, composed in 1778, she reveals that she still thought the classical matrons lived sedentary lives, devoted to domestic tasks but yet enjoying the esteem of contemporaries because they formed courageous, virtuous men of heroic stature.[34] Yet this vision no longer intensified either content (as in 1774) or discontent (as in 1776). The reason is simple: she no longer desired, at least not so eagerly, to emulate the Spartan matrons, for her conception of ideal married life had changed. No longer does she write Sophie of marriage as a *corvée* to be endured only because it offered a career of virtue directly as a wife and indirectly as a mother of extraordinary sons. Rather, she speaks of how happiness will come from living with a congenial mate, from attempting to make another happy.[35]

[32] To Sophie, June 24, 1776, *ibid.*, I, 425; October 2, 1776, I, 490; February 7, 1777, II, 29; March 15, 1777, II, 45-47; April 12, 1777, II, 61-62; July 1, 1777, II, 91; to Henriette, July 21, 1776, I, 443-45.

[33] In part, this is based on inference. In her essay on "How the Education of Women Could Help To Make Men Better," to describe the lives of the women in republics, she employed those same phrases she had once used, over three or four years before, to describe the life of Spartan and Roman matrons. Hence, it may be inferred that the general description found in her essay had an obvious reference to the customs of classical republics, and that her conception of these customs had remained the same.

[34] Mme Roland, *Mémoires* (ed. Faugère; Paris, 1864), II, 352, 356; to Sophie, January 14, 1777, *Lettres*, II, 13; June 21, 1777, II, 84; to Henriette, July 22, 1778, II, 301; July 26, 1778, II, 310.

[35] To Sophie, September 1, 1776, *Lettres*, I, 467; May 31, 1777, II, 74; August 27, 1777, II, 121; September 5, 1777, II, 126; February 17, 1778, II, 198, 200.

In 1780, by her marriage with a governmental official, M. Roland, Manon was given an opportunity to realize her dreams. Henceforth, until the Revolution, she could seek happiness in attempting to make another happy. During the early years of her marriage she found contentment in the attempt. But as her domestic tasks became more monotonous, her husband's relatives more exasperating, and her husband more difficult, contentment sometimes changed to resignation; and she was compelled to console herself with the thought that her life was, after all, the one most "favorable to the practice of virtue," and to find an escape in the writings of Rousseau.

She and her husband, however, nearly always had one bond of common interest: she was interested in him, and he was interested in himself. She was interested, therefore, in his work; and she would read the proofs of his book, revise his articles, and in time write some of his addresses. His career became her career, and eventually she came to know "what," according to Barrie, "every woman knows." Such a life usually had its "severe happiness," as well as its moments of satisfaction. Such a life fulfilled both her wish to try to make another happy and her wish for a career of virtue. Whether contented or resigned, she could cease to voice the regret that she had not been born a Spartan or a Roman.

Now and then, it is true, she expressed dissatisfaction with, and criticism of, the existing order, and found other societies more ideal. But dissatisfaction with French institutions in the present never was coupled with a conviction that they could be radically improved in the future, for she accepted them as a matter of course.[36] Until the Revolu-

---

[36] *Mémoires*, I, ix; *Lettres* (1780–93), I, 653; Madelein Clemenceau-Jacquemaire, *Madame Roland* (Paris, 1929), I, 190; and letters to M. Roland, May 21, 1784, *Lettres*, I, 425; November 20, 1785, I, 546.

tion therefore, she never was a revolutionary or a reformer, not even in spirit. Even her dissatisfaction with present institutions, moreover, was, after her marriage, unrelated to an interest in antiquity or in the classics, for after her marriage her interest in both apparently declined. Her epistolary references to antiquity are infrequent, casual, and confined to bits of rhetoric to illustrate her thought. Her letters, moreover, which record much of her reading, indicate that her attention was directed toward English, French, and Italian classics, and especially toward Rousseau. Lucian and fragments of Sophocles, Anacreon, and Sappho were the only classics of antiquity that were mentioned.[37] Plutarch, it is true, is still a favorite, and she dreams of how in a peaceful old age she will reread him; but apparently she does not read him through now.[38] When her husband spoke a little piece on Plutarch before a local learned academy, she praised, copied, and revised it,[39] and inserted phrases which had already appeared in her letters and which will reappear in her *Mémoires*. She had her husband say that Plutarch's "vehemence of heart attaches you strongly to things, but still more particularly to men, with whom you identify yourself to the extent of thinking yourself capable of the virtue which they exemplify." But it is obvious from this phrase and from others like them, and indeed from the entire essay, that the Rolands treasured Plutarch because he was Virtue, teaching by example, and not because he portrayed in flattering terms a republican society.[40] Judging from the available

---

[37] To Roland, January 27, 1783, *Lettres*, I, 216; also to Roland, December 13, 1786, in *Lettres 1767–1780*, II, 491.

[38] To Roland, January 13, 1787, *Lettres*, I, 662; *Mémoires*, I, 37.

[39] To Roland, December 22, 1786, *Lettres*, I, 649.

[40] Bibliothèque nationale, nouvelles acquisitions, Papiers Roland, 6243, fols. 89–90.

sources, it was a present, not a past, example—the unjust administration in France, or the examples of England, Switzerland, and perhaps of the United States, or perhaps a reading of Rousseau—which reminded Mme Roland, after her marriage, that she was dissatisfied with the existing order, that in theory, at least, she was a sentimental liberal with an academic liking for a republic.

If, therefore, for convenience, the "revolutionary spirit" may be resolved into a discontent with the existing order, an ideal of what a new order should be like, and a belief that this ideal could and should be made actual, it is plain that until the Revolution Mme Roland always lacked the third element. It is no less clear that her interest in antiquity had little, and less and less, to do with the inception and occasional outbursts of her discontent. Only in connection with her picture of an ideal order, in connection with her academic preference for a republic, did her interest in antiquity play a part; and that part apparently diminished in significance as she grew older.

To both her and Brissot, the classics had served as a source of knowledge when the two had wanted knowledge, and had afforded an escape when the two had wanted an escape; but both as sources of knowledge and as an escape, the classics had been overshadowed in importance by French books. At the root of the cult of antiquity of both the French woman and the French man lay a sturdy self-esteem which no failure could enfeeble; a self-esteem which told Mme Roland that, had she been in the position of her heroes or in similar circumstances, she would have acted as her heroes had acted, and that she had, in fact, once or twice acted as they had acted; a self-esteem which told both her and Brissot that they could, in the present, find a career in emulating the ancient dead, and that for them the past was something to regret since there such a career would indeed have been theirs. And if the careers they desired and regretted were different, if their views of antiquity stressed different sectors of the past, if Brissot looked to Cicero while Mme Roland looked to the matrons of early Sparta and Rome, it was simply because Brissot was a man while Mme Roland was a woman; and the attention of both, as they regarded the present and the past, was held by those careers most open to their sex.

When they thought their careers thwarted, both blamed, to a certain extent, the existing society. But while Brissot, believing that matters could be remedied by reform, agitated for a change and even set up antiquity as a Heavenly City toward which society should tend, Mme Roland, believing that radical innovation was impossible, that neither French society nor her position in it could be cured, accepted both as something to be endured, and never set up antiquity as a Heavenly City toward which society could tend. Antiquity, therefore, had played a greater rôle in strengthening Brissot's full-fledged reforming spirit than it had in developing even the embryo of such a spirit in Mme Roland; but in neither case was antiquity in this respect of surpassing significance, and its significance tended to diminish as the Revolution approached.

# CHAPTER V

## THE *PHILOSOPHE* VIEW IS ACCEPTED

IN LAST analysis, Manon Phlipon regretted antiquity because she knew that the institutions which would have given her a career and happiness in the past could not be revived in the present. She knew that this was true because two *philosophes*, Montesquieu and Rousseau, had told her that it was so. For she, like Brissot, Marat, and Robespierre, accepted both the *philosophe* picture of the classical past and the *philosophe* theories concerning that past. With the picture, we are already acquainted. Antiquity (that is, early Rome and Sparta) was liberty, equality, and virtue; poverty, austerity, frugality, and courage; and a self-sacrificing love of country, of equality, and of liberty. It was a glamorous Garden of Eden which called forth from one contemporary the following praise—praise which our four revolutionaries-to-be would not have found extravagant. This contemporary, Servan, wrote:

> Lovely Athens charms my senses; but virtuous Sparta touches my soul. Age of the fine arts, brilliant days of Augustus and of Vergil, you are surpassed by those days of liberty and of virtue, by that sacred age of Regulus, of Camillus, and of Scipio. . . . . If I could have seen Athens and Rome in their days of glory, I would not have visited first of all the Capitol or the Jupiter of Phidias, but the home of Aristides and of Cato. There, in those simple sanctuaries of virtue . . . . with their children about them, I would have desired to look upon these men so virtuous and so great.[1]

The *philosophe* theory assumed that virtue like this was indispensable in a republic. Two chief *philosophes*, Mon-

[1] "Discours de M. Servan sur les mœurs," in Brissot, *Bibliothèque philosophique* (Paris, 1782), VII, 19-20.

tesquieu and Rousseau, had learned from history that in Sparta and Rome liberty, political equality, and the republic had declined when political virtue (love of country, of the republic, of equality) had decayed; that political virtue had decayed when private virtue (frugality, austerity, simplicity) had disappeared and when extreme wealth, luxury, and inequality of fortune had entered. Montesquieu and Rousseau also knew that republics had endured only in states of small area and of small population; that when Rome grew large, the republic fell. Generalizing from particular cases like these, they assumed that republican institutions, liberty, and equality would, in the long run, thrive and endure only in states that were "petits et pauvres" and inhabited by the virtuous. It naturally followed that republican institutions such as existed in antiquity would not endure in large, opulent, depraved France. Only a monarchy was suitable for Frenchmen.[2]

This reasoning Manon Phlipon, Brissot, Marat, and probably Robespierre accepted.[3] They might juggle about the elements of the logic. They might, like Brissot, for example, argue positively that a small area and a small population means poverty, that poverty means no luxury, no luxury means virtue, and virtue the possibility of republican liberty and equality. Or they might, like Manon and Marat, reason negatively that a good soil and climate leads to wealth, wealth to luxury, luxury to immorality, immo-

[2] Montesquieu, *Esprit des lois*, pp. 19-21, 31, 34, 37-39, 42, 83-84, 89, 94-98, 100-105; Rousseau, *Du contrat social*, pp. 248-49, 264, 266, 273, 281, 286-87, 302, 334-35.

[3] Mme Roland, *Œuvres* (Paris, l'an VIII), III, 123-26, 170-74; Brissot, *Théorie des loix criminelles* (Berlin, 1781), pp. 44-47, 106 n. 46, 208-10; *Les moyens d'adoucir la rigueur des loix pénales* (Châlons-sur-Marne, 1781), pp. 7-9, 12, 72; *Testament d'Angleterre* (1780), pp. 52, 103; "Recherches philosophiques sur le droit de propriété et sur le vol," *Bibliothèque philosophique*, VI, 291, 292-93; *ibid.*, IX, 9. Marat, *Chaînes d'esclavage*, pp. 25, 28, 79 n. 1; Robespierre, *Œuvres complètes*, pp. 24-26.

rality to the fall of liberty. But however they might differ in details, they all reached the same conclusion: for France, radical imitation of republican antiquity was beyond the reach of hope. As a result Manon doubtless found an additional reason to believe that the society which she had regretted could not be revived; Brissot, despite his belief that a republic after the classical model surpassed a monarchy and that Lycurgan equality of fortune was a legislative masterpiece, yet was forced to conclude that neither the republic nor equality was practicable in large, commercial France;[4] while Marat became the curious case of a man whom history taught to believe what he did not want to believe. During 1774 he was in England, struggling to rouse the British electorate to the necessity of preserving their liberty. Yet even as he agitated, he saw that commerce had enriched the British, had created an extreme inequality of wealth, and had softened by luxury their former austere morals; and in accordance with what classical history had taught him, he gloomily felt that the liberty for which he was struggling must eventually succumb before a depraved morality.[5]

The theory of Montesquieu and Rousseau thus discouraged radical innovation through radical imitation of antiquity. It did not, however, close the door on moderate reform. Their theory assumed, it is true, that within a given country only the form of government adapted to certain fundamental conditions would endure. For that reason the theory doomed the French reformer to accept the monarchy. But the theory also presupposed that only the most perfect adaptation will bring the greatest possible amount of happiness. It thus left the way open in France

[4] *Théorie des loix criminelles*, p. 106, n. 46, and pp. 44–46; *Les moyens d'adoucir*, pp. 7–9.

[5] Marat, *op. cit.*, pp. 83, 346, 355, 357–58.

for reforms effecting a more perfect monarchical adaptation. But Brissot, Marat, and Condorcet soon noted, sometimes with sorrow, that antiquity, with its laws adapted to conditions necessitating a republic, had nothing to teach men seeking a more perfect monarchical adjustment. Brissot, for example, interested in crime and punishment, considered the revival in France of the censorships, the severe penalties for adultery, and the rigorous sumptuary laws of antiquity. He concluded, however, that while these laws and institutions had been adapted to the poverty and virtue of small Sparta and Rome, it would be useless and uselessly cruel to reproduce them in France. No punishment, however severe, could check luxury or immorality in a large commercial state; no law or institution—alas!—could resurrect the Roman virtue.[6] Brissot's conclusion in regard to the censorship was shared by Marat. Institutions like these, said the latter, were suited only to a small, virtuous state; powerless to make men virtuous in large, depraved France, they are too "sublime" for "our little souls."[7]

Brissot's conclusion in regard to sumptuary legislation was, for a time, shared by Condorcet. The latter, one of the few revolutionaries-to-be who seemed conscious of the Battle of the Ancients and the Moderns, early believed that in poetry, the theater, learning, scholarship, and in law the moderns were superior to the ancients.[8] Only in the field of politics, and then only in 1776–77, did he put in a good word for the latter. He then praised the simplic-

[6] *Théorie des loix criminelles*, pp. 208–10, 232, 235, 264; *Les moyens d'adoucir*, pp. 71–72.

[7] *Plan de législation criminelle* (1790), pp. 28–29, 124.

[8] Condorcet, "Eloge de Blondel," *Œuvres*, II, 41; "Eloge de M. Fontaine," *ibid.*, II, 139–40; "Seconde lettre d'un théologien," *ibid.*, V, 325; "Réflexions sur l'esclavage des nègres," *ibid.*, VII, 97–99; "Discours prononcé dans l'Académie française" (1782–84), *ibid.*, I, 403–4, 446–47.

ity and power of their legislation, and the virtue of their legislators. He thought the condition of early Rome, with agriculture supreme, luxury unknown, ideal. But he censured any attempt to revive the sumptuary laws of Rome; they were suited only to peoples where the desire to obey the law was sufficiently strong to secure obedience.[9]

As the Revolution approached, even the hypothetical questions involving the possibility of radical or moderate imitation of antiquity ceased to occupy these revolutionaries-to-be. As we have seen, after her marriage in 1780, Mme Roland's interest in the classics and in antiquity declined. Judging from the sources (which admittedly are rather reticent) Robespierre's view of the classical past from 1784 to 1789 did little to maintain his reforming spirit. During the 1780's, as Marat became interested less in man than in nature, less in politics than in color, light, and electricity, his interest in the classical past appears only in a few passages in his brief *Eloge de Montesquieu*. His preoccupation with classical history and his interest in, as distinguished from his admiration of, antiquity declined in the decade immediately preceding the Revolution.

With Condorcet and Brissot not even this admiration remained. During the latter half of the 1770's, the American Revolution taught Condorcet that even in politics some moderns surpassed the ancients. After 1780, he would mention the institutions of the latter only with contempt and disdain. Upon Brissot the American example exerted a similar effect. In the years 1783–84 he found in Thomas Paine's *Common Sense* and in Crevecœur's *Letters from an American Farmer* the picture of an unalloyed, American golden age—a picture, furthermore, so exact a confirmation of his dreams that he did not question its

---

[9] "Eloge de l'Hôpital," *Œuvres*, III, 534-35, 551; "Réflexions sur le Commerce des blés," *ibid.*, XI, 157-58, 185.

accuracy.[10] Besides this glamorous perfection, antiquity seemed coarse and imperfect. Already in 1783 enthusiasm for classical institutions waned as he compared them with those of Pennsylvania.[11] By 1784 the American example had undermined his belief that republics were adapted only to countries of small area. He now explained that, if the republican form of government had declined in antiquity as a republic's territory expanded, it was because "nations were not then sufficiently mature," "political science was not then sufficiently advanced," the people were then "ignorant and fierce," and because the institutions of particular republics were defective.[12] Indeed, no ancient republic deserved consideration as a model. Even Rome, as he remarked two years later, had its defect. In answer to Chatellux, Brissot wrote:

You believe you honor the Americans greatly by having them resemble the Romans and the Greeks; but I think them greatly superior to these ancients. . . . I confine myself to stating this proposition, which I will prove elsewhere, to show you that the men of today, far from being degenerate, will be capable of surpassing their ancestors when the circumstances are favorable. . . . .

How is it that you cited the terms "plebeian" and "patrician," those fatal class distinctions which caused all the misfortunes, all the convulsions of the Roman Republic, distinctions which dragged Rome into perpetual quarrels, into a mania for conquest, and into despotism? If Rome had known of, and had adopted, the natural and sacred equality of the Americans . . . . without a doubt her existence would have been of longer duration; and it was from this point of view that I just remarked that the Americans were very much superior to the Romans.[13]

[10] *Licée de Londres*, I (April, 1784), 27; II (November, 1784), 287.

[11] "Réflexions sur le code de Pennsylvanie," *Bibliothèque philosophique*, III, 239, 243.

[12] *Licée de Londres*, II (September, 1784), 147. For other criticism and faint praise of antiquity during 1784, see *ibid.*, I (January, 1784), 23; II (September, 1784), 154. For other hosannas in praise of America during 1784 see *ibid.*, I (January, 1784), 27; II (November, 1784), 287.

[13] *Examen de Chatellux* (London, 1786), pp. 106–8.

Thus by 1784, and certainly by 1786, his comparison of American institutions with those of antiquity had led him to condemn the latter.[14] As a result, his revolutionary spirit, from 1784 to the Revolution, will be nourished by the contemplation, not of the classical, but of the American example.[15]

In the minds of contemporaries and historians, both the juvenile and the more mature sympathy with republican antiquity acquired in retrospect an exaggerated significance. This sympathy, it was thought, had helped to bring on the Revolution—the Revolution which, to quote Chateaubriand, "was accomplished before it occurred"; the one which, to quote Mr. Becker, "was accomplished in men's minds before they made it the work of their hands";[16] a Revolution which made men dissatisfied with the existing society, gave them some idea of what a new one should be like, and assured them that such a new order was practica-

---

[14] On further praise of America for its liberalism during the period September, 1784, to February, 1789, see, for example, *Licée de Londres*, II (September, 1784), 154; II (November, 1784), 287; *Examen de Chatellux*, pp. 2, 23–24, 76, 102–8, 111; *Lettre à l'empereur sur l'atrocité des supplices* (Brussels, 1787), p. 13; *Lettre à l'auteur du Mercure* (Bouillon, 1787), pp. 27–28; *Point de banqueroute*, première partie (London, 1787), p. 18; *Observations d'un républicain*, p. 162. In contrast to frequent, redundant, and fervid praise of America are the casual references to antiquity: *Un défenseur du peuple à l'Empereur Joseph* (Dublin, 1785), p. 7; *Point de banqueroute*, première partie, p. 14, n. 1; *Examen de Chatellux*, pp. 24, 128–29; *Mémoire sur les noirs* (Paris, 1789), p. 9.

[15] Before the Revolution two other noted revolutionaries-to-be, Barère and Vergniaud, revealed a mature interest in antiquity. But their interest was almost entirely rhetorical, as they found in classical history literary allusions to adorn their prose. With Barère, it is true, the innumerable allusions betray a tendency to accept the conventional view of republican antiquity as the home of liberty and of virtue. But this view was apparently unrelated to any reforming spirit in Barère. See: Barère, *Eloges académiques* (Paris, 1806), pp. 124, 127, 128, 141, 145, 148, 149, 151, 154, 163, 169, 176 n. 9, 226, 236, 244, 257, 263–64, 280, 285, 287, 291–93, 295, 298, 299, 300, 305, 310, 312, 315, 319; *Eloge de Louis XII* (1782), pp. 17, 57; *Eloge de Furgole* (Toulouse, 1783), pp. 6, 8, 27. For Vergniaud see: Vatel, *Vergniaud*, I, 183; II, 37, 48; Vergniaud, "Lettres et vers," *Archives historiques du département de la Gironde*, XVIII (1878), 553–55.

[16] *The Declaration of Independence* (New York, 1922), p. 30. (Quoted with author's permission).

ble. Even though we may not admit that sympathy with republican antiquity directly promoted this psychological change, yet it could be argued that indirectly it played a part. Mme Roland said, with some truth, perhaps, that Plutarch, by giving her certain impressions and ideas, had disposed her to become in time (perhaps she meant with the Revolution) a republican. Jean de Bry made the same reflection in regard to the reading of the classics in general. This reading disposed men, it could be inferred, to become, not only revolutionaries when the Revolution arrived, but also agitating reformers before it occurred. A sympathetic study of classical history (for instance, in the case of Brissot, Robespierre, and Marat) may have prepared them for an early sympathetic acceptance of the liberal *philosophe* view. In fact, it might be surmised, with what truth I do not know, that as the twig of youthful sympathy with the classical commonwealths was bent, so the tree of more mature liberalism may have been inclined.

It could be reasoned, indeed, that a vision of a faultless past had directly helped to maintain, if not to create, dissatisfaction with a defective present. With Brissot and Mme Roland, as we have seen, this may have been the case. And, indeed, so splendid was this vision of the past that it was likely to promote, in nearly anyone, dissatisfaction with nearly any present society; for what society would not seem mean and imperfect when set alongside this heroic perfection? Yet this very perfection, which fitted the vision to arouse dissatisfaction and to become with Rousseau and his imitators an instrument of attack, unfitted it to become a principle of reconstruction. Since classical commonwealths were conceived to be so perfect in comparison with the present, imitation of their example meant radical change. But not one of the reformers-to-be whom we have studied believed such change was imminent or possible, so permanent did the existing order seem. Such a belief would tend to inhibit, it seems to me, any desire to set up these commonwealths as models for France to imitate.

The perfection of the vision, however, will not alone explain its failure to nourish in reformers-to-be a revolutionary spirit. After all, America, as Brissot and other devotees envisaged it, was as faultless as the antiquity of Marat, for example. Yet the example of America helped to sustain in Brissot and others a spirit of radical reform. The reason is simple: the American Revolution had occurred in the present in a large country. Its example gave some assurance, therefore, that radical reform, looking, if not to a republic, at least to more liberty, was possible even in large eighteenth-century France. It gave some faith that, if ever those in power became wiser or weaker, wrongs could be righted and a radically better world would be possible—a faith without which a revolutionary spirit is dead, without which, indeed, it is never born.

But the examples of ancient republics gave no such assurance; indeed, they tended to dim such faith. To more than one eighteenth-century reformer-to-be their examples taught that their institutions which had brought liberty and some equality were adapted only to small populations of lofty morals and a simple life. The very perfection of the ancient republics, the knowledge that these institutions even in glorious Sparta and Rome could not survive the entrance of luxury in either, or the expansion of the latter would tend only to strengthen this conception. How, therefore in the face of such evidence could any intelligent eighteenth-century liberal have faith that these institutions which he admired were practicable in large, luxury-loving, depraved eighteenth-century France? How could he propose them as models to imitate? Despite his longing for liberty, he could not, interpreting history as he did, make such a proposal or have such a faith. The ideas of men concerning history here constituted, as they so often do, a barrier, rather than a stimulus, to human aspiration. If, however, these two inhibiting conceptions—one of the present and the other of the past—should ever disappear; if men ever came to believe that radical change and a republic were possible in France, then admiration for the classical commonwealths might cease to be sterile. Republican antiquity would cease to be a retrospective Utopia that was too Utopian, a Garden of Eden to admire and to regret, and might then become in the minds of men a Heavenly City which could be realized on earth.

# CHAPTER VI

## A RADICAL REQUESTS RADICAL
## IMITATION (1789)

IN ANY chronological survey of the interest in antiquity during the French Revolution, Camille Desmoulins should be considered first. He was the first to manifest (as early as July, 1789) a full-fledged revolutionary cult of antiquity. In addition, during the first two years of the Revolution he was the only one on whom antiquity exerted a decisive influence. It was natural that he should be, in these respects, a leader, for in him those inhibiting conceptions which still led others to believe that a republic was impossible in France had already died away. The early revolutionary events of May and June, 1789, apparently revealing the weakness of the court and the Frenchman's fitness for liberty, had taught him that, though he might admire antiquity, to regret it was no longer necessary, since a radical innovation comprising the imitation of classical republics now was possible. In the first, fine careless rapture which attended these discoveries, at the dawn of the Revolution, he who had regretted that he had not "been born a Greek or Roman" now exclaimed: "I give thanks unto thee, O Heaven, for having placed my birth at the end of this century."[1]

Desmoulins, it may be remembered, opened his revolutionary career on July 12, 1789, by springing to a table in the Palais Royal to announce that the popular finance minister, Necker, had been dismissed, to cry "To arms!" and to initiate thus the three-day uprising which eventu-

[1] *La France libre*, I, 74; see also p. 127.

ated in the capture of the Bastille. He followed up this exploit by the publication of two brochures, *La France libre* and the *Discours de la lanterne*, which attracted the attention of Mirabeau, who invited him to Versailles. Of the resulting visit, Desmoulins wrote home:

> For eight days past I have been staying at Versailles with Mirabeau. Every instant he takes my hand, he pats me on the back; he then goes to the assembly, regains his dignity on entering the vestibule, and does wonders; after that, he returns to dine with excellent company and sometimes his mistress, and we drink excellent wines. I feel that his table, too delicate and too overloaded, will corrupt me. His burgundies and maraschino have an attraction which I seek vainly to hide from myself, and I have all the difficulty in the world to regain my republican austerity and to detest the aristocrats whose crime it is to enjoy these dinners.[2]

Desmoulins, however, need not have feared that he would lose his "republican austerity," for one cannot lose what one has never possessed. Indeed, it may be suspected that, if he had had such excellent dinners, such burgundy and maraschino, and such pats on the back before, rather than during, the Revolution, he might have forgotten his ardor for liberty inspired perhaps by the classics. Whatever would have been the result had he attained early success, the fact remains that in the spring of 1789, he was still a struggling, stammering, petty, and not very successful lawyer in Paris, unappreciated by his home townsmen in Picardy (a fact which rankled in his mind almost to his death), rather futilely in love with a beautiful heiress, and dissatisfied with the existing order.

No doubt, to a certain extent, a view of contemporary evils lay at the root both of this dissatisfaction and of his agitation for the abolition of those restrictions which curbed liberty to publish; of those favors which reserved offices and careers to the privileged; and of that monarchy which had spawned kings that were corrupt, extortionate,

---

[2] Desmoulins to his father, September 29, 1789, *Œuvres*, II, 344–45.

cruel, and oppressive.[3] But the view of present evils, personal and political, will not alone explain the reforms of
Desmoulins. For this explanation does not entirely answer
the question why certain particular evils were selected for
condemnation and cure. Why didn't Desmoulins go farther than he did? The vision of the unequal distribution of
taxes led him to propose their more equal apportionment
among all the citizens according to their means. Why
didn't the vision of the evils resulting from the unequal
distribution of property, which Babeuf was about to de-
nounce, lead him to propose that property also be more
equally apportioned among all the citizens?[4] Why, furthermore, did he go so much farther than his contemporaries and propose the abolition of the monarchy and the
creation of a republic?

To the last question the answer conceivably could be:
the influence of Rousseau or of the American example.
But while both assured Desmoulins that a republic was
possible, they did not give the initial republican "slant."
Rather, if we believe his confessions, which his writings
confirm, he became a republican partly because from a
reading of the classics in *collège* he had gained a certain
vision of republican Rome and Athens and because this
vision so affected him that during the Revolution he hated
kings and dreamed of republics. Why he gained such a
vision while some others who read the same classics did
not, is not clear. Nor is it clear why his knowledge of history did not influence him to go farther, to hate property
inequalities, and to dream of a Spartan communist state.
But it does seem that when the Revolution arrived, and
perhaps before, condemnation of a monarchical present

[3] Desmoulins, *La France libre*, I, 93, 95–119, 122, 127–29; "Discours de la
lanterne aux Parisiens," *Œuvres*, I, 147–48, 167, 173 and n. 1; "Reclamation en
faveur de Marquis de Saint-Hurugue," *ibid.*, pp. 203–4.

[4] Desmoulins opposed such a redistribution. See *La France libre*, I, 84–85.

arose both from a view of present evils and, as he himself remarked, from admiration of a republican past. As if to illustrate how past and present conceptions united to produce such an effect, Desmoulins recalled his feelings upon viewing in his youth an entry of the queen to Paris:

> The memory of those triumphal chariots of the Romans, where a man of high rank was given to understand by a slave at his side that he was, after all, only a citizen; here, on the contrary, the profound sentiment of their pride, of their scorn for the nation; that extravagant idea which I thought I read in their faces, that it was to God and to their swords, and not to us that they owed their elevation to a position of honor; the comparison of their individual insignificance with that inflated grandeur . . . . all these pictures filled me with an indescribable indignation, and my hatred of royalty brought on a fever, the only one I have ever had.[5]

Some of that hatred of royalty, in brief, which possessed the Romans, who groaned when Antony offered Caesar the crown—some of the hate of tyranny which appeared in Brutus' act and in Cicero's *Second Philippic* (the oration most quoted by Desmoulins)—seems to have entered into his attitudes.[6]

If his principles and his vision of Rome led Desmoulins to detest royalty, his tastes and his vision of Athens told him what were the "sweets of liberty." At Athens, he informed his fellow-citizens, liberty meant rewards for the talented; civic crowns for the virtuous; and equality before the law. Nor was liberty an enemy of the good things of life. On the contrary, at Athens, politics, the art of governing men, was employed in making them happy, in using "the liberty and the arts, these gifts of heaven, to make enchanting the dream of life." There liberty had brought a flourishing commerce and luxury, had subsidized the theater, and had been friendly to Aspasia. There, instead of a gloomy, austere religion, enemy of joy and natural

---

[5] *Ibid.*, I, 120–21.

[6] *Ibid.*, pp. 71, 118, 119; *Révolutions de France et de Brabant*, No. 11, p. 490; No. 14, p. 10; No. 16, p. 138; No. 17, p. 149.

desire, the Athenian worship was gay, friendly to woman
and to liberty, and encouraged celebration by frolick-
ing dance and festival. It was a past where Desmoulins'
wish for a career, a good time, and domestic joy would
have been gratified. It was a vision which aided him to
believe that the "tree of liberty" bore a delicious fruit and
thus helped to sustain the easily dispirited Desmoulins in
his endeavor to have that tree transplanted to France.
Is it any wonder that with this vision in mind and with
his somewhat epicurean tastes he should conclude that
the republican government of Athens was in general the
one most suitable for France? A republic which would not
only do away with the crimes of kings and the iniquities
of privilege but would also bring to France, as to Athens,
careers open to talent, equality before the law, prosperity,
luxury, happiness, and joy.[7]

But though he might urge his countrymen to have, like
the Athenians, a republic, he did not advocate detailed
imitation of Athenian institutions. Indeed, he held up the
institutions of no people for complete, circumstantial
aping.[8] He appeared to want, not a republic such as the
ancients had possessed, but one that French legislators
could construct when "aided by the enlightenment of the

[7] On the vision of Athens and its transplanting to France, see Desmoulins,
*La France libre*, I, 90–91, 93, 122, 165 n. 2, 176, 178, 180; *Réclamation en faveur du
Marquis de Saint-Huruque*, I, 203–4; *Révolutions de France*, No. 20, pp. 306–7;
No. 32, pp. 378–80.

[8] It is true that occasionally in casual asides he remarks that certain institutions in antiquity and in America should be transplanted to France. He suggests,
for example, that in France, as in Rome, the tenure of office should be brief. But
in cases like these it is difficult to demonstrate that the proposed institution was
suggested by an antique example; present circumstances may have prompted the
proposal. Furthermore, even when such asides are gathered together, they do
not show that he wished the French constitution to be a complete, servile copy of
the institutions either of America or of antiquity. See, for some of the asides,
*Révolutions de France*, No. 5, pp. 231–32; No. 14, p. 3; No. 18, pp. 219–20; No. 19,
p. 243; No. 22, p. 395; No. 32, pp. 378–80; No. 53, p. 20; No. 55, pp. 103, 107–9;
No. 78, pp. 604–7, 610.

century and the impulsion of the moment."[9] Nevertheless, one proposal to which he constantly recurs was perhaps inspired by an antique example as mediated by the
classics or Rousseau. The analogy between the ward meetings of the Parisians and the forum assemblages of the
Romans perhaps suggested to him that Frenchmen assembled in their wards should, like the Romans, approve
or veto legislation. In effect, his was a proposal for repeated referendum by public meetings.[10]

Rounding out his argument in favor of this specific reform and of his general proposal for a republic, Desmoulins answered certain familiar objections. In reply to the
familiar talk that the many were too incapable, corrupt,
and immoral to rule, he cited the wisdom of the people in
Greece, Switzerland, and America. "How," he asked, "can
you reply to these examples?"[11] Later, his illusions (if they
were illusions) concerning the nobility and sagacity of the
many were corroded away by the observation of the ingratitude, blindness, and immorality of the multitude.[12]
He will then argue that depravity in private matters does
not mean depravity in public action and that the people are
politically incorruptible because no one has enough money
to bribe them.[13]

[9] *Ibid.*, No. 27, pp. 618–19.

[10] *Ibid.*, No. 17, p. 166; No. 25, pp. 548–49; No. 45, p. 262; No. 68, pp. 120-
21; No. 81, pp. 114–15.

[11] *La France libre*, I, 124.

[12] With Desmoulins, disillusionment regarding the character of the people
came gradually. For a time, praise of the people still mingled with blame
(*Révolutions de France*, No. 2, pp. 88–89; No. 3, pp. 111–12; No. 8, p. 368; No. 12,
p. 565; No. 14, pp. 7–8; No. 15, pp. 88–89; No. 43, p. 167; No. 49, pp. 450–51,
455–59; No. 64, pp. 562–63; No. 65, pp. 606–7; No. 78, pp. 611–15).

[13] *Ibid.*, No. 41, pp. 55, 60; No. 74, pp. 397–98; No. 78, pp. 611–15. For
another argument, this time drawn from Rousseau, see also No. 28, p. 202; No.
58, pp. 251–52; still later, a letter by Desmoulins in *Chronique de Paris*, No. 30
(January 30, 1792), Supplément.

To silence those who objected that France was too large for a republic, he pointed to America.[14] To answer those who still held that the Frenchman's love of luxury made impossible a durable French republic, Desmoulins observed that some believe:

> No liberty, no equality, is possible without the institutions of Lycurgus, who forbade Sparta to have furniture not made with hatchet and saw . . . . , who inspired love of frugality with his cheese and detestable sauce, who cured the husbands of jealousy by honoring cuckoldy, and who cured ambition with his table d'hôte at ten sous per meal.[15]

Naturally, Desmoulins, whose taste ran to excellent dinners, burgundy, and maraschino, found this Lenten régime of Lycurgan Sparta detestable; and he comments: "Mably finds all this admirable; but . . . . Lycurgus is a doctor who keeps you healthy with dieting and water. But what sickness worse than such a régime of eternal dieting and water."[16]

Naturally, furthermore, since he desired both liberty and the good things of life, it was easy for Desmoulins to discover that the liberty of Sparta had not depended on the absence of the luxuries he relished. He writes:

> The Lacedaemonians, superstitious about the laws of their Lycurgus, . . . . had got the idea that they would cease to be free . . . . when they no longer lived on black porridge and cheese. But it was not their drink, the water of the Eurotas, which could inspire in them the taste for equality and independence; for no one looks upon kings and nobles with so much contempt as a drunk.[17]

Besides, he continues, there is the example of republican Athens with its gardens, theaters, and commerce to prove that luxury and liberty are compatible,[18] to help Desmoulins have faith that liberty and a republic were possible in a France that was luxury-loving, and to assure him

[14] *La France libre*, I, 124.

[15] *Révolutions de France*, No. 20, pp. 304–5.

[16] *Ibid.*, p. 305.      [17] *Ibid.*, pp. 304–5.      [18] *Ibid.*, pp. 306–7.

that he could drink his wine and eat his cake and have his freedom too.

In last analysis, perhaps, Desmoulins believed that liberty and luxury were compatible simply because he wished to enjoy both. In other words, it was because he wished to place so few inhibitions on his physical appetites that he lacked those inhibiting intellectual conceptions concerning the necessity of virtue and the simple life in a republic. Now, just because Desmoulins lacked these inhibiting intellectual conceptions, he became a republican and an exponent of the republican, revolutionary imitation of republican antiquity. For that reason we arrive at the paradox that, if Camille was unique among Frenchmen in being a republican and the possessor of a revolutionary cult of antiquity, it was by reason of that quality in which he was least unique—his love of wine and women, for he was not alone among Frenchmen in this respect. But, like most paradoxes, this one ignores more than half the truth. Though it recognizes the part his tastes played in inducing him to believe in the feasibility of a French republic, it ignores those other factors—the American instance, the logic of Rousseau, the invective of Cicero, the dream of Athens, and the view of present ills, personal and political, which contributed to the making of this republican.

But, while his early republicanism was for a long time unique, possibly during the succeeding months his attitude toward antiquity became typical. We may ask, therefore, whether in the persistence of his admiration, the dying-away of his regret, and in the request for general and specific imitation of antiquity he became a representative figure? We may inquire whether in these respects he was, during 1789–91, representative of the conservatives, of the liberals, of the radical republicans, or of the still more radical communists of 1790–91?

# CHAPTER VII

## CONSERVATIVES CONDEMN IMITATION
### (1789–90)

FROM 1789 to 1795 three legislatures met in France. The first, meeting from 1789 to 1791, drew up a constitution for France, and hence is known as the "Constituent Assembly." The second, meeting from 1791 to 1792, passed legislation under this constitution, and hence is known as the "Legislative Assembly." The third met from 1792 to 1795 to draw up a new constitution for France; accordingly, it has been called the "National Convention," or more simply the "Convention."

While these legislatures were in session, we may imagine for Paris a panorama of unceasing activity: legislators at their lodgings chatting with friends, conferring with allies, or at their desk preparing a speech or committee report; legislators in the assembly hall, reading or improvising a speech, interrupted perhaps by objections from the floor, by heckling from the gallery, or by applause; reporters in their alcove feverishly striving to keep up with the speaker, hurriedly preparing copy for the next edition; printers in their shop, setting in type the assembly news, fitting words, lines, and articles to a given space, and ever haunted by the pitiless approach of the deadline; and finally the readers, gullible, ignorant, and prejudiced, on the street, in the cafés, or at their homes, engrossed by the news.

In all this activity, interest in antiquity counted for something and came to count for more and more. Even during the Constituent, not a few orators and journalists were fond of drawing analogies between present policies and those that had been followed in antiquity. Not that such analogies could always be found. For this reason, no doubt, in the Constituent debates concerning ecclesiastical or financial programs, few classical allusions appear. But when a legal question arose, as, for example, "Should capital punishment be continued in France?" or when political or constitutional problems were posed, as, for example, "Should the king have the power to veto legislation, to appoint ministers and judges, and to declare war and conclude peace?" then some orator or pamphleteer was apt to observe: since such and such a policy had been followed in antiquity with beneficial (or harmful) results, it should be imitated (or avoided) now. Thus, in the debate on whether judges should be elected by the people, the foremost orator of the extreme conservatives, Cazalès, took the negative, and asked his colleagues, since their own experience was limited, to consult that of others. He said:

If history rises before us to uphold incontestable principles, by what strange temerity should we, legislators of a day, we, to whom, until this moment, every question of political science has been unknown, cast aside the lesson of experience? Do we not know that the past is the school of the present as well as of the future? . . . . If I were to describe to you the popular factions, the fatal effects of intrigues, and of the prestige of eloquence; if I were to name those who, like Socrates, Lycurgus, Aristides, and Solon, were immolated by the people; if I were to cite those illustrious victims of the errors and the violence of the people; if I were to remind you that Coriolanus was banished, that Camillus was exiled, that the Gracchi were sacrificed at the foot of the tribunal; if I were to tell you that the assemblies of the Roman people were merely conjurations; if I were to show you the public place transformed into a battlefield; if I were to tell you that there was not one election, not one law, not one judgment which did not entail a civil war, you would agree that there are some inconveniences in popular government. . . . . Perhaps this faithful picture of the disorders of a republic which earned the admiration of all nations, and which was the mistress of the universe, will doubtless produce some effect on your mind, or upon your heart. And do not think that this digression is irrelevant; every nation which holds elections will be subject to the same inconveniences.[1]

[1] *A.P.*, XV (May 7, 1790), 419.

To the modern American, unused to seeing his own legislators take historical precedents seriously, such allusions
might seem nothing more than bits of oratorical window-
dressing selected solely for their ability to move the listen-
er, and not necessarily because they represented the orator's conviction. No doubt this was the case with some
allusions, with those, for example, of l'Abbé Maury, who
was ever keen to make a speech in style. His classical tags
were usually rhetorical bric-a-brac:, casual, brief, and contradictory. He cried up antiquity when its examples supported his policy and cried it down when it did not. From
allusions like those of Maury how can one establish the
orator's view of the past.[2]

The allusions of Cazalès and of many others were not of
this nature. Some apparently expressed the real conviction
of the speaker. Unlike those of Maury, they were neither
casual, nor brief, nor contradictory. Indeed, in many
cases, when the scattered allusions of each orator are compared, it is seen that they agree and together form with each
man a plausible, consistent vision of antiquity. More particularly, in the case of Cazalès,[3] the same vision of antiquity which appears in the foregoing quotation from a
public oration when he was out to convince an audience
also appears eight months later in a more private conversa-

---

[2] *Ibid.*, IX (October 30, 1789), 610; XI (January 2, 1790), 64; XI (January 11,
1790), 154, 160; XV (May 5, 1790), 396; XV (May 18, 1790), 566, 567, 573; XVI
(June 19, 1790), 375, 377; XVII (July 9, 1790), 12; XVII (July 15, 1790), 90;
XVII (August 10, 1790), 698; XIX (September 28, 1790), 296; XIX (October 17,
1790), 676, 680; XX (November 20, 1790), 568; XXII (January 4, 1791), 15;
XXIV (March 22, 1791), 275; XXVI (May 24, 1791), 375, 378; XXVI (June 3,
1791), 728.

[3] In addition to the example of Cazalès, that of Mirabeau may be cited.
After using a glowing eulogy of the Athenian example to support a proposal to
register all youths when they reach twenty-one, Mirabeau, in his correspondence,
again refers with praise to "cette belle idée antique" as though his eulogy had
been sincere. See *Courrier de Provence*, IV, No. 40 (October 28-29, 1789), 33,
*Point du jour*, No. 119 (October 29, 1789), p. 477.

tion concerning a policy already settled upon—in circumstances, therefore, where insincerity arising from a desire to show off or to move an audience would be less likely to develop.[4] In addition many of the references were developed at length, filling a page of the debates, several pages in a newspaper, and sometimes chapters in a book. Many were refuted at length. And in not a few, as in the quotation from Cazalès, appeared that philosophy taught in the *collèges* and in the classics, a philosophy which said that history is a school where statesmen might gain wisdom. All this suggests that the orator, his opponent, and perhaps his listeners, took these allusions more seriously than mere fugitive figures of speech are usually taken.

In last analysis, why did orators like Cazalès refer to the examples of antiquity? Simply because the problems now facing French statesmen were more nearly analogous than formerly to problems ancient legislators had tried to solve. As a result, a number, conservatives and liberals alike, began to feel that the successful or unsuccessful solutions worked out by the classical peoples might teach wisdom. The problem then became: Should they ask Frenchmen to admire and imitate or to condemn and avoid the practices, social and political, of republican antiquity?

A study of the Constituent Assembly debates from mid-August, 1789, to June 20, 1791, reveals at once a tendency for parties to differ in their answer to this question. For that period, the speeches of Cazalès, Maury, Montlosier, and the Vicomte de Mirabeau have been taken as representative of the Extreme Right. The words of Mounier, Malouet, Clermont-Tonnerre, Lally Tollendal, Desèze,

---

[4] *L'ami du roi* (Royou), No. 239 (January 24, 1791), p. 3. On p. 4 of the January 28 issue of this newspaper, Cazalès protests against the publication of the details of a private conversation. The fact that he does not protest on the ground that the reported details were inaccurate suggests that they were correctly given.

and Virieux have been taken to represent the Right, or Anglophiles. The speeches of Bureaux de Pusy, Desmeuniers, Dupont de Nemours, Le Chapelier, Liancourt, Mirabeau, Rabaut, and Thouret have been studied for the sentiments of Right Center and of Left Center. The orations of Barnave, Barère, Brevet de Beaujour, Dinocheau, Dubois-Crancé, Duport, Gossin, Goupil de Préfeln, Gouy d'Arsy, Merlin, Mougins de Roquefort, and Rewbell have been examined for the attitudes of the Left; and those of Buzot, Robespierre, and Pétion for the Extreme Left.[5] From an analysis of the references to Greece and Rome appearing in these speeches the following generalizations may be made. Though the examples of antiquity possessed prestige, though they were something to conjure with, yet in the speeches of the two parties of the Right, the references requesting that the republican antiquity be condemned and avoided outnumbered those requesting admiration and imitation by nearly two to one. In the speeches of the Center, the reverse was true. In those of the Left and of the Extreme Left, the references requesting admiration and imitation outnumbered those asking condemnation and avoidance by four to one and three to one, respectively.

[5] Since, with the possible exception of the Anglophiles, no formal parties with well-defined party leadership, program, and discipline existed in this Assembly, and since no roll calls were taken, any attempt to determine party association is a bit hazardous. The foregoing division has been made after consulting certain biographical studies mentioned below; the party distribution given in the newspaper entitled the *Actes des apôtres;* the position of the leaders on the power of the king to veto legislation and declare war; the lists of members of the following clubs: le Club des impartiaux (Right), le Club des amis de la constitution monarchique (Right), la Société de 1789 (Center), le Club des feuillants (Center and Left), and the Jacobins. See *Actes des apôtres,* Nos. 166–67, pp. 39–45; A. Challamel, *Les Clubs contre-révolutionnaires* (Paris, 1895), pp. 92, 96, 99, 105–7, 151–58, 173, 217–23, 286–320, 337, 391, 400–417; R. Launay, *Barère de Vieuzac* (Paris, 1929), pp. 56–57, 66, 76, 78; C. Du Bus, *Clermont-Tonnerre* (Paris, 1931), pp. 103, 112–14, 328; Bougler, *Mouvement provincial en 1789,* I, 252–53; L. Cahen, *Condorcet* (Paris, 1904), p. 239.

To the legislators of the Right, both Extreme and Anglophile, may be added certain conservative editors: Durosy of the *Gazette de Paris;* Montjoie of the *Ami du roi;* Royou of a rival *Ami du roi;* and the editors of *Actes des apôtres.* In regard to antiquity, the attitudes of these journalists (except Royou) and of the above-mentioned legislators of the Right (except Maury and the younger Mirabeau) tended to be alike, just as in a general way their views of present policy tended to be similar. They all tended, furthermore, to believe that the experience of the classical past had something to teach. Some even retailed to their listeners the philosophy of history which held that history in general taught lessons.[6] Thus Mounier observed that, since the passions of men remain the same throughout the ages, "one is able to predict by what men have achieved in the past, what they could still achieve under the same circumstances; so that the past is always the best guide for the future."[7]

The radical Desmoulins also probably entertained this opinion concerning the use of history. But in nearly every other respect his views were the antithesis of those of the conservatives and moderates. He stood for government by the people, without a monarch. They wished for government by the wise and good—and hence, of course, by the few, for are the many ever wise or good? These men thought not. Having recently beheld a great beast of a populace unleashed in Paris, roaring its menace against those conservative suspects it could not reach while it lynched a few that it could, these conservative journalists and legislators

---

[6] *Gazette de Paris*, April 7, 1790, p. 1; June 11, 1791, p. 1; *A.P.*, XV (May 3, 1790), 379–80; XV (May 7, 1790), 419.

[7] J. J. Mounier, *Recherches sur les causes qui ont empêché les français de devenir libre* (Genève, 1792), I, 145; see also pp. 216–17.

distrusted the multitude and wished to grant the king large powers that he might hold it in check.

Desmoulins, furthermore, in July, 1789, insisted that the power which liberty had given the Athenians had been wielded to elect the wisest and best, to reward the talented and the virtuous, and to give festivals and a good time to all. More conservative Frenchmen, beginning in August, 1789, perhaps in reply to Camille, portrayed how the Athenians had used their power to elect the incapable and the corrupt, to penalize outstanding virtue by ostracism or death, and to bring misfortune and sorrow to Athens. With vehemence these conservatives enlarged upon the fitful fury, the folly, and the fickleness of an Athenian populace which willed, and then mourned, the death of Socrates; banished, and then recalled, Aristides the Just; and hearkened not unto Desmosthenes but to demagogues corrupted by the gold of Macedon.[8] Nor in the opinion of a number were the Romans, who banished Camillus and hearkened to the tribunes, much better than the Athenians.[9]

Using their knowledge of the Athenian past and of present passions to foretell the future, the conservatives predicted that similar evils would visit France if unrestricted power were given the populace. In addition a few used the division of Greece into warring commonwealths and the

[8] *A.P.*, VIII (August 12, 1789), 408; IX (September 21, 1789), 89; XI (February 23, 1790), 684; XV (May 7, 1790), 419; XV (May 18, 1790), 562; *Point du jour*, No. 306 (May 18, 1790), p. 88; *Gazette de Paris*, December 9, 1789, p. 1; March 12, 1790, p. 3; June 5, 1790, p. 1; June 6, 1790, p. 1; October 4, 1790, p. 3; November 30, 1791, p. 2; January 6, 1792, p. 2; *Actes des apôtres*, I, No. 36, 7; V, Introduction, 36–38; V, No. 130, 11; *Ami du roi*, No. 71 (August 10, 1790); *Ami du roi* (Montjoie), No. 117 (September 25, 1790), p. 479; No. 154 (November 11, 1790), p. 675; Mounier, *op. cit.*, II, 154–55, 187.

[9] *Ami du roi* (Royou), No. 239 (January 24, 1791), p. 3; *A.P.*, XV (May 7, 1790), 419; *Gazette de Paris*, April 3, 1790, p. 1; November 30, 1791, p. 2; *Ami du roi* (Montjoie), No. 126 (October 4, 1790), p. 513.

submission of Rome to a despot after the Roman Republic expanded and then fell to demonstrate the impossibility of a large republic in France. Extreme liberty or a republic, they predicted, would splinter France into warring fragments or bring a despotism.[10]

Supported by these predictions, a few, like Cazalès, fought the creation of elective offices. Others, like Mounier, advocated the separation of powers. All argued for granting the king extensive veto, war, and peace powers, and judicial authority to bridle the multitude. All were for shunning the more republican and democratic features of republican antiquity.[11]

In the golden age of Athenian liberty, it may be remarked, there was, as in every age, some gold and some alloy; and Plutarch's account, apparently the source of Desmoulins and probably that of the conservatives, depicted both. But while Desmoulins stressed exclusively the gold of this golden age, these other Frenchmen stressed the alloy, the hardness of humanity, for they also had a cult of antiquity, the cult of its seamy side. A later generation would have remarked that these conservatives were "debunking" history; would have said, somewhat flatteringly, that they were giving a realistic view, and would have noted that they had made the Athenians more "human," as if only those qualities that are hard are human. We may note that each—Desmoulins as well as the conservative—

[10] *A.P.*, XI (February 23, 1790), 684–85; XXVIII (July 13, 1791), 250; *Gazette de Paris*, June 5, 1790, p. 2; July 15, 1790, p. 1; May 20, 1791, p. 1; *Ami du roi* (Montjoie), No. 154 (June 3, 1791), p. 613; *Actes des apôtres*, V, Introduction, pp. 33–34; *Ami du roi*, No. 18 (June 18, 1790), p. 71; Mounier, *op. cit.*, II, 195–98.

[11] *A.P.*, VIII (August 12, 1789), 409, 410; VIII (August 31, 1789), 518; IX (September 21, 1789), 89; XI (February 20, 1790), 657; XI (February 23, 1790), 684–85; XV (May 7, 1790), 419; XV (May 17, 1790), 547; XV (May 18, 1790), 562; *Point du jour*, No. 306 (May 18, 1790), p. 88; *Gazette de Paris*, December 9, 1789, p. 1; *Ami du roi* (Royou), No. 239 (January 24, 1791), p. 3.

framed, as was natural, his vision of the past in accordance with his present hopes or fears and in harmony with his present principles. Each found, it may be guessed, his own hopes, fears, and principles strengthened by this vision of the Athenian past; and, to complete the circle, with his hopes and fears and principles thus strengthened, each, it may be surmised, held his conception of Athenian life all the more strongly.

# CHAPTER VIII

## LIBERALS CEASE TO REGRET AND SOME-
## TIMES TO ADMIRE (1789–90)

MONG the liberals, any tendency to regret antiquity was removed by the Revolution. By opening careers to the talents of all we have studied, and by enabling some to play in affairs of consequence the Roman or the Spartan, the Revolution removed for all that frustration of the desire for a career which had caused some to regret antiquity. Thus, while Marat, Desmoulins, and Brissot could now acquire notable reputations as journalists, and Robespierre could attain eminence as deputy to the Constituent, Mme Roland could write for the press and (through her husband) make a stir in local politics. At the same time, Robespierre could think of himself and of his colleagues as imitating Lycurgus when they abdicated their power after drafting a constitution; Brissot could consider himself a sternly independent Cato, sparing no guilty one in his denunciations;[1] while Marat, because he had perhaps stopped a royalist detachment from crossing a Parisian bridge, could compare himself to Horatius Cocles blocking Porsenna's vast array.[2] These men could now enjoy, to a fuller measure than before, the thrill of heightened self-esteem which comes with the discovery by imagination or the creation by imitation of some analogy between ourselves and the ancient great.

Nor were such careers limited to mature men. Striplings

[1] Brissot, *Le patriote français*, No. 475 (November 26, 1790), p. 3; No. 482 (December 3, 1790), pp. 2–3.

[2] Brissot, *Mémoires*, I, 206.

like Saint-Just, the famous Terrorist-to-be, could also act the Roman. By so acting, Saint-Just revealed one feature of his mature interest in antiquity, which, like that of Brissot, Mme Roland, and of Robespierre, developed in his early twenties. Like some of these others, Saint-Just, conscious of his abilities and consumed by ambition, dreamed of a career open to his talents, was eager to play the Lycurgus or the Brutus when he should become of age, and fumed at his youth, which prevented him from achieving a legislative career at once.[3] But his experience also indicates how this mature interest could be transformed by the Revolution. Unlike the others, he did not curse the century and the country of his birth, or weep that he had not been born a Greek or a Roman, for within a limited sphere the Revolution already offered the opportunity to carve out a career as a local politician, to mimic Tarquin, and to play the Scaevola. Thus, when the count of Laraguais was "not at home" to receive him and some accompanying peasants, Saint-Just boasted to Desmoulins that "I acted like Tarquin . . . . , cut the head of a fern which happened to be near me . . . . and without saying a word turned about."[4] Shortly after, in May, 1790, at the public burning in his native town of some counter-revolutionary pamphlets, "Saint-Just [so run the minutes of the meeting], his hand over the libelous fire, pronounced the oath to die for his fatherland and for the National Assembly and to perish

[3] C. Vellay, "Lettres inédites de Saint-Just," *Revue historique de la Révolution française*, I (1910), 481, 484–87; see also Saint-Just to Daubigny, July 20, 1792, Saint-Just, *Œuvres*, I, 349.

[4] *Œuvres*, I, 221. The act of Tarquin to which Saint-Just referred was the following: According to Livy, when Tarquin's son Sextus had gained the confidence of the Gabians, enemies of Rome, Sextus sent a courier to his father to ask what he should do. To the courier, Tarquin gave no verbal answer, but, walking in the garden of the palace, struck off the heads of the tallest poppies with his staff. Upon being told by the messenger what Tarquin had done, Sextus, taking the hint, put to death the most eminent Gabians. See Livy i 54.

rather than forget his oath. These words brought tears to the eyes of all."[5]

But regret for antiquity, however, had included regret, not only

1. For classical careers, but also
2. For classical institutions because
    a) They were admired;
    b) French institutions were disliked; and because
    c) The future held no hope for radical improvement of French institutions since
        (1) The existing order seemed so stable and since
        (2) Men thought republican liberty would not endure in France inasmuch as
            (a) France was too large (had not the Roman Republic fallen when Rome grew large?) and
            (b) Frenchmen were luxury-loving and depraved (and without the simple life, private virtue was, of course, nonexistent; while without private virtue, public virtue—love of country, liberty, and of equality—could not endure [had not Athenian, Spartan, and Roman liberty declined when liking for the simple, non-luxury-loving life decayed?].

Not every liberal we studied held all these ideas. Yet before 1789 every liberal in question harbored a sufficient number to induce him to admire and to regret the past. After 1789 the Revolution, it is true, did not sweep from men's minds all these conceptions. Yet in time it swept away a sufficient number for liberals to cease to regret, and sometimes to admire, antiquity. But, just as before the Revolution, liberals differed in the number of these ideas which they cherished, so, during the Revolution, they differed in the number which they abandoned and in the rapidity with which they shed them. Liberals differed in the persistence with which they clung to the old probably because of the differing immobility of their minds, the

[5] Quoted in Nover, *Saint-Just* (an unpublished thesis at Cornell University), p. 14.

sometimes dissimilar interpretation they put on the Revolution, and the diverse ways that the Revolution affected them.

No one equaled Desmoulins in the number of conceptions abandoned and in the speed with which they were shed. The Revolution was scarcely under way when he dropped whatever beliefs he may have held concerning the stability of the existing order, the unsuitability of a republic in a large country, and the unfitness of Frenchmen for liberty. A year passed, and he was assuming, as we have seen, that a love of luxury did not mean a low private virtue. In addition he was proclaiming that a simple life and private virtue were not essential to maintain public virtue, thriving liberty, or a prosperous republic. Not content with these changes, he altered the customary interpretation of classical history. He denied that Spartan liberty endured because of the simple virtuous life of the Spartans, and refused to believe that Athenian liberty fell because Athenians loved luxury. Of the old eighteenth-century complex he retained only his admiration for republican antiquity. Admiration, however, no longer fed a defeatist resignation but swelled a new hopefulness. Admiration, when coupled with a persuasion that imitation of antiquity was possible, now helped him to believe that the glorious vision which he had once regretted would now be realized, and that all the ills that have ever afflicted mankind would disappear from France.

Farthest removed from Desmoulins stood a very few liberals, still believing that to copy classical institutions would be futile and dangerous. Thus, when the question arose: "Who should prosecute criminals?" Brevet de Beaujour, deputy to the Constituent, reasoned that Frenchmen—alas!—were so depraved that the Roman practice of leaving the prosecution to any citizen who cared could not be revived in France. Cowardly, self-seeking, and careless of the public interest, Frenchmen would never overcome their fear or their indifference to prosecute influential or audacious criminals.[6]

Marat, too, clung to the notion that Frenchmen were vile and vicious. For this reason he was prone to despair of any durable resurrection of liberty such as it had once existed in antiquity.[7] Since, furthermore, he still admired antiquity and did not believe that the Constituent was drafting a free constitution, he was usually still possessed by those three emotional states—dissatisfaction with the present, lack of hope for the future, admiration of past—which before 1789 had been the ground or regret for antiquity.[8]

The youthful Saint-Just, too, at this time clung to the notions, though not to the sentiments, of the old régime. In his work, the *Esprit de la constitution*, he tended, indeed, to relate so many of the political practices of the republics of antiquity (their republican government, their severe legislation, their ardent morality) to their small area that he made it logically impossible for him to contend that France, large of size, should imitate much of what he admired in antiquity.[9] At the same time he supposed that the equality of wealth and the communistic life obtaining in Sparta were related to its poverty, while some of its educational institutions (like public gymnastics) were

[6] *A.P.*, XVII (August 9, 1790), 665–66.

[7] Marat, *L'ami du peuple*, No. 9 (September 18, 1789), p. 84; No. 81 (December 29, 1789), p. 7; No. 91 (January 8, 1790), pp. 3–5; No. 427 (April 12, 1791), p. 6.

[8] Even Marat, however, occasionally manifested a new spirit, as his continuing gloom was shot with gleams of hope. Then he would look forward to the return of the fine days of Athens and of Rome. See *ibid.*, No. 96 (January 13, 1790), p. 2; No. 284 (November 18, 1790), p. 8; also *Plan de la législation criminelle*, p. 84, n. 1.

[9] Saint-Just, "Esprit de la constitution," *Œuvres*, I, 263–65.

adapted to its virtue. As a result he could not propose, he
felt, that France, wealthy and depraved, should copy
either the equality of wealth or the gymnastics he admired.[10]

Yet this conclusion that the institutions of antiquity
must be ignored did not occasion any great distress of
spirit. The reason is simple: Unlike Marat, he was neither
dissatisfied with the present nor without hope for the future. He felt that the new French constitution was, on the
whole, a satisfactory way to organize a liberal government.
He was confident, furthermore, that liberty thus organized
would in twenty years make a new, more moral man of the
old depraved Frenchman.[11]

At this time, however, from the opening of the Revolution until the flight of the king, neither Brevet, Marat, nor
Saint-Just in their attitudes toward antiquity were typical
Frenchmen. If we ignore a casual aside apiece by the deputy De Wimpfen[12] and by the editors of the *Courrier de
Provence*,[13] then it may be said that Marat was the only
important journalist, and Brevet was the only deputy, to
signify both admiration and regret. And if we except a
casual remark each by Brissot and Marat,[14] the only prominent Frenchman to manifest the disposition to admire and
yet to ignore the institutions of republican antiquity was
Saint-Just.

For, unlike the latter, most liberals did not now believe
that France's size or immorality should prevent it from
copying certain specific classical institutions. Indeed, in

---

[10] *Ibid.*, pp. 266, 287.

[11] *Ibid.*, pp. 263–65, 269, 271, 283, 291, 325.

[12] *A.P.*, XI (December 31, 1789), 54.

[13] *Courrier de Provence*, No. 52, p. 368.

[14] Marat, *Supplément de l'Offrande à la patrie* (au Temple de la liberté, 1789),
pp. 18–20; Brissot, *Le patriote française*, No. 75 (October 21, 1789), p. 2.

the opinion of some deputies on the Left and Extreme Left, and of the journalists Gorsas, Loustalot, Desmoulins, and, sometimes Brissot, France could and should imitate the classical commonwealths in their provision for such various reforms as a brief office-tenure; a referendum; rapid voting; no property qualification required of voters; a citizen army; the election of army officers and ambassadors by the people; the deciding on war and peace by the people's representatives; and the opening of the practice of law to all, trained or untrained.[15]

But as indications of any positive influence exerted by the classical past, let us not take these requests for imitation too seriously. Save for one or two, all read as if the author either thought: "How can I improve this speech by a brief classical tag?" or reasoned: "What classical example will help win my listeners to my excellent proposal for a specific extension of democracy?" Only in one instance— Mougin's motion to pattern the French jury system after the Roman and not the English model—can we be sure that the orator thought: "That was a good institution in antiquity, let's duplicate it in France." Even in this case, the past example, though it stirred up some debate, exerted no lasting influence, since Mougin's motion failed.[16] Most liberals, therefore, at this time requested imitation of classical institutions simply because it was easy for democrats to find rhetorical support for democratic proposals in a democratic past. In so far, however, as these rhetorical

[15] See, for example: *A.P.*, XV (May 17, 1790), 540; XV (May 25, 1790), 670; XX (November 9, 1790), 337; XXI (December 14, 1790), 467; XXIV (April 6, 1791), 610; Gorsas, *Courrier*, III (September 4, 1789), 53; XXI (February 18, 1791), 275, n. 1; *Révolutions de Paris*, No. 11 (September 19, 1789), pp. 4, 11; No. 57 (August 7, 1790), p. 219; No. 68 (October 23, 1790), p. 77; No. 72 (November 20, 1790), p. 337; No. 75 (December 11, 1790), p. 514; *Point du jour*, No. 95 (October 1, 1789), p. 167.

[16] *A.P.*, XII (April, 1790), 547; XV (April 20, 1790), 327; XXI (December 21, 1790), 682.

references represented the sincere conviction of the speaker, they suggest that the typical liberal admirer of antiquity now was hopeful that imitation of many radical classical institutions was possible and perhaps imminent. Accordingly, he had little reason to regret the institutions of antiquity.

A last tinge of regret caused by a persuasion that a republic was impossible in France nevertheless may have lingered. Only with Desmoulins, whom we have discussed, and with Brissot can we be sure that this last cause of regret was extinguished. Brissot, moreover, had a double reason for not regretting antiquity. He had some hope that eventually in France a republic would be possible;[17] and he had long ago ceased to admire antiquity.[18] It was the American Revolution (it may be recalled) which, by bringing forth a superior constitution, had taught him to disdain the seemingly inferior governmental organization of too democratic Athens and too aristocratic Rome. What the American Revolution did for Brissot, the French Revolution did for others. By creating, or giving high promise of creating, a people and a constitution that seemed superior to classical peoples and to classical constitutions, the French Revolution taught not a few that regenerated Frenchmen need no longer admire republican antiquity.

Desmoulins, for example, about the end of May, 1790, praised the fine moderation displayed by Frenchmen during the Revolution. It proved, he said, that they would never be so cruel as the Athenians and Romans. For let us say this for Frenchmen, he continued:

[17] *Le patriote français*, No. 412 (September 24, 1790), p. 2; No. 439 (October, 21, 1790), p. 4.

[18] *Ibid.*, No. 74 (October 20, 1789), p. 2; No. 301 (June 5, 1790), p. 4; No. 634 (May 4, 1791), p. 484.

All these peoples did not equal the Frenchmen of this century, at least the contemporary Frenchmen, the authors of this revolution. No, history presents nothing so honorable to any people as this mass of testimony offered by our revolution.[19]

Thus, just as early revolutionary events had taught Desmoulins that the Frenchman was the equal of the ancients and hence could imitate them, so now the progress of the Revolution taught him that Frenchmen were superiors of the ancients and hence could look down upon them. Desmoulins had come a long way since the time he had regretted that he "had not been born a Greek or a Roman."

In this respect his experience was not unique. Shortly, after, in that ecstasy of exhilaration which accompanied the celebration of the "Federation" of July 14, 1790, Mme Roland, who also had lamented that she had not been born a Spartan or a Roman, now exclaimed:

I remember with tenderness those moments of my youth when, nourishing my spirit, in silence and seclusion, with the study of ancient history, I wept for spite at not having been born a Spartan or a Roman. I no longer have any cause to envy the ancient republics: we are being enlightened by a purer day, philosophy has extended the knowledge of the rights and duties of man, and we shall be citizens without being the enemies of the unfortunates who do not partake of the benefits of our country.[20]

At this time, Mme Roland and Desmoulins were not alone in believing that what Frenchmen were accomplishing eclipsed what the ancients had achieved. During the first year and a quarter of the Revolution, when liberals were still rich in hope and not yet disillusioned by disappointment, the pamphleteers Condorcet and Manuel, the legislators Rabaut de Saint-Etienne, Sieyes, and Barère, and the editorial writers Garat of the *Journal de Paris*, Loustalot of the *Révolutions de Paris*, Barère of the *Point du jour*, and those of the *Courrier de Provence* occasionally

[19] *Révolutions de France*, No. 28, p. 203.
[20] *Lettres*, II, 107–8, July 18, 1790.

ranked the political achievements of their countrymen above those of the ancients.[21] Broadly speaking, all of these individuals, including Desmoulins and Mme Roland, were liberals, not conservatives. This was natural, for only liberals found the political accomplishment of the day admirable. Only they, therefore, could draw from these reforms a belief that French political achievements were superior to those of antiquity.

Too much, however, must not be made of the occasional, casual remarks of these men. With most, they are an expression not of permanent, fundamental attitudes but of a transient, surface sentiment. Probably only with Condorcet, Sieyes, and Barère are they traces of a carefully considered point of view. Only with respect to the first two are they traces of a philosophy by whose precepts they acted. But with these two, and especially with Condorcet, so ingrained was this tendency to rank antiquity low, so important did it become in coloring their intellectual make-up, that it constituted in these French disdainfuls a veritable superiority complex.

With Mme Roland and Desmoulins the transient feeling of superiority had grown out of the events of the French Revolution. With Condorcet this was not so. Even before 1789 as we have seen, he believed that in the Battle of the Ancients and the Moderns, the latter had won on nearly all fronts. Only in the field of politics, and then only before 1776, did he put in a good word for the ancients. In 1776, however, the Revolution in America taught him how, even in this field, some moderns surpassed the ancients. The

---

[21] Desmoulins, *Révolutions de France*, No. 30, p. 287; *A.P.*, X (November 12, 1789), 38; "Discours préliminaire," pp. i–iv of *Point du jour*, No. 103 (October 10, 1789), p. 267, No. 259 (April 1, 1790), p. 268; *Courrier de Provence*, No. 19 (September 5–7, 1789), p. 416, No. 76, pp. 364–65; No. 211 (December 15–17, 1790), p. 57; *Révolutions de Paris*, No. 27 (January 9–15, 1790), pp. 34–35; *Journal de Paris*, No. 239 (August 27, 1789), p. 1077.

events of the first revolutionary year in France confirmed
what the American example had taught. In a spirit of arro-
gant condescension Condorcet now seemed to say that no
doubt, considering their century, the ancients had done
fairly well. But really they had no true notions of natural
liberty, equality, or the rights of man. Their vaunted love
of liberty was not a "generous passion for independence
and equality but a fever of ambition and pride"; liberty itself they made to consist solely in having no king or no
overpowerful senate; equality existed at best only among
citizens, while many were enslaved; and the governments
were dominated by an aristocratic spirit and by the rich
who ignored the rights of the ignorant poor. When society
was just being born, when only prejudice and error could
exist, and when no printing press diffused among the common people the few suspected truths, much of this error
was, of course, excusable. But what have we who have no
slaves other than the printing press, who have advanced so
much farther along the path of truth, and who have diffused that truth among the many to learn from barbarous
and ignorant antiquity?[22] He did not share Desmoulins'
opinion that antiquity was a Heavenly City to admire and
to imitate. On the contrary, he requested his contemporaries coldly to disdain and to ignore the institutions of republican antiquity.

It may be guessed that by 1790 Condorcet's faith in
progress and his general scorn for the ancients determined
that he should disdain and ignore the political institutions
of republican antiquity, while his liberalism told him which
of these institutions he should ignore and disdain. Conceivably, had he not been the high priest of the cult of

[22] Condorcet, "Eloge de Franklin," Œuvres, III, 372, 374, 382–83, 402–3;
"Sur l'instruction publique," ibid., VII, 197–98, 202–3, 268–69, 278–79, 374–75,
417–18, 444; Journal de la société de 1789, Prospectus (June 5, 1790), pp. 2–3;
No. 10 (August 7, 1790), p. 2.

progress, he would (like other liberals) have found something to admire in this distant past. Conceivably, had he been a conservative he might have disdained not government by the few but a government too weak to check the multitude. In a sense his attitude (and that of others who came to share it) was the liberal counterpart of the conservative tendency to condemn and to avoid the institutions of republican antiquity. But while the conservatives condemned classical liberty because it *was* liberty, though it might be equal to any France could produce, Condorcet condemned classical liberty because it was inferior to the modern product, though it might have been the best possible for that time. The views of both the conservative and Condorcet were representative of two current attitudes that at times became so prominent and so prevalent that much of the remaining history of the cult of antiquity could be written in terms of how the tendency to admire and imitate fought for adherents against these two other tendencies to condemn and avoid and to disdain and ignore.

In his negative tendency not to regret antiquity, Condorcet was typical of that larger drift of French radical opinion which set in as a consequence of the Revolution. By opening careers to those who thought they had talent, by furnishing them the opportunity to play the Roman on the public stage, and by enabling them to participate in a glorious endeavor to realize ideals that seemed worth while, this Revolution had given success and significance to the activity of most radical reformers, reconciled them to their status and to their life in the present, and extinguished in them any personal reasons for grieving that they had not been born in a distant past. In a somewhat similar fashion, by initiating along democratic lines a radical alteration of the *ancien régime*, the events of the first revolutionary year reconciled most radicals to the government under which they lived, and removed, in all but a few, any reason to regret the institutions of antiquity. Not that radicals were entirely satisfied with the new order which the Constituent Assembly was creating. On the contrary, many a reformer thought the liberty already achieved to be incomplete and imperfect. But the shortcomings of reform seldom aroused keen discontent, for the speedy conquest of even this imperfect liberty encouraged men to hope that even more liberty, and hence a happier world, could soon be secured. To a certain extent, therefore, satisfaction with the present and extinction of regret for the past proceeded from this hope that the dawn of liberty really meant the coming of a better day.

So firmly did reformers believe in the imminence of a millennium that they did not allow the spectacle of the unhappy tumult, which (according to the conservatives) accompanied classical liberty, to moderate their vast expectation. In a general way this was in contrast with the pre-Revolution tendency to allow the examples of the classical republics to dim any hope that radical reform could bring permanent good to France. But, if the classical examples no longer diminished, they did not, as yet, augment human expectation. Only with Desmoulins did they help to swell a new hopefulness, for only he believed that imitation of classical republics on an extensive scale and in their most republican features was on the way. This belief was not shared, however, by Saint-Just, who deemed such imitation to be impracticable in France; or by Brissot and Condorcet and the like, who thought such a resurrection undesirable; or by those many liberals who probably believed that at best only the duplication of a few scattered classical institutions was feasible, worth while, and perhaps imminent. In any case, since not one, save Desmoulins, believed that imitation of the classical republics was impending, the vision men had of these commonwealths was unrelated to any hope that the millennium was rapidly drawing nigh. Indeed, it may be said, that arousing, as it did, regret in only a few and hope in but one, the image of the classical institutions momentarily seemed unrelated, on the whole, to the revolutionary spirit and activities of men.

# CHAPTER IX

## THE REPUBLICAN MOVEMENT

FOR over a year Demoulins stood alone in openly avowing a desire to see France a republic. But in time he was joined by others: in September, 1790, by Lavicomterie, a man of letters, afterward a deputy from Paris to the Convention, and whose second republican book, *Crimes des rois de France* (1791), made a sensation; and in October, 1790, by the Roberts, husband and wife, who praised Lavicomterie's first republican work, struck up a friendship with him, and made their newspaper, the *Mercure national*, a republican sheet. Then, in June, 1791, after the king had fled from Paris, only to be stopped at the frontier, a number of others, hoping that Parisian exasperation with the monarch might be directed against the monarchy, came out for the republic. Among these were Brissot, Condorcet, the American enthusiast Achille du Châtelet, the editors of the *Révolutions de Paris*, and Billaud-Varenne, an indefatigable pamphleteer who eventually rose, in 1793–94, to be one of the leaders of the Terror. Finally, during August and September, 1792, after the king had been suspended from office for blocking effective defense against the invading Prussians and Austrians, many others became republicans. Among them were the three obscure, unimportant pamphleteers of the second republican movement—Lefevre, Dumouchet, and Psaume. Whatever may have been the pre-Revolution convictions of these men, each one now believed that a republic was possible in France. Since this was so, republican antiquity could now become, in the minds of these men, what it had

already become in the mind of Desmoulins—a Heavenly
City which they wished to see realized on earth. Accordingly, we may first ask whether antiquity did indeed play
such a rôle. We may also inquire whether, in their endeav-
or to believe and to make others believe that a republic
would be most excellent for France, these republicans
found the classical examples a help or a hindrance, a stimulus or a stumbling-block.

During the summer of 1791, when the king's flight had
made the republican controversy acute, the republicans
were opposed not only by the old conservative groups,
represented by men like Cazalès and Malouet, but also by
the old Center and the Liberal Left, led by the Lameths
and Barnave, who thought that the Revolution had gone
far enough and who feared that the abolition of the monarchy would mean the abolition of the suffrage privileges
of the middle classes. Anxious, therefore, to use all possible
means to discredit the republicans and the democrats, these
liberals who had turned conservative sometimes drew on
classical history for their arguments. By most republican
publicists of note, except Robert and Achille du Châtelet,
these arguments were soon answered—sometimes answered, indeed, before they were presented. For, since the
typical conservative merely rehashed the antirepublican
objections of the eighteenth century, republicans had already felt it necessary to combat such views.

On the one side of the controversy, the conservatives
held up republican antiquity as an example to condemn
and avoid; enlarged upon the mischief wrought in classical
commonwealths by the blind and impetuous multitude;
and dwelt on the anarchy and civil conflict that had dis-
turbed these republics. They found the causes of this tumult and confusion, unhappiness and mischief, in the republican and democratic institutions of antiquity, in the

two facts that the multitude was unchecked by a king and deliberated not through representatives but in large public gatherings.[1] They then predicted that similar tumult would prevail in France if French republicans abolished the monarchy and established universal suffrage and a democratic referendum on the constitution and on all legislation. Most conservatives, however, stressed not the troubles agitating these republics when they were small, poor, and virtuous. Most emphasized the fact that when the Roman Republic expanded and grew large and powerful, rich and corrupt, civil war and the fall of the Republic ensued.[2] What had happened in Rome would, conservatives warned, happen in large and wealthy France if a republic were established there.[3] French national unity would be threatened; civil war between ambitious leaders, unchecked, as they were, by a king, would break out; a despotism would eventually be established; persons and possessions would be insecure; and liberty—that is, security of life and of property—would be at an end. The Roman instance thus helped conservative publicists to con-

[1] *Postillon par Calais*, No. 570, pp. 5-6; *ibid.*, "Observations," July 22, 1791, pp. 1-4; *ibid.*, July 29, 1791, pp. 1-4; Drouet, *Voilà ce qu'il faut faire du roi* (Chez Guilhemat), p. 24; Anonyme, *Le roi traité comme il le mérite* (Paris), pp. 2-3; *A.P.*, XXVIII (July 13, 1791), 250.

[2] "Observations," *Postillon par Calais*, June 27, 1791, pp. 1-3; June 29, 1791, pp. 1-2; June 30, 1791, pp. 3-4; July 5, 1791, pp. 1-4; *L'ami des patriotes*, No. 31 (June 25, 1791), p. 423, n. 1; *A.P.*, XXVIII (July 13, 1791), 250; Anonyme, *Discours prononcé aux Jacobins sur la question suivante: Que faut-il faire dans les circonstances actuelles*, pp. 3-4.

[3] Quite a few conservatives referred to the familiar argument that France was too large for a republic, but without referring to the Roman example on which this argument, in the minds of most, was based. See: Anonyme, *Opinion d'un ami de la constitution sur l'enlèvement du roi* (1791), p. 2; Anonyme, *Avis aux Français par un patriote raisonnable* (n.d.), p. 2; Coué-Lanne, *Adresse aux Français* (n.d.), p. 2; Anonyme, *Réflexions sur la situation critique du roi, de l'Assemblée nationale, et de la France* (Paris, 1791), p. 31; Anonyme, *Avis aux amis de la constitution* (n.d.), pp. 2-3; Anonyme, *Nous ne mordrons point à une grappe empoisonnée* (n.d.), pp. 3-4; also see Barnave, *Œuvres*, II, 45, 380.

jure up a bugaboo well calculated to frighten any well-to-do bourgeois into the arms of the king.

In reply, a few republicans made bold to turn the Roman instance to the profit of their own republican cause. Lavicomterie, for example, before the king's flight, like Condorcet and Carra after that event, observed that before the Roman Republic fell it ruled, and ruled gloriously, for centuries over a territory as large as, and sometimes larger than, France.[4] Why couldn't Frenchmen do what the Romans had done?

Most republicans, however, did not find in antiquity a reassuring example. Most were still held in thrall by the conservative picture of the classical past. They still believed that the classical republics had been something of a failure. They still accepted as fact that tumults and injustices had repeatedly disfigured the story of republican antiquity, and that after it grew large the Roman Republic fell. Such stubborn facts (as stubborn, that is, as any historical fact can be) were difficult to bend to a conformity with a belief that a republic was just the thing for large, populous France. Perhaps for this reason, more than one republican seemed to feel the classical past to be an embarrassing presence of which he would like to be rid. But to rid himself of his embarrassment, to explain away past failures, and to refute the lessons these failures apparently taught, whither could be turn? To authority? But authority (that is, Montesquieu, Rousseau, Mably, and Voltaire) said that a republican form of government was adapted only to countries small in size. To example? But the examples of Switzerland, Holland, and the Renaissance republics of Italy only confirmed what classical history taught; while the American republic, as conservatives ob-

---

[4] *Le Républicain*, No. 4, p. 75; Carra, "A ses concitoyens de tous les départements," *A.P.*, LXXV (October 3, 1793), 595–96; Lavicomterie, *Du peuple et des rois*, pp. 17–18.

served, was too young to demonstrate that a large republic could endure for long without tumult.

As a result, one or two republicans, put to it to answer the conservatives, fell back on the argument that, after all, the tumult and injustices in republican antiquity hadn't been so bad; that they might have been worse; that they would have been worse under a monarchy.[5] Other writers prepared a more convincing argument. Yes, these latter conceded, there had been in republican antiquity tumults and injustices and a fall of the Roman Republic. Such disorder and disintegration, however, had arisen not from the absence of a monarchy but from the presence of other defects. With an occasional tinge of critical disdain, publicists like Brissot, Pétion, Condorcet, and Psaume (1792) explained that the disorder and the injustice to the wisest and best had arisen from the direct democracy of antiquity, from the division of the ancients into privileged and unprivileged, into conquering city and subject people, and from the nonexistence of periodical amending conventions which peacefully adapt constitutions to changing conditions.[6] Likewise, Lavicomterie, Billaud-Varenne, and Lefevre (1792) explained that the eventual downfall of the Roman Republic had also been caused by defects in governmental organization: the selection of magistrates from a privileged class; the framing of legislation not in accord with the eternal verities; the failure to make the law supreme over all who exercised the executive power; the failure to have a national guard strong enough to quell

---

[5] Billaud-Varenne, *L'Acéphocratie, ou le gouvernement fédératif* (Paris, 1791), pp. 47–49.

[6] *Le patriote français*, No. 696 (July 5, 1791), p. 19; No. 699 (July 9, 1791), p. 36; No. 707 (July 17, 1791), p. 72; *A.P.*, XXVIII (July 14, 1791), 273; XXX (August 29, 1791), 54; Condorcet, "De la république," *Œuvres*, XII, 233–34; Condorcet, "Discours sur les Conventions nationales," *ibid.*, X, 209; Psaume, *Réponse aux objections des monarchistes* (Paris, 1792), pp. 16, 20–22; Aulard, *La Société des Jacobins*, II, 609.

Caesar's rebellion; and in general the tendency to establish
the dominion of their government not on right but on
might, on conquest.[7] But, said the republicans, our French
republic will have the latest, most modern improvements—
representative government, equality between all citizens,
and periodical conventions to amend the constitution. The
insecurity of life and possessions which obtained in antiquity will not, therefore, obtain in France. Since, furthermore, not one of the defects which appeared in Rome
will appear in our matchless constitution, drafted by intelligent Frenchmen enlightened by a century of true
philosophy, why should any thinking person believe that a
French republic will fall as the Roman Republic fell? Some
non-thinking individuals have, it is true, laid the fall of
Rome's liberty in part to increasing depravity; have then
decided that depravity and a lasting republican liberty are
incompatible; have noticed that Frenchmen are still, to a
certain extent, depraved; and have finally concluded
against a French republic. But, said Lavicomterie, Billaud-Varenne, Carra, and Brissot, while we agree to the
reasoning, we combat the conclusion. We maintain that
the liberty already secured or to be acquired will so regenerate Frenchmen that a republic will endure.[8]

All this logic, of course, made a brave showing when it
was spread over pages in a pamphlet or chapters in a book.
But in last analysis, logic, as so often happens, was largely
based on a shifting emotion, in this case on hope—hope
that Frenchmen would cease to be depraved; hope that the
republic of France would not relive the disorders of that of

[7] F. N. Lefevre, *Ce que doit faire la Convention nationale* (Paris, 1792), pp. 16–
17; Lavicomterie, *op. cit.*, pp. 17, 31–33; Billaud-Varenne, *op. cit.*, pp. 66–67.
The Roberts, husband and wife, likewise found the Roman governmental organization defective. See *Mercure nationale*, seconde année, No. IV (January 14,
1791), p. 226 (incorrectly numbered; this should be p. 126).

[8] Carra, *op. cit.*, pp. 595–96; *Le patriote française*, No. 739 (August 18, 1791)
p. 204; Lavicomterie, *op. cit.*, p. 95; Billaud-Varenne, *op. cit.*, pp. 44, 71–72.

Rome; hope, in brief, that a republic was both possible and desirable for France. Yet its being founded upon this emotion was the very strength of this reasoning. It would naturally appeal to great numbers of Frenchmen to whom recent revolutionary achievement had given greater hope for the future, as well as greater disdain for the past. It is somewhat curious to note, however, that the more this logic was developed, the more impossible it became to use past examples to strengthen the slender foundation of hope on which it was based. Logic demanded a search for flaws in classical institutions. And in this search the republicans were eminently successful. As a result they strengthened their argument that such disorder and disintegration would not recur in France, whose government would not possess these defects. But they also destroyed their opportunity to use republican antiquity as a glorious flawless vision capable of inclining the hopes and hearts of men toward a republic. What they gained in logic, therefore, they lost in emotional appeal. It is true that, if their interpretation were accepted, the classical past could no longer serve as a conservative bugaboo arousing needless fear. But neither could it be a Heavenly City fitted to sustain legitimate expectation. Nor could it become a model suggesting concretely how hope for a better world could be fulfilled by specific imitation of the institutions of antiquity. This was true because the pressure of controversy forced republicans first to underline the shortcomings of these institutions and then to say, "We don't want a republic after a classical model; we plan to set up something different which will endure without tumult because it will be different." Under these circumstances it was difficult for any republican who still accepted the conservative opinion that classical republics had been a failure logically to set up antiquity as a pattern of excellence to imitate.

Not all republicans, however, accepted the conservative opinion; and of those who did, one or two turned and twisted their thought until it escaped the conclusion which the controversy apparently forced upon it. Lavicomterie, for example, could not deny that the Roman liberty had fallen after the Roman domain was extended. He attributed this fall, therefore, to the hodgepodge character of Roman legislation, inspired not by the eternal verities but by the expediency of the moment. Yet, when he perceived that prospects for abolition of the French monarchy were still unpromising, he proposed for France what confessedly amounted to a similar hodgepodge, inspired by expediency and Rousseau. What is more, his proposal, elaborated through two long chapters, provided for the duplication (with, it is true, slight improvements taken from Rousseau) of the Roman tribunate and of the Roman censors, the tribunes, by their absolute veto, to check any act of the executive or of the legislature to enlarge their powers, and the censors, by their public blame of immoral acts, to maintain a pure morality. He justified the setting-up of institutions he recognized to be defective by copying (without credit) Rousseau's defense of the tribunate.[9] He also added that, though such institutions had not prevented the ultimate fall of Roman liberty and morals, yet they had delayed that fall and might perform a similar service for France.[10]

Billaud-Varenne, convinced that "all immoderate power is an absorbent caustic," had also ascribed the fall of the Roman Republic to structural flaws which allowed chiefs of the government (like Caesar) to become stronger than

[9] Rousseau, *Contrat social*, Livre IV, chap. v, first lines; Lavicomterie, *op. cit.*, p. 78, Lavicomterie's copy reads: "Puisqu' on ne peut établir une exacte proportion entre les parties constitutives de l'état, puisque des causes rebelles en altèrent sans cesse les rapports," the tribunate is needed.

[10] Lavicomterie, *op. cit.*, pp. 78, 80–85, 87, 91, 94–95, 97, 100.

the government itself. Yet, in another section of his work, he denies that the Republic fell because of constitutional defects. Indeed, he there praises its constitution for successfully preventing the concentration of power in the hands of the few. He there finds the secret of its success in the lack of a central unifying authority and in the diffusion of power among a large senate, two consuls, and two tribunes. A similar successful diffusion in Sparta, in all the republics of Greece, and in Carthage, as in Rome, demonstrates, he adds, that such division of power should be revived in France. In the detailed working-out of his proposal, however, he eschewed servile imitation of any classical model. He would divide legislative power between a central legislature, which would propose laws, and the departmental administration bodies, which would then pass upon them; and he would distribute executive power among the districts, the municipalities, and the courts. There are those, he observes, who will object that such a government is impossible in a large empire. But, he counters, "antiquity furnishes two examples which prove that even for a warlike nation this objection is without foundation." These examples were Carthage and Rome.[11]

Dumouchet, too (in 1792), thought Rome had not been a complete failure. Finding that the Roman Republic had flourished for four centuries, he ignored the discussion about its fall, and attributed its long prosperity to the two consulships whose annual election kindled emulation among aspirants and whose short term of office stimulated the occupants to win triumphs on the double-quick. He then proposed that, like the Romans, the French annually elect two consuls; and with unspeakable delight he foresaw what glories these elections would bring:

[11] Billaud-Varenne, *op. cit.*, pp. 15–20, 64–69.

What emulation . . . . ! What an abundant source of talents and virtues! All the citizens will become inflamed with this love of the public welfare, which transcended all jealousies and surpassed every private interest.[12]

But neither Dumouchet nor Lavicomterie nor Billaud-Varenne valued the imitation of antiquity as an end, but only as a means. They prized it solely because it promised to revive and preserve in France the liberty, the passion for public good, the candor, humanity, and right-dealing, the exalted virtue—in brief—of antiquity. And they did not doubt that this virtue would bring happiness.[13]

Scarcely had the first republican movement of 1791 failed, than Babeuf (the leading equalitarian of the Revolution) was writing that even its success would not have brought a millennium. Only equal ownership of landed property would, he intimated, relieve the misery of the many. With this reform in mind, with his hopes for the realization of radical reform lifted high by recent liberal successes, he regarded with interest what he thought had been attempts to establish property equality in the past. The heroes of the alleged attempts—Lycurgus, the Gracchi, and Camillus—became his heroes; and he took the name of the latter. The code of the Spartan lawgiver and the agrarian laws of the Gracchi now, in a general way, became models which he would have France imitate. And past examples now raised his hopes for immediate radical reform when he discovered that it was in just such circumstances as existed in France, with extreme inequality of wealth prevalent and a constitution under discussion, that property equality had been instituted in the past.[14]

[12] Dumouchet, *Opinion sur la royauté* (Paris, 1792), p. 14; also see pp. 2, 3, 6–10, 13.

[13] Dumouchet, *op. cit.*, pp. 3, 5, 14; Billaud-Varenne, *op. cit.*, pp. 47–48; Lavicomterie, *op. cit.*, pp. 84, 87, 100.

[14] A. Espinas, *La philosophie sociale du XVIIIe siècle et la Révolution* (Paris, 1898), pp. 404–5, 409; Advielle, *Histoire de Gracchus Babeuf*, I, 66–67.

In 1789 and 1791, others besides Babeuf used the Spartan instance to give their equalitarian dreams an air of prestige and possibility. For in the success of the Lycurgan code, Bonneville, associate of the socialistic Abbé Fauchet, found support for the view that property equality brings power, virtue, and happiness to states;[15] Boissel noted an example which showed that even imperfect equalitarian institutions promoted health and banished avarice, cupidity, and corrupting luxuries;[16] while l'Abbé Cournand, a radical professor of the *collège* de France, and his echo, the newspaper known as the *Révolutions de Paris*, discovered a rejoinder to those who maintained economic equality was only a crazy chimera. Indeed, the work of ancient legislators like Lycurgus indicated, l'Abbé and the *Révolutions* hinted, that equality of fortune was "the surest way of so organizing society that all men were good and happy."[17]

Though an active interest in antiquity possessed three republicans and three or more equalitarians, the influence this interest exerted on them, or indirectly through them on the course of the Revolution (1790–92), must not be exaggerated. A reading of the *philosophes*, a view of contemporary inequality, and not a vision of Sparta, may have inspired the equalitarian projects. In any case, these projects did not now occasion much stir; and they never were realized in fact. If, furthermore, the dreams of republicans were realized, if in 1792 a republic came to France, it was because events—the advance of the enemy and the king's disloyalty—pushed Frenchmen into abolishing the monarchy, and not because republican theory

[15] Based on inference from the following passages: *De l'esprit des religions* (Paris, 1791), I, 77; II, 25, 82; see also I, 52–54, 56.

[16] *Le catéchisme du genre humain* (1789), pp. 56, 122–23.

[17] L'Abbé Cournand, *De la propriété* (Paris, 1791), pp. 44–45; *Révolutions de Paris*, VIII, No. 96 (May 7–14, 1791), 243–44.

and republican past example exerted an irresistible attraction. Even in the first republican movement of 1791, events again—chiefly the king's disloyalty—supplied reasons which brought men into line, though here theory and example also played a notable part. But here it was chiefly the example, not of Rome, but of America, which moved men like Condorcet, Brissot, Achille du Châtelet, and D'Izarn-Valady. For most, as we have seen, the examples of antiquity were something to explain away.

Nevertheless, in the thought of those equalitarians and of those republicans who still admired the classical past, antiquity had its function. It suggested to them detailed measures of policy to be proposed, like the creation of tribunes, censors, and consuls. It supplied them with arguments that spoke to the imagination and hopes of men— arguments tending to prove that, since a republic or property equality had brought happiness in the past, it would do so in the future; and it perhaps helped them to give some prestige, authority, and an air of respectable antiquity and reassuring familiarity to projects which might otherwise have seemed utterly crack-brained and imprudently novel. So much can be gathered from the more obvious features of the works of these reformers.

From their works, however, we are led to guess that past example also operated in ways more obscure upon the disposition of these men. We are led to surmise that the vision of the happy virtue obtaining in antiquity encouraged them to dream of reviving such virtuous felicity in France; that the mere fact that a republic or property equality had once existed and had brought happiness in the classical past encouraged them to hope that the establishment of either was practical and would indeed restore happiness in the present; and we are led to assume that, by thus teaching them that their projected reform was both feasible and worth while, antiquity helped to sustain them in their apparently fruitless endeavor to realize their projects. We are thus led to conclude that with them antiquity no longer worked to dishearten by offering the vision of some unattainable good, but now helped to keep their spirit level with their hopes and their hopes level with their dreams.

# CHAPTER X

# FLOWERS OF RHETORIC

WITH the failure of the first republican movement, republicans deferred their hopes for immediate realization of institutional reform.[1] In this they did not differ from their contemporaries who readily put up with the work of the Constituent Assembly until further change (either reactionary or radical) seemed possible. With this the dominant mood, the new representative body—the Legislative Assembly—did not concern itself greatly with the reform of institutions. It concentrated on problems of daily policy involving the *émigrés*, non-juring priests, finances, and, later, the war with Austria. Questions like these were little suited to evoke references to the institutional life of antiquity. They had not evoked such allusions in the Constituent Assembly when such problems had been considered. They were even less likely to occasion such allusions in the Legislative Assembly, where the "disdain-and-ignore" attitude typified by Condorcet[2] was now shared by some others. Kersaint, for example, a leading member of the liberal, Girondin party, declared that it was with nations as with men: in their youth they imitate examples; in their maturity they give examples to be imitated. France was now mature and need no longer imitate the classical past.[3] Codet, an obscure deputy, with true Gallic cockiness, crowed that since their regener-

[1] *Chronique de Paris*, No. 278 (October 5, 1791), p. 1120; No. 290 (October 17, 1791), p. 1168; No. 330 (November 26, 1791), p. 1327; No. 355 (December 21, 1791), p. 1427; Desmoulins, *Tribune des patriotes*, No. 1 (April 30, 1792), p. 15; Hamel, *Robespierre*, II, 140.

[2] *A.P.*, XLII (April 21, 1792), 228–29.     [3] *Ibid.*, XLII (May 1, 1792), 587.

ation the French can be compared to no other people; they resemble no one but themselves; hence they cannot learn either from Athens, Sparta, Rome, or England.[4] It was the boast of Lacépède that the French constitution was founded on natural rights. "What," he asked, "could the French learn from the Spartans with their unnatural laws and institutions?"[5] This inclination to glorify things French, though not necessarily to disdain things classical, was expressed by most speakers. It is not surprising, therefore, to discover that in this Assembly the tendency to admire and to regret had totally disappeared. Since, furthermore, classical institutions seldom were discussed and since (as in the Constituent) all parties agreed in admiring classical heroes, the tendency to condemn and avoid antiquity and the party divisions over classical history (both so prominent in the Constituent) did not, on the whole, appear in the Legislative Assembly.

The references to the heroes of antiquity, moreover, were so casual and so brief, the emotional charge coloring their statements seems so small, the historical philosophy that is behind them is so meagerly developed—they are, in brief, so unlike many of the references amplified during the Constituent Assembly that they seem what in fact they probably are merely rhetorical devices to render the argument more lucid, more vivid, and more compelling. Indeed, with the classical tags of Vergniaud, the foremost orator of the Legislative Assembly, it is known that such was actually the case. From the notes of his projected speech at his trial it is known, and from an examination of his other orations it can be guessed, how in his outline he would set down the classical allusions he intended to employ as summaries of a preceding argument; and how he revised his notes to secure allusions so familiar and yet so

[4] *Ibid.*, XLIV (May 25, 1792), 103.    [5] *Ibid.*, XLV (June 29, 1792), 670.

striking that his hearers could forget neither the allusions
nor the argument they contained.[6]

A number of allusions of Vergniaud and one-fourth of
those appearing in the debates of the Legislative Assembly
were only labels affixed to exalt and to encourage the orator
and his friends, or to shame his enemies. Orators would
exlaim: "The *émigrés* are Catilines"; "The invading Aus-
trian hosts resemble the liberticide hordes of despotic
Xerxes"; "The French armies are lionhearted Romans, or
they are Spartans and Athenians, ready to die at Ther-
mopylae or to conquer at Marathon."[7] When finally, in the
course of events, the general of these Romans, Lafayette,
left his army for Paris and lectured the Assembly on the
Jacobins, seven legislators later discussed (in passing)
whether he resembled Caesar, who had also tried to dictate
laws to constituted authorities. Six out of seven agreed
that Lafayette was not a Julius Caesar, since, as his friends
said, he was more virtuous; since, as his enemies said, he
was more incapable and stupid.[8] No one, however, was
cynical enough to suggest that if he was more virtuous it
was perhaps because he was more stupid.

[6] Vatel, *Vergniaud*, I, xi–xii; II, 255, 260–61, 313; Aulard, *Orateurs de la Convention*, I, 380–81, 383; *A.P.*, XXXIV (October 25, 1791), 401–2; XXXVI (December 27, 1791), 442; XXXVII (January 18, 1792), 490, 493; XL (March 19,
1792), 153; XLVI (July 3, 1792), 81–83.

[7] See, for example, *A.P.*, XXXIV (October 25, 1791), 401, 405; XXXIV
(October 28, 1791), 483; XXXIV (November 9, 1791), 716; XXXVI (December
13, 1791), 88; XXXVI (January 1, 1792), 727, 736; XXXVII (January 2, 1792),
3; XXXVII (January 18, 1792), 490; XXXVIII (February 12, 1792), 460; XL
(March 30, 1792), 705; XLII (April 30, 1792), 572; XLIII (May 22, 1792), 670;
XLIV (June 6, 1792), 640; XLV (June 17, 1792), 327; XLVI (July 3, 1792), 83;
XLVI (July 11, 1792), 351; XLVII (July 25, 1792), 124; *Chronique de Paris*,
No. 365 (December 31, 1791), 1467; No. 38 (February 7, 1792), 150; No. 260
(September 5, 1792), 993.

[8] *A.P.*, XLV (June 30, 1792), 712–13; XLVII (July 21, 1792), 12, 16; XLVII
(August 8, 1792), 566, 572, 588; see also Billaud-Varenne, *Discours sur notre
situation actuelle prononcé aux Jacobins à la séance du 29 juin, 1792* (Paris, 1792),
p. 11; Robespierre, *Défenseur de la constitution*, No. 8, 404; No. 9, 451–52.

# CHAPTER XI

## THE PROBLEM OF REGENERATION
## (SEPTEMBER, 1792—OCTOBER, 1793)

IN APRIL, 1792, the Legislative Assembly declared war on Austria. From the first the war went against the French. The armies of Austria and of Prussia, her ally, invaded France; and there seemed nothing to prevent their march into Paris. The crisis was rendered more acute by the fact that the king, Louis XVI, refused to co-operate loyally in the nation's defense. Therefore, to secure united action against the enemy, the Legislative Assembly suspended the king from his functions and (as the Constitution required) ordered the election of a National Convention to meet in September. When it met, the Convention, while its armies threw back the enemy, abolished the monarchy, set up a republic, and executed the monarch. As a result of these actions, the Conventionnels now found themselves committed to a republic, for they felt that, should a Bourbon ever become king of France, he would in revenge end their lives and their careers. No wonder, therefore, with life and a life's work at stake, the Conventionnels wished to establish a republic that would endure. No wonder the doubts that Rome's history had hitherto raised concerning the possibility of a large republic were no longer allowed to inhibit republican endeavor. Indeed, doubt itself was not permitted, as the Conventionnel, a sport of circumstance, now proclaimed that he was master of his fate, invincible to the foreign foe and omnipotent as a legislator.

This strength of spirit was quite different from the old

pre-1789 feeling of impotence and resignation in the face of ills that could not be cured. In consequence of this change of feeling, radical imitation of antiquity, hitherto a remote impossibility, could now become, in the minds of many, an imminent, practical reality.[1] Those conceptions, further-more, which had formerly inhibited, could now stimulate radical action. The belief that without virtue a republic could not endure, and the opinion that most Frenchmen were still degenerate and depraved, now stimulated every admirer of classical institutions (except Desmoulins) to propose the regeneration of Frenchmen through carefully planned institutional reform.

Nor was this plan so absurd as might seem. Before 1789 the life of the absolute monarchy had been insecure in part because the revolution in men's heads had outrun the revo-lution in facts; now, in 1792, the life of the republic was uncertain in part because the revolution in facts had out-run the revolution in men's heads. Frenchmen now rallied to the republic, writes Aulard, partly because it was bring-ing victory out of defeat. Would they continue to support it when victory gave way to defeat? To assure that they would indeed continue their support, the Convention thought it necessary to arouse a love of country, of liberty, of fraternity, of equality, and of the republic. We would call this love "patriotism," "loyalty to the flag," "devo-tion to democratic principles and institutions." The Con-ventionnels called it "virtue," "political virtue"—and with reason, since their love of country, etc., implied a more Spartan sacrifice of self to country than our terms im-ply. In addition, a few Conventionnels thought it necessary to revive the private virtue, the simplicity, frugality, and austere morality that had existed in republican antiquity.

[1] Contemporaries realized this; see, for example, *A.P.*, L (August 20, 1792), 668.

In any case, the problem was to determine what institutions they should create. For the machinery of government, constitution-makers could, of course, rely on a deroyalized, more democratic variation of the work of the Constituent Assembly; and in any case, to the governing of a large populous empire, antiquity, with its direct democracy, had little to contribute. But for the unprecedented, unattempted task of improving and then maintaining the virtue of a people, where could they find guidance? Most turned to Montesquieu, Rousseau, and sometimes to Mably. Habit and prestige alone would naturally have directed attention to the works of these men. And once attention was so directed, it was held by the fact that these works discussed in detail the problem (of how and why republics endured) which legislators were attempting to solve, and discussed it in terms of those preconceptions (the relation between virtue and a republic) which even a Revolution had not undermined. Furthermore, now, that legislators were prepared to ignore the *philosophe* caution that only small countries of virtuous inhabitants could be republics, the entire *philosophe* discussion of classical republican legislation, hitherto academic and irrelevant, became pertinent and practical. As to a legislative guidebook, therefore, a few legislators could now turn to Mably's discussion of Athenian and Spartan institutions in his *Entretiens de Phocion*. "It is there," Rabaut de Saint-Etienne wrote, "that, in the austere manners and morals of the Spartans, you will learn how a republic is constituted."[2] More consulted Montesquieu, also in the spirit of Rabaut, who wrote:

Montesquieu thoroughly understood the spirit of the various governments, and that of the republic in particular; it is from his book that legislators may draw the laws of a sound democracy and the institutions which it should be given in order to make it durable. . . . .

[2] *Chronique de Paris*, No. 3 (January 3, 1793), p. 11.

Our legislator considers a few of the methods employed in several [ancient] republics to maintain the original manners and morals . . . . which alone can assure the stability of the laws . . . . ; he finds them in paternal authority . . . . in the authority of elders, in the various bodies of censors established in various democracies.[3]

Still more, perhaps, communed with Rousseau, who, in his *Contrat social* and in his *Considérations sur le gouvernement de Pologne*, discussed the means to establish firmly the constitution of the republican or semipopular state. There he advised the creation of a tribunate, a board of censors, an occasional dictatorship, a civil religion, and a system of public education, all to be more or less patterned after a Roman or a Spartan model. But no matter which of these three French authorities the legislators consulted, they would always find the institutions of antiquity praised and recommended for a republican state. No wonder a number of Conventionnels should be partial to the duplication of these institutions, whenever duplication seemed feasible.

Still other reasons help to explain why legislators were so inclined. For one thing, the oratorical and journalistic practice of mentioning the schools, the festivals, and the moral censorships of antiquity had kept alive the memory of the classical past from 1789 to the Convention. Then, too, independent of extra luster reflected upon them by the commendation of *philosophes* and of orators, the classical examples possessed a prestige all their own. Rabaut de Saint-Etienne again expressed what was in the minds of a number when he wrote:

These laws of the classical republics were often the fruit of great wisdom, either because the legislator was gifted with a superior genius for observation, and had studied the workings of the human heart, or because the concurrence of the people in making laws for themselves was often more skilful than experience.[4]

The classical republics, finally, were now without a serious rival in bidding for the admiration of men. Before the

---

[3] *Ibid.*, No. 124 (May 4, 1793), p. 3.    [4] *Ibid.*, No. 6 (January 6, 1793), p. 22.

Revolution, for this admiration republican antiquity had competed with the French medieval monarchy as ideally portrayed by Boulainvilliers, l'Abbé Dubos, Montesquieu, and Mably; with the liberal limited monarchy of England sympathetically described by Voltaire and Montesquieu; and with the new American republic. During the revolutionary years, in swaying the minds of men, each of these societies had its day: the old French monarchy in 1788 to 1789, when men were trying to find in the French medieval past the kind of Estates-General they wished to revive; the English monarchy in late summer of 1789, when the Constituent committee on the constitution proposed a governmental organization after the English model; the American example during the first republican movement. And then, as respect for each society became engulfed in the current of disdain which grew out of the French superiority complex, the following of each society was reduced to a few like-minded souls whose tastes and principles its example best supported, the French medieval monarchy drawing its faithful from the reactionaries, the English monarchy from the moderate conservatives, and the American republic from the liberal Girondists. By the time each of these groups had disappeared from the revolutionary scene, the reactionaries after the close of the Constituent, the Anglomaniacs after the suspension of the king,[5] and the Girondists on June 2, 1793,[6] the cult for each

[5] For the gradually mounting tide of disdain for the English constitution, see, for example: Marat, *Chaînes de l'esclavage*, p. 324; *Journal de Paris*, II, No. 239 (August 27, 1789), 1077; Gorsas, *Courrier de Versailles*, III, No. 59 (September 4, 1789), 58; Gorsas, *Courrier des départements*, I, No. 2 (September 23, 1792), 25; *Chronique de Paris*, No. 278 (October 5, 1791), p. 1120; No. 355 (December 22, 1792), p. 1425; *A.P.*, XXXV (December 2, 1791), 511; *Le patriote française*, No. 967 (April 3, 1792), p. 378; Billaud-Varenne, *Discours à la séance du 29 juin, 1792*, p. 5; *Moniteur*, No. 100 (December 30, 1793), p. 77; No. 115 (January 14, 1794), p. 200; No. 116 (January 15, 1794), p. 206; No. 125 (January 24, 1794), p. 279; No. 136 (February 4, 1794), p. 373.

[6] Faÿ, *L'esprit révolutionnaire en France et aux Etats Unis à la fin du XVIII⁰ siècle* (Paris, 1925), p. 221.

of these societies had likewise disappeared. Even before June, 1793, however, and sometimes even among Girondists, American prestige had suffered a decline.[7] Accordingly, even when the Convention opened, the classical republics constituted the only societies to command an undiminished admiration. As a result, there was no longer any society outside modern France that could by a more surpassing brilliance shadow, and thus discredit, the brilliance of antiquity, as before the Revolution in the mind of Brissot America had discredited Rome. If, furthermore, legislators were to seek for guidance through imitation of the example of another, their own low opinion of English, American, and medieval French societies, when combined with high regard for those of antiquity, left them no choice. They had to turn to republican antiquity.

For various reasons, therefore, a number of Conventionnels looked with favor upon any duplication of classical institutions. Such imitation was recommended by authority, by former legislators, by its feasibility, by the prestige which enveloped these institutions, and by the fact that imitation would solve the perplexing problem of the regeneration of Frenchmen and would thus assure the foundation of a republic that would endure. It was no wonder, therefore, that Rabaut de Saint-Etienne now wrote:

. . . . the citizens . . . . take pleasure in recalling the laws which served to govern the ancient republics; they like to hope that our legislators will mediate the means of reforming us on these happy models.[8]

Nor is it astonishing that a number of legislators were ready to follow Rabaut's advice by advocating the duplica-

[7] Condorcet, "Esquisse d'un tableau historique des progrès de l'esprit humain, Première partie" (1793–94), Œuvres, VI, 201–2; Chronique de Paris, No. 364 (December 31, 1792), pp. 1461–62; No. 48 (February 17, 1793), p. 171; No. 61 (March 2, 1793), p. 242; A.P., LXII (April 15, 1793), 158; LXII (April 17, 1793), 434; LXIII (April 26, 1793), 392; LXIV (May 15, 1793), 698.

[8] Chronique de Paris, No. 6 (January 6, 1793), p. 22.

tion of the censorships,[9] the festivals, and the educational
practices of antiquity.

In the case of the censorships, the Roman instance
directed the thought of legislators; in the case of education
by school and by festival, it was largely the Greek example, and especially that of Plutarchian Sparta. Plutarch,
it may be recalled, in his life of Lycurgus, noted that, to
preserve his reform, the Spartan lawgiver relied on his system of education, thinking that his laws, "being imprinted
on the hearts of their youth by good discipline, would be
sure to remain." What this discipline was, everyone
knows. Children, taken from their parents at the age of
seven, were placed in lodgings where, submitted to the
same discipline, they shared the same hard fare, wore the
same plain, scanty clothing, did their exercises and took
their play together, all to the end that they might learn
to love and to serve Sparta with Spartan rigor. To further
this end, moreover, they were instructed in music and
verse, that they might participate in solemn public festivals and sing songs inspiring ardor for patriotic action.
Furthermore, when they became adult, education in service and love of country did not cease, for all their time,
when not engaged in a campaign, "was taken up by the
choral dances and the festivals, in hunting and in attendance on the exercise grounds and places of public conversation." Citizens so bred, Plutarch concluded, "made themselves one with the public good, [were] . . . . devoted
wholly to their country."[10]

Montesquieu and Rousseau, like Plutarch, thought the
Spartan system admirably suited to arouse political virtue,
to win men to a love of country and of its laws—to do, in

---

[9] *A.P.*, LXII (April 17, 1793), 425–26; LXIV (May 10, 1793), 516–18;
LXVII (June 24, 1793), 200–201, 315, 388, 390, 417.

[10] Plutarch, *"Parallel Lives,"* I, 78, 79, 87, 88, 90, 91; hereafter the 1900 translation of Plutarch is referred to; see Bibliography.

brief, what education in a republic ought to do. In fact, in Spartan state-regulated education, where all children were raised in common and in equality, instructed in the laws of the state, and surrounded with examples and objects which spoke of the country that nourished, loved, and cared for them—in this system which had produced miracles of patriotism in Crete, Persia, and Sparta—Rousseau found his ideal of public education. He maintained, indeed, that the necessity of a system like this was a fundamental maxim of popular government, adding that the Roman republic endured without it only because Rome was a continual miracle anyway.[11] When, furthermore, he came to advise the Polish on constitutional reform, he advocated establishing a state-regulated system of *collège* education imbued with a Spartan spirit. Students would live in common and in equality, be won to a love of country by a study of its laws and its heroic history, and be accustomed, by competitive games and gymnastics witnessed by elders, to fraternity, equality, regulation, and a desire for public approval. Save, however, for these games in common, which were required of all children, this semi-Spartan régime was to be neither compulsory nor gratuitous. Nor does Rousseau discuss whether it should be extended to the primary level. In these respects he departed from the Spartan ideal.[12] Perhaps like Montesquieu, Rousseau felt, as indeed he elsewhere remarked, that the compulsory, universal, and free Spartan education was not entirely practicable in modern nations too large to be well governed.[13]

During the first three and a half years of the Revolu-

---

[11] Rousseau, *L'économie politique*, pp. 390–91.

[12] Rousseau, *Considérations sur le gouvernement de Pologne*, pp. 435–36, 437, 438–39, 440–41.

[13] Rousseau, *L'économie politique*, p. 391.

tion, legislators had been more inclined than Rousseau to ignore, and indeed to condemn, the radical implications of the Spartan example. Thus, the author of Mirabeau's discourse on education condemned the attempt by classical legislators like Lycurgus to give a particular bent, a particular distortion, to citizens.[14] Talleyrand, in his report to the Constituent, censured the Spartan compulsory education of all children away from home as a violation of parental rights.[15] To Condorcet, the expert on education in the Legislative, the boasted Spartan absolute equality in the education of citizens appeared possible only where the iniquitous inequalities of slavery existed.[16] And the two major plans reported out of the Convention's Committee of Public Instruction before July, 1793, ignored any suggestions the Spartan instance had to give.

Not all Conventionnels were in sympathy with the two plans of the Committee. It was in disapproval of its first plan, in so far as it concerned primary education, that Lepeletier in December, 1792, and in January, 1793, shortly before his assassination by a royalist, conceived and wrote his educational project,[17] which has gone down in history as an outstanding example of Spartan influence. It was in disapproval of the Committee's second plan that Robespierre, as a member of the Commission (not Committee) of Public Instruction, read and championed Lepeletier's posthumous report to the Convention on July 13, 1793. Shortly before this date, a certain Alexandre De-

---

[14] *A.P.*, XXX (September 10, 1791), 512–13.

[15] *Ibid.*, p. 454.

[16] Condorcet, "Sur l'instruction publique," *Œuvres*, VII, 197–98; for somewhat similar sentiments, see *Révolutions de Paris*, No. 170 (October 6–13, 1792), pp. 104–5.

[17] France, Convention nationale, Comité d'instruction publique, *Procès-verbaux du Comité d'instruction publique de la Convention* (ed. M. J. Guillaume; Paris, 1891–1907), I, 263, n. 1. (Referred to hereafter as "Guillaume.")

leyre also spun out an educational dream which in part stemmed more obviously from the Spartan example. Of the two "Spartan" projects—Lepeletier's and Deleyre's— that of the first is more celebrated. It was the work of a revolutionary martyr; the fight for its adoption was led by Robespierre;[18] it stirred up quite a debate; and (with compulsory attendance ruled out) it was in principle adopted by the Convention.[19] But a peculiar interest also attaches to the plan of Deleyre, written, as it was, by a friend of Rousseau and by a thinker who seeks to harmonize his every thought and word with the word and spirit of his friend and master.

In premises and in fundamentals, the projects of the two Conventionnels did not greatly differ. Both assumed that the coming of the republic had necessitated the regeneration of Frenchmen. "Laws have been made for the nation; it is now a question of making the nation for the laws." Both reasoned that complete regeneration of the nation could be accomplished only when children were taken from their parents and lodged together in communal *maisons d'éducation*. There, uncontaminated by parental influence, they would never escape the given pedagogical mold.[20]

But once fundamentals were disposed of, resemblance between the two projects ceased. Lepeletier would take the child from his home at the age of five and return him at the age of twelve. To prolong the period of compulsory communal education to the end of adolescence, Lepeletier said, is "a lovely dream." He went on to say:

We have occasionally dreamed of it deliciously with Plato; sometimes we have read of it with enthusiasm, realized in the annals of Lace-

[18] *Ibid.*, I, 558–59; II, xvii, xix, xxv, xliv, 63, 88, 278.

[19] *Ibid.*, II, xxv, 88.

[20] *Ibid.*, I, 645, 649–50; II, 35, 37, 38, 45, 52.

daemon; sometimes we have found an insipid caricature of it in our *collèges;* but Plato created only philosophers, Lycurgus made only soldiers, and our professors produced only scholars.[21]

The French Republic, he continued, has need of farmers, merchants, and artisans, who must learn their calling in adolescence and away from home.

Deleyre, however, was willing deliciously to dream with Plato and Lycurgus. He did not, it is true, make schooling compulsory; but he did expect that eventually every youth would attend his *maisons.* The children who came would remain from the age of seven to that of eighteen, the very ages that Spartan instruction began and ended.[22] They would be submitted to a régime dictated in part by Deleyre's admiration for the Sparta of Plutarch and of Rousseau. Leading "la vie fraternelle des Spartiates," they would live in common and in equality, dressed, fed, and instructed alike.[23] To excite their love of country, they would be required to read Plutarch; and while they read, they would listen to warlike marches so that the insitutions of Lycurgus might be better engraved in their hearts.[24] As recommended by Rousseau, himself inspired by antiquity, much of their time would be filled with performing physical exercises, gymnastics, and warlike dances set to music.[25] And since, as in Sparta, girls, as well as boys, were to be educated, the boys, with their female contemporaries as spectators, would on occasion go through "the evolutions of a Pyrrhic or warlike dance," while the girls would respond with "a virginal dance, which would recall the ancient festivals of Diana."[26] As indications of a state of mind, these minor projects for the imitation of Sparta give sense to the speculation that

[21] *Ibid.*, II, 39.          [22] *Ibid.*, I, 650.          [23] *Ibid.*, p. 654.
[24] *Ibid.*, 662; see also pp. 648, 658, 659, 661, 663–64.
[25] *Ibid.*, p. 654.          [26] *Ibid.*, pp. 669–70, 671.

Deleyre's major proposal to place children and adolescents in common houses apart from their parents was also inspired by the Spartan example.

With Lepeletier, little foundation can be found for such a speculation. A possible, hypothetical Spartan influence is betrayed only by the suggestion that the children shall share alike, eating plain food and wearing simple clothing, and by the proposal that recalcitrant fathers refusing to surrender their children should lose their citizen rights.[27] And even here we may doubt. For, in truth, his spirit is addressed to the present and not to the past. He did not stress—indeed, he did not mention—the chief Lycurgan end of education: the kindling of a love of country. He did not emphasize, though he mentioned, a prime Lycurgan means—gymnastics.[28] And he refused to allow the prestige of Lycurgus to seduce him into advocating the extension of communal education beyond the age of twelve, into proposing, in brief, what seemed contrary to the present interests of agricultural and commercial France. In fact, his entire project seemed dictated by present circumstance, chiefly by the need to secure absolute equality of educational opportunity to all—to the rural child who lived too far from day schools, to the city street gamin who must earn his bread, as well as to the children of the well-to-do. In addition, the necessity of eventual self-support compelled a truly non-Lycurgan emphasis on accustoming the children to work, especially to agricultural labor.[29]

If admiration for antiquity came to be regarded as the motive of Lepeletier, it was doubtless because his chief critics—Grégoire, Masuyer, Duhem, and Chénier—anxious to discredit his project, started the hue and cry that he was madly proposing to mold the education of large, popu-

---

[27] *Ibid.*, II, 38, 40, 42.

[28] *Ibid.*, p. 42.     [29] *Ibid.*, pp. 36–37; 53; see also p. 278.

lous, enlightened, commercial France after that which had
existed in the tiny, primitive, agricultural, slave-holding
Spartan community.[30] But if the positive influence exerted by antiquity on Lepeletier was slight, the influence of
the negative argument drawn from Sparta was nil. As it
did not prevent the Convention from decreeing that communal *maisons d'éducation* (attendance not compulsory) be
set up, it probably had little to do with the repeal of the
decree.[31] Not until later does the example of Spartan education of youths exert a more obvious and more potent
influence on the thought and action of a few legislators.

Spartan education, however, as described by Plutarch,
did not end with adolescence but continued, as we have
seen, throughout life. So brief, though, were Plutarch's
passages concerning this adult education in part by public
festival that during the Revolution its existence might
have been ignored but for Rousseau. The latter, in design-
ing a government for Poland, observed that to be stable
the fundamental laws must reign in the hearts of the citizens, must have not only their approval and obedience
but also their love. To inspire this love (which also in-
volves a love of country) Lycurgus, undertaking "to found
a nation already degraded by servitude and its attendant
vices," had attached citizens to their country and to each
other in part by games witnessed by the assembled citizenry, by public exercises which augmented their strength
and their self-esteem, by spectacles recalling the history of
their ancestors, and by festivals reminding them of their
country. Similar, though not like, *divertissements* Rousseau
would have the Polish invent for themselves: for example,
a decennial festival to commemorate the patriotic heroism

---

[30] Ibid., I, 148 and n. 1; II, 134, 173, 674, 754; Grégoire, *Mémoires*, I, 344;
see also, for a reply Guillaume, *op. cit.*, pp. 675, n. 2, 681, 682.

[31] Guillaume, *op. cit.*, II, xliv.

of the historically famous Confederation of Bar; public games; and spectacles involving, for instance, the handling of horses and public recompense of patriotic valor. Apparently in these festivals there was a classical institution that Rousseau believed could be revived in the modern state.[32]

Anyone who doubted that this institution could be revived must have had his doubts dispelled in 1790. In that year there sprang up throughout France spontaneous local celebrations of revolutionary progress (festivals known as "federations"), culminating in the great national Federation of July 14, and all keyed to a most elevated strain of patriotic exaltation. Impressed by the prodigies of emotion thus aroused, haunted by classical reminiscences, legislators, journalists, and pamphleteers—men like Mirabeau, Talleyrand, Viénot-Vaublanc, Francais de Nantes— soon were wishing consciously to imitate the policy of classical governments.[33] They would give a formal, legal, more permanent organization to this fluid crowd phenomenon. They vaguely hoped it would prove a potent instrument of adult education. While in the meantime, the French festivals, which continued, themselves sometimes assumed a classical dress, as David designed, for example, classical costumes and drapery, and a *char antique* for the translation of the remains of Voltaire.[34] They sometimes

[32] Rousseau, *Considérations sur le gouvernement de Pologne*, pp. 421, 423-24, 427, 429-31.

[33] *Chronique de Paris*, No. 186 (July 5, 1791), p. 745; No. 335 (December 1, 1791), Supplément; No. 350 (December 16, 1791), 1407; No. 254 (August 30, 1792), p. 971; *A.P.*, XXXVII (January 28, 1792), 720-22; *Le patriote français*, No. 902 (January 29, 1792), p. 114; Mathiez, *Les cultes révolutionnaires* (Paris, 1904), pp. 79-81.

[34] Gorsas, *Courrier*, XXVI (July 13, 1791), 179-80, 188-89; *L'ami du roi* (Montjoie), No. 194 (July 12, 1791), p. 775; see also *Chronique de Paris*, No. 87 (March 27, 1792), p. 347; No. 109 (April 17, 1792), p. 431; No. 155 (June 2, 1792), p. 615; *Révolutions de Paris*, No. 145 (April 14-21, 1792), p. 101; No. 152 (June 29, 1792), pp. 451, 453.

assumed a vaguely classical form, as we read, for instance, how on July 14, 1791, at Boulogne-sur-Mer in a festival "worthy of the fairest days of Lacedaemon," all the "elders" not "selfish celibates" were publicly dined. Then, we are told, toward the end of the meal

a troup of children was introduced. This bringing-together of the two ages excited the liveliest interest. Tears of joy flowed from all eyes at the moment when these young pupils of the fatherland scattered flowers about the veterans, while lavishing upon them the most tender caresses.[35]

Indorsed in this fashion by French notables, proved by present example, recommended by Rousseau, and described by Plutarch, these classical festivals had all that was necessary to win from the Convention a favorable hearing for any proposal to revive them in France. During the first year and a half of its life, the Convention listened to numerous proposals of this sort. Of these, the most significant were those of Rabaut de Saint-Etienne, Sieyes, Chénier, and Robespierre. Those of the first three may be considered here; that of the fourth, later. In all four cases, the influence of antiquity, whether mediated by the *philosophes* or the classics, was great and perhaps decisive in determing the thought of these men; while their thought, in turn, eventually affected the action of the Convention.

The first proposal of significance came, as we have said, in December, 1792, from Rabaut. The problem facing the Convention, he said, was how to communicate immediately to all Frenchmen a uniform enthusiasm for liberty, equality, and fraternity.[36] Possibly to effect this communication he had meditated "on the means of applying" something of the Cretan and Spartan national public education. But he was forced to pay it the tribute of regret

[35] Gorsas, *Courrier*, XXVI (July 20, 1791), 317.

[36] Guillaume, *op. cit.*, I, 231, 233.

when he discerned that "too many differences from these peoples and their times forbid us to aspire so high." Such unremitting, continuous education, which, during every waking hour, from the cradle to the grave, kept every citizen occupied with his country and exercised in all the virtues, was possible only in a society founded on agriculture and on slavery.[37]

Nevertheless, Rabaut's meditations were not in vain. In the instruments of this national adult education of Sparta and of Crete, in their gymnastics, public games, and national festivals, marked by "the fraternal competition of all ages . . . . and the sweet and imposing spectacle of an assembled human society"—in these festival institutions, in brief, "so well known by the ancients"—he found the means to make of the French "a new people." He therefore proposed that each canton should have a *temple national*, to be used both as a school building and as an assembly hall for citizens. There, each Sunday, citizens will gather; listen to a lesson in ethics and to a reading of the declaration of rights; and sing hymns in honor of country, liberty, equality, and fraternity, and suited "to form citizens in all the virtues." In fair weather in the inclosure around the *temple*, they will engage in gymnastics, public games, and military exercises. The costume of the citizens, their arms, their exercises—all the "festival equipage"— will be determined by the legislature. At these fêtes, the elders of over sixty will sit apart. They have the right to censure any child for any misdemeanor. In addition, they elect a few of their number to form a senate, which will censure, by public reprimand, the bad children and will reward, by public praise and prize-giving, the good. The children will wear a costume prescribed by the legislature;

[37] *Ibid.*, p. 232.

will learn (after the age of ten) gymnastics and public exercises; and will memorize a catechism on constitutional
principles as well as the declaration of rights and duties.
Once a year, on the day known as the *Fête des enfants*, all
the ten-year-olds will be examined for their knowledge
both of this declaration and of the civil hymns. On another
day, named the *Fête des adolescents*, the fifteen-year-olds
will be examined on the civil catechism. The public gymnastics, the military exercises, the civil hymns, the uniform dress for children, their censure by "elders," the
senate of "elders" over sixty, were all, it may be noted,
found in Plutarchian Sparta. What Rabaut proposed in
brief was to make Spartans out of Frenchmen every
Sunday.[38]

Rabaut's colleagues interrupted him with frequent applause, invited him to join the Committee of Public Instruction, and in future sessions of the Convention repeated or developed his proposals.[39] Indeed, to a limited extent, the official plan of the Committee of Public Instruction, drawn up by Sieyes, resembles that of Rabaut. Like
that of Rabaut, this plan, presented to the Convention on
June 25, 1793, provided for a public building (here called
*un théâtre national*) where citizens might assemble to perform military evolutions, go through gymnastics, play
music, engage in the dance, and also act out amateur spectacles representing the history of mankind and of the
French Revolution. In addition, perhaps taking the hint of
Rousseau, who had praised those classical celebrations
where Homer was recited and Aeschylus and Sophocles
were performed, the projected decree would open the

[38] *Ibid.*, pp. 233–35.

[39] *Ibid.*, pp. 229–30; see, for example, the speeches of Bancal, Jeanbon Saint-
André, and the project of Lepeletier: *ibid.*, pp. 249, 280; II, 57.

*théâtres nationaux* to those who wished to try out their talents as poets, orators, artists, or readers. Developing Rousseau's suggestion that, as in antiquity, prizes be given to those who excel, the plan provided for competitions between people within cantons, between cantons, between districts, and between departments, with prizes (in the canton awarded by a tribunal of elders) to victors.[40]

All this, said Sieyes, was to be created to moralize men, to police peoples, and to inspire individuals and communities with "a commendable rivalry of esteem and of glory."[41] What is noticeable in this statement of purpose—indeed, what distinguished his project from the schemes of Rousseau, Durand-Maillane, Masuyer, Rabaut, and Jeanbon Saint-André—is the absence of emphasis on the need to kindle and to maintain a somewhat Spartan love of country. It is true that, like Rabaut, Sieyes appears to look to the Greeks. He evidently hopes to transplant snatches of their celebrations (the military evolutions, the gymnastics, the music, the dancing, the competition between poets); he declares that, if his project is carried through, "we shall no longer have any cause to envy ancient Greece";[42] while his ally in the Committee of Public Instruction, Daunou, in defense of Sieyes, exclaims: "Oh, recreate within the bosom of France those brilliant solemnities which formerly offered to the assembled communes of Greece the thrilling spectacle of every pleasure, every talent, and every glory."[43] But the Greece of Daunou and of Sieyes was not that of Sparta but that of Athens and of the Olympic festivities, where competition in the games and in the arts inspired, as Sieyes said his fêtes would inspire, "a com-

[40] *Ibid.*, I, 513–16; it must be added that many of the details of this project were not inspired by antiquity.

[41] *Ibid.*, p. 570.     [42] *Ibid.*     [43] *Ibid.*, p. 582.

mendable rivalry of esteem and of glory, which is the mother of progress."

The plan of Sieyes for festivals was merely part of a larger scheme for public education as a whole. When that scheme was discarded, his plan shared its fate. Indeed, the entire discussion regarding public festivals was put over until its revival four months later by Marie-Joseph Chénier. Speaking when worship of country, of the republic, and of liberty was becoming a cult, Chénier for the moment became its prophet. To his colleagues he said:

> You will know how to found, on the ruins of dethroned superstitions, the only universal religion . . . . whose only dogma is equality, whose laws are the oracles, whose magistrates are the pontiffs, and which burns the incense of the great human family only before the altar of the country, that common mother and divinity.[44]

But a new cult requires new ceremonies; a new state of feeling demands new forms of expression. Chénier found them, so he thought, in an adaptation of the institutions of antiquity—the public games and gymnastics, where prizes were awarded to the most skilful; the recompense of useful virtue and useful deed with an oak leaf to the citizen "qui a bien mérité de la patrie"; and finally the public festivals. These latter would be dedicated to liberty. Eloquence would celebrate its heroes; poetry sing its praises; music and the dance enliven its triumphs; while hymns, emblems, and indeed the entire ceremony, would commemorate the history of the French Revolution. All of these republican institutions made Greece great, causing the little town of Athens to produce in a century and a half more great men than all Europe has seen in fourteen centuries. They will make France equally great and will surround Frenchmen with a triple rampart of patriotism.[45]

[44] *Ibid.*, II, 757.        [45] *Ibid.*, pp. 756-59.

In this fashion, Chénier, like Rabaut and Sieyes, were encouraged by antiquity to hope that by a few holiday parades, processions, orations, community singing, and community gymnastics, they could accomplish the tremendous task of remaking the nature of the French people. Indeed, all three men seem somewhat naïvely to expect so much of so little. But perhaps such faith with regard to the future, along with discontent with the present, is the essence of the revolutionary spirit.

# CHAPTER XII

## THE CULT GOES DEMOCRATIC

IN THE course of years, to symbolize his patriotism and his attachment for liberty, the American has developed a number of devices—the flag, the national anthem, the Declaration of Independence, the Constitution, and the names of Washington and Lincoln. In the course of time the Frenchman has done likewise. But during the early stages of the Revolution, when French patriotism and love of liberty were just being born, and before many symbols had been developed, the Frenchman was sometimes forced to borrow symbols from other countries and from other times, and especially from antiquity.

Even before Chénier had spoken, therefore, the legislators and artists had associated antiquity with the new cult of liberty and of country. This cult too, like every religious phenomenon, had its saints and martyrs—Marat and Lepeletier—but also Scaevola, and especially Brutus, since to symbolize a love of liberty and of country Frenchmen had popularly adopted some of those classical heroes who had manifested a similar love. With an equal partiality Frenchmen now bracketed the names of these ancient and modern martyrs in the same rhetorical reference and placed their busts side by side. Thus, if the first Brutus could have visited the Convention, he would have seen his bust (along with that of Lepeletier) prominently displayed near the orator's tribune; would have constantly heard his example, his spirit, and his inflexible love of liberty held up for admiration and emulation; would have read the decree (later repealed) ordering the printing of his image,

along with that of Cato and Publicola, on certain assignats;[1] and would have learned perhaps that Fouché had
celebrated a *Fête de Brutus* in the Cathedral of Nevers.[2] In
addition he might have noted how at public festivals, to
symbolize a love of liberty, Frenchmen ever since 1790 had
borrowed the classical Phrygian cap.[3] And he might have
observed that all this, the work of the leaders of opinion,
gave to this cap, to his name, and, to a lesser extent, to the
names of other classical heroes a certain prestige in the
eyes of the masses.

Partly as a consequence of this prestige, in March, 1792,
two years after the Phrygian cap had first appeared in a
public festival, the Parisians made of its wearing a popular
fad. They were told, wrote the *Révolutions de Paris*, that

this woollen cap was, in Greece and in Rome, the emblem of the de-
liverance of all enemies of despotism. That is enough. From this moment each citizen wants to have this cap. Jealously proud of wearing
it, he becomes more eloquent in the tribune of the clubs.[4]

Then a year and a half later, in the autumn of 1793,
about the time Chénier made his speech, there swept
through urban France the "dechristianisation" movement
—a manifestation of a desire to obliterate all traces of
Catholicism. Partly as a result of this desire, partly because of the prestige the leaders of opinion had given antiquity, some men and some towns whose names savored of
Catholicism exchanged them for classical ones. This was
the case of Babeuf, who substituted for his three Chris-

[1] *A.P.*, LXVI (June 6, 1793), 99.

[2] Guillaume, *Procès-verbaux du Comité d'instruction publique de la Convention
Nationale*, II, lxxviii.

[3] Mathiez, *Les cultes révolutionnaires*, p. 30; *Le patriote française*, No. 1045
(June 20, 1792), p. 685.

[4] *Révolutions de Paris*, XI, No. 141 (March 17–24, 1792), 534; see also
*Chronique de Paris*, No. 75 (March 15, 1792), p. 300; No. 76 (March 16, 1792),
p. 301; *Le patriote français*, No. 954 (March 21, 1792), p. 324.

tian names, François-Noël Toussaint Nicaisse, first the name of Camillus and then that of Caïus Gracchus. He later defended the changes in the following terms:

> I had the moral purpose, in taking as my patron saints, the most honorable men, in my opinion, of the Roman republic . . . . of intimating that I should desire this happiness as strongly as they, although by different means. . . . . To erase the traces of royalism, of aristocracy, and of fanaticism we have given republican names to our districts, cities, streets, and to everything that bore the imprint of these three types of tyranny. . . . . Why wish to force me always to preserve "St. Joseph" as my patron saint and model? I want nothing of the virtues of that fine fellow. The decree rendered by the legislature by which it was permissible to declare by a legal act that one no longer wished to be called "Roch" or "Nicodème," but preferred to take as patron and model of imitation "Brutus" or "Agis"; that decree was wise and moral. . . . . In the midst of free opinion, it is repugnant to me still to bear the second name of "Toussaint." And "Nicaisse," the third and last happy saint whom my beloved sponsor gave me for imitation, has a tone which I do not at all like; and if some day my head falls, I have no intention of walking about carrying it in my hands. I should rather die outright like the Gracchi, whose life also pleases me, and under whose tutelage I henceforth place myself exclusively.[5]

This non-Catholic spirit also animated the town of Ris, whose deputation told the Convention: "Our patron was Saint Blaise; but a young volunteer spoke to us of Brutus; he related his actions to us, and suddenly Saint Blaise was dislodged and Brutus put in his place."[6] Finally, the petition of the town of Saint-Maximin, inspired, it is said, by Lucien Bonaparte, indicates how memory of the ancient and modern heroes of liberty and of country, when combined with the willingness to extinguish all signs of Catholicism, brought about an alteration of the town's name. The petition reads:

REPRESENTATIVES: You have decreed that the cities which bear superstitious names are to change them.

The *sans-culottes* of Saint-Maximin have always avidly seized upon

---

[5] *Tribun du peuple*, No. 23, p. 1, n. 1.

[6] *Moniteur*, No. 42 (November 2, 1793), p. 314.

anything that can contribute to the ruin of religious and royalist prejudices: . . . .

Marathon is the name we have taken; this sacred name recalls to us the Athenian plain which became the tomb of a hundred thousand satellites, but it recalls to us with still greater sweetness the memory of the Friend of the People. Marat has fallen a victim of federalists and intriguers. May the name which we adopt contribute to immortalize his virtue and civism.[7]

In certain sections of France, this classical nomenclature became the rage. As a result, if a Frenchman lived outside of Paris, he might inhabit, for example, the town of Mont-fort-le-Brutus, formerly Montfort-l'Amaury, or the town of Brutus-le-Magnanime, formerly Saint-Pierre-le-Moutier.[8] Within Paris he might find himself in the section of Mucius Scaevola or in that named after Brutus.[9] While, if he moved just cater-corner across the street from the latter section into that named after Mirabeau, he might have found his address to be Rue de Brutus, de Scaevola, des Gracques, de Manlius, de Franklin, de l'Egalité, de la Liberté, de William Tell, de Cato, de Fabius, de Décius, de Socrates, de la République, or de Regulus, as the case might be.[10] If he followed the latest craze, he would have exchanged his own good Christian French name of Pierre, François, or Jean for that of Aristides, Socrates, or Scaevola and would have given a classical praenomen to his newborn.[11] Perhaps the name of his son was among those counted by the erudite Vatel when the latter discovered that, on the average, according to the registers *de l'état civil de la Seine*, out of four hundred praenomens of this

[7] Guillaume, *op. cit.*, III, 629–30.

[8] Aulard, "Les noms révolutionnaires des communes," *La Révolution française*, LXXIX (January–December, 1926), 303.

[9] *Moniteur*, No. 298 (July 16, 1794), p. 217.

[10] *Révolutions de Paris*, XIV, No. 175 (November 10–17, 1792), 359.

[11] E. Lévy, *Le manuel des prénoms* (Paris, 1922), pp. 281–97.

sort, there were three hundred Bruti.[12] Indeed, he may have been the father of Brutus Marat Lepeletier, or perhaps he was the cabinetmaker who christened his infant son Solon Brutus Weber, or the *commissaire du comité civil de la section du Mail* who named his infant Régénéré Anatole Pierre Lycurgue Combert.[13]

In any case, so many Phocions, Horaces, Scaevolas, and the like began again to walk among men that the Convention was asked to prohibit the "usurpation of classical names." The Convention at this time, however, refused to do so, perhaps partly because, as it was remarked, the practice was so common.[14] Indeed, the Convention itself participated in the craze by decreeing, on the motion of Barère, that copies of the bust of Brutus which adorned its meeting place should be multiplied and sold by the porcelain works at Sèvres.[15]

Except perhaps for the wearing of the Phrygian cap, not all Frenchmen—indeed, not the great majority—participated in this classical masquerade. The giving of classical names to the newborn was only a city, not a rural, phenomenon. It appeared, furthermore, only in certain cities where republicanism was strong—not, for example, in Bordeaux but in Paris. Nineteen-twentieths of the infants, therefore, it has been estimated, continued to be named Paul, Pierre, and Jean, etc.; and of the remaining twentieth, some received not classical names but those of revolutionary martyrs—Marat and Lepeletier.[16] Doubt-

---

[12] E. Biré, "La Révolution et l'enfance," *Revue de la Révolution*, I (1883), 68.

[13] *Ibid.*, pp. 69-70; Lévy, *op. cit.*, pp. 281-87 (2d carton).

[14] *A.P.*, LXXXI (December 8, 1793), 142; see also Vilate, *Causes secrètes de la journée du 9 au 10 thermidor* (Paris, 1825), p. 176; Claretie, *Camille Desmoulins, Lucile Desmoulins*, p. 415.

[15] *A.P.*, LXXXIII (December 25, 1793), 309.

[16] Lévy, *op. cit.*, pp. 220, 298.

less, in general, the same proportions apply to the alteration of the names of towns and of sections. Nevertheless, in Paris at least, these external trappings to the interest in antiquity—the rhetorical gasconading in popular addresses concerning how France would crush England as Rome crushed Carthage, the sudden popularity of the name of Brutus, the spread of his busts and portraits, the wearing of the Phrygian cap, the festivals decorated by David—these were sufficiently widespread and prominent that they might have led any visitor to Paris to conclude that when in France one should do as the Romans did.

These phenomena also gave to that interest in the antiquity which had begun as a thing of spirit among a few the formal outward semblances of a religious cult. Like every religion, the cult of antiquity now had its Bible—Plutarch and Livy; its Garden of Eden—the golden age of Greece and Rome; its hope of redemption after falling from this ancient state of grace; its saints and martyrs—Aristides, Socrates, Phocion, Cato, and Brutus; its images of saints— the busts of Brutus and the statues (in the Convention Hall) of Lycurgus, Solon, Camillus, and Cincinnatus; its miracle plays—Voltaire's *Brutus* and his *La mort de César*, Chénier's *Caïus Gracchus*, and others; its symbolism—the Phrygian cap and the fasces; its seminaries—the *collèges;* its philosophy of history—imitation of the good and avoidance of the bad past example; and, as we shall see, its sectarian division—namely, whether Solon or Lycurgus was the prophet to follow.

But, if classical nomenclature and the wearing of the Phrygian cap became a fad, it was not because admiration of antiquity had become, among the many, a religious sentiment. Nor was it because the multitude was guilty of an erudite knowledge of history. Rather, other reasons explain this widespread aping of antiquity. For one thing, such imitation was open to those of meanest capacity; for who was so poor that he could not sport a common laborer's *bonnet de laine*, thought to resemble the ancient cap of liberty, or who so mean as not to have a name to change. Then, too, as spectators of David's processions, of Voltaire's dramas, and of sessions of revolutionary oratory, man had come to know that such a *bonnet* and such names had in the past, in some vague way, stood for liberty. And, of course, once the fashion was well started, innumerable motives would further its spread. The desire to be conspicuous, to be in style, to feel grand and important,[17] to curry favor with a local Jacobin official,[18] to display contempt for Catholicism and hatred of the enemies of liberty, to conceal aristocratic conduct behind a liberty-loving façade,[19] or the wish to feel they were participating (if only by symbolic act) in the glorious struggle for liberty—all these desires would have led men to boast a cap of liberty or a high-sounding praenomen.

[17] *Révolutions de Paris*, XI, No. 141 (March 17–24, 1792), 534; *Le patriote français*, No. 1300 (March 4, 1793), p. 261.

[18] Lévy, *op. cit.*, p. 307; Biré, *op. cit.*, p. 67.

[19] *Révolutions de Paris*, XVIII, No. 220 (6–14 nivôse, l'an 2), 380; Lenôtre, *A Gascon Royalist in Revolutionary Paris* (New York, 1910), p. 34, n. 1; *Moniteur*, No. 174 (March 14, 1794), p. 687.

# CHAPTER XIII

## SOLON OR LYCURGUS

### I

WHEN Plutarch wrote his *Parallel Lives* he paired, as everyone knows, a Greek with a Roman, Theseus with Romulus, Lycurgus with Numa, Solon with Publicola. Had he not been bound by this pattern, he might well have joined and contrasted the two practical lawgivers of Greece, Solon and Lycurgus, the moderate and the radical, as typical of differences that sometimes exist among reformers. The moderate was of Athens, a man of modest station, rising from the people to be a model lawgiver unto his countrymen: not giving them the best laws in the world, but "the best they would receive"; not adapting the situation to the laws but the laws to the situation; not aiming at absolute equality among all citizens but hoping to preserve for them some liberty; not relying on force but on persuasion to preserve his work. The radical was of Sparta, a king for many years, giving to his countrymen, so said the Delphic oracle, the best constitution in the world—a constitution which adapted conditions to its laws rather than vice versa, which established equality among citizens while destroying their liberty, and which itself had to be established by force rather than by persuasion.[1]

What Plutarch failed to join, the French National Convention put together. When that Assembly moved on May 10, 1793, into its new hall in the Tuileries, its mem-

---

[1] On these points see *Plutarch, "Parallel Lives,"* I, 217–19, 443, 447, 465.

bers found themselves arranged in a rising tier of benches facing the orator on his tribune, the president, and the two secretaries behind their desks, and above, on an indented ledge which ran around the room, full-length statues of Solon and Lycurgus. In addition, on this same ledge stood Plato and Demosthenes; while against the opposite wall, above and behind the amphitheater in which the deputies sat, these four Greeks were matched by statues of Camillus, V. Publicola, J. Brutus, and Cincinnatus—Romans all. With plaster, cloth, paper, and paint the interior decorator of the hall had done his best to make these eight strangers feel at home. He suspended over the head of each of them an imitation crown of laurel, formerly among Greeks a mark of distinction. With rich silks he draped the president's chair *à la romaine*. He painted the plaster walls an imitation yellow marble, relieved by various ornaments of different colors. Among the ornaments most frequently repeated were the crowns of laurel and also the fasces, formerly carried by Roman lictors. The president's desk and the orator's rostrum were painted a *vert antique* and adorned with supporting pilasters colored a *jaune antique*. Altogether the effect in general was, so a contemporary tells us, that of pure and noble simplicity, *dans le style du bel antique*. True, the acoustics of the hall were wretched, and the means of ventilation scanty, with the result that if the speaker spoke softly he was not heard, if he spoke loudly he was not understood, while if he spoke late in the day he might find that stale and stuffy air had dulled the minds of his listeners.[2] But of what importance were these material lacks when one had all the properties

[2] These facts are largely taken from a contemporary account by a journalist named Dulaure, who described the hall in *Le thermomètre du jour*, May 13, 1793, quoted in Lenôtre, *Paris révolutionnaire*, p. 107.

for enacting a classical tragedy, or when one could grandly refer to Solon and Lycurgus, who were looking on?[3]

After the expulsion of the leading Girondists, the two Conventionnels who probably took this antique atmosphere most seriously were two personal enemies, Camille Desmoulins and Saint-Just—one a liberal, the other a radical; one an admirer of Solon and Athens, the other devoted to Lycurgus and Sparta. With the early revolutionary career of Desmoulins as a republican opponent of the monarchy we are already acquainted. We now find him in the summer and autumn of 1793 again in the opposition, but this time with hostility directed against the dread Committee of Public Safety and against its policy of terror. His personal relationships—for example, with the royalist Dillon, the anti-Terrorist Fabre d'Eglantine, and with Danton, who now was proposing that "the blood of men should be spared"; his own newly developed horror of bloodletting (at the trial of the Girondists, whose fall he had abetted, he was nearly overcome by pity and stabbing remorse); and his professional conviction that liberty of the press must be maintained—all conspired to turn him against this régime which crushed freedom of the press, arrested friends of his, like Dillon, and cut off men's heads by the basketful.

But what could he, a feeble orator and a member of no influential committee, hope to do to end the régime he disliked? Open attack in the press would only lead to arrest. In his newspaper, the *Vieux cordelier*, he resorted, therefore, to irony—that last refuge of the impotent intellectual. Under the pretense of giving a literal translation of Tacitus, and under the guise of describing the suspicious cruelties of Tiberius, of Nero, and of Caligula, who

[3] For such oratorical references, first by Danton, then by Barère, see *A.P.*, LXV (May 18, 1793), 65; LXV (May 29, 1793), 578.

had executed the innocent on the denunciations of inform-
ers, Desmoulins traced a terrible picture of a similar
slaughter under the tyrants of the Terror—all the while
gravely protesting that he was depicting what had happened under the Roman Empire merely to show what horrors would visit France if a monarchy returned; all the
while gravely maintaining with wide-eyed innocence that
it was not he who was speaking but History, or rather
Tacitus. This "method of covert allusions and perfidious
irony" was not new; it was, it has been observed, that of
the Encyclopedists.[4] Nor was the use of Tacitus to describe and to damn revolutionary horrors novel; the reactionary *Actes des apôtres* under the Constituent Assembly
had already published a translated paragraph or two from
the *Histories* for that very purpose.[5] Indeed, throughout
the Revolution, in private and sometimes in public, it was
the fashion, if you felt ill used or oppressed, to identify
your opponent with Tiberius or Nero and yourself with
their victims. In this way you identified your oppressor
with Vice and yourself with Virtue; you sustained the evil
opinion you had of his political morality and you kept a
good conceit of yourself. Desmoulins' essay made it possible for the great number to accomplish this pleasant identification. Indeed, perhaps the popularity of his essay may
in part be explained by the fact that, while aristocrats and
bourgeois could chuckle over its irony and relish its attack
on the unpopular Terror, they could also find in it high
authority—that of Tacitus and of history—to confirm
their private estimate of their oppressors and of themselves.

Desmoulins soon abandoned, however, his ironical pretense and began more openly to have it out with the Terror

4 Mathiez, *The French Revolution* (New York, 1928), 433.

5 *Actes des apôtres*, IV, No. 115, p. 3.

and its supporters. So much bloodletting, he says, is unwise. Though we need to arouse in the citizenry a love for the Republic, yet the Terror, by alienating the condemned and their relations, is arousing fear and hate and is thus undermining the institutions it is supposed to establish. Besides, the Terror is unnecessary. There is no need to kindle in citizens an austere love of frugality and simplicity. All that is needed to maintain a republic is liberty, that is, the observance of the principles of the declaration of rights, the cessation of arbitrary arrest and imprisonment, and, above all, the maintenance of liberty of the press.[6] Liberty thus conceived and thus defined would, he promised, bring happiness.

To give content and collateral to his promise, he again cited, as in 1789, the good times free Athenians once had had.[7] Had his newspaper not been suppressed, he would have continued these tactics and would have given the Athenian vision added content as a changing controversy led him to find new things in old sources. The intolerance with which the Terror government treated criticism of itself would have led him to extol at length the freedom allowed Athenian playwrights to satirize generals, ministers, and committees. The repeated reflections cast on his love of women and wine by more austere fellow-republicans would have induced him to exclaim:

What a charming democracy is that of Athens! There Solon did not pass for a dandy; . . . . though he made no difficulty of confessing his penchant for wine, women, and song . . . . he was, nonetheless, regarded as a model legislator.[8]

[6] *Vieux cordelier*, No. 3 (December 15, 1793), p. 45; No. 4 (December 20, 1793), pp. 51–52; No. 5 (December 25, 1793), p. 90; No. 6 (December 30, 1793), p. 103. But the dates printed on the newspaper do not correspond to the dates on which the numbers appeared: No. 5 came out on January 5, 1794; No. 6 came out in February.

[7] *Ibid.*, No. 6, pp. 110–11; see also pp. 109, 112.

[8] *Ibid.*, No. 7 (posthumous publication), in Desmoulins, *Œuvres*, II, 273.

His new conservative moderation and the attempts by radical Terrorists to realize by force a seemingly impossible, unpopular ideal would have caused him to praise Solon's maxim: "The legislator who works on material of a rebellious nature should give to his country not the laws which are best in theory but the best laws the people will tolerate."[9] While he had already thought in May, 1793, that the detailed institutions Athenians once had received would also do very well for France: free theater tickets for the poor; the prytanaeum for those who had served their country well; the enrolment of men of the same region in the same regiment; exemption from military service of those who equipped a cavalryman; and a taxation system which would be easy on Desmoulins' new intimates, the well-to-do.[10]

In this way in 1793, as in 1789, Desmoulins brought before the public this vision of Athenian life to assure others, as it had assured himself, that his tastes, principles, and policies were correct. It was natural that he should do so. For by 1793 he cherished a philosophy of style which told him that, "to give clearness to the ideas of an author, there is nothing like comparisons and images." He also harbored a philosophy of history which taught him that examples from ancient history taught lessons, that history was the sole teacher of those who wish to learn the art of governing. In addition, he held a philosophy of propaganda which told him that, to gain supporters, he must so picture his republic that men would believe its realization meant happiness. All three philosophies encouraged him to use past examples. But naturally he picked for use that example which clarified his ideas as he wished them clarified, taught those lessons he wished history to teach, and

[9] *Ibid.*, p. 251.

[10] *A.P.*, LXXV (October 3, 1793), 633-34.

indicated that liberty would bring to men those satisfactions he imagined they craved. In his conception of Athens he found the classical instance which did all these things—which, as an instrument of propaganda, served him well.

## II

While Camille Desmoulins turned to the institutions of Athens, his chief oratorical opponents—Saint-Just, perhaps Robespierre, and to a lesser extent Billaud-Varenne—preferred those of Sparta. Of the three, Saint-Just was most prone to think, like Camille, in terms of the imitation of antiquity. But in many other respects he was the antithesis of Desmoulins. While the latter admired the prosperity and good living of Athens, Saint-Just esteemed the stern virtue of early Rome, and especially of Sparta. Along with, or perhaps behind, this difference in emphasis lay a difference in tastes. For, while Camille was a good liver, if not a loose one, Saint-Just was that strange creature, a Puritan in Paris, living up to his puritanical code of austerity, self-denial, and severe simplicity.[11]

Saint-Just, however, had not always been so exemplary a character. Though probably never the scamp that conservatives had pictured, yet before the Revolution he possibly did run off with, and sell, his mother's silver, while in his published poem *Organt* he occasionally rhymed an obscene tale. After 1789, however, ambitious, as always, to cut a figure in the world, but now specifically stimulated by the opportunity the Revolution offered to be the noble patriot in great events, he became a new, more virtuous character. Indeed, he appeared to remake himself into a man, until by 1794 he had subjugated all his passions (if we may believe his friend Gatteaux) to his love of coun-

[11] Saint-Just, *Œuvres*, I, xi; Barère, *Mémoires*, IV, 408-9.

try.[12] But though the Revolution gave the stimulus, it may be surmised that classical heroes gave the model for this transformation. Evidence to support this guess, however, is scanty. Yet he was ever fashioning himself—his style of writing, thinking, and acting—closely after the pattern set by illustrious men whom he admired (Voltaire, Montesquieu, Scaevola, Lycurgus), sometimes impregnating his own spirit with that of another.[13] It may also be observed that the admiration for "virtuous and simple antiquity" existed before his reformation occurred;[14] and that the conception of virtue he adopted, the ideal patriot he himself once described,[15] and the character he became, were all in the approved Plutarchian pattern—a compound of austerity, simplicity, and forgetfulness of self in devotion to country.

At all events, as early as 1790, Virtue thus conceived was his ideal. He admired it in the past, in the republican heroes of antiquity; he deplored its lack in the present, in luxury-loving, depraved, egoistic France;[16] he entreated members of the Constituent to revive it in the future. "O Legislators! Give us laws which force us to love them; . . . . forgetfulness of self and love of country is the source of all good."[17] And he was hopeful that, ere his age was doubled (he was then twenty-two), he would see French private morals regenerated by free institutions.[18]

This hope and this entreaty presupposed faith in the

[12] Saint-Just, *op. cit.*, I, xii.

[13] Nover, *Saint-Just*, pp. 7, 14; L. Lévi, "Saint-Just était-il un disciple de Robespierre?" *La Révolution française*, LXXII (1919), 392–93.

[14] Saint-Just, "Organt," *op. cit.*, I, 81.

[15] *Moniteur*, No. 207 (April 16, 1794), p. 221.

[16] Saint-Just, *Esprit de la Constitution*, I, 283, 287, 291, 292.

[17] *Ibid.*, p. 292.          [18] *Ibid.*, p. 291.

power of institutions and of their creator, the lawgiver. This faith Saint-Just did not lack. In 1790 he concludes, from the Lycurgan example, that "when the legislator has bent to his uses the possible virtues of the people, he has done all,"[19] implying that this feat was in the power of man, and indicating what was to become more apparent, that his faith in the might of the legislator was sustained and probably inspired by the example of Lycurgus. But the legislator, though powerful, is not omnipotent. He can bend only the possible virtues. In France he cannot, on the whole, imitate that "virtuous and simple antiquity" so full "of institutions which resemble madness but which attest its lovely simplicity";[20] he cannot revive immodest Spartan gymnastics ("I regret that they appear so strange to us, and that we are so nice only because we are so corrupt");[21] nor can the legislator set up a republic that would endure ("When Rome expanded, she had need of magistrates whose authority was immense").[22] Circumstance, as interpreted by Saint-Just's logic, itself based in part on conceptions of classical history, thus set bounds to what the legislator could do.

But as circumstances changed, imitation of antiquity came within the reach of hope. The first step in this direction was taken when Saint-Just, as a member of the Convention, felt himself obliged to plan for the creation of a French republic that would endure. The belief that a large republic was impossible naturally now became, in more senses than one, "ancient history." The second step toward imitation was not taken until the Terror. For until then, though he believed he possessed the power of a Lycurgus,[23] he used it with the gentle discretion and the pol-

[19] *Ibid.*, p. 282; see also pp. 283, 288.

[20] *Ibid.*, p. 287.                    [22] *Ibid.*, p. 264.

[21] *Ibid.*                              [23] *A.P.*, LXIII (April 24, 1793), 201.

itic moderation of a Solon. To accomplish the regeneration
of Frenchmen, he then thought that constraint would not
be needed, force should not be used, and legislation could
be keyed to a judicious adaptability to things as they are.[24]
For in reforming a people just emerging from corruption,
"One must yield to their weaknesses, . . . . and fit the laws
to the people, not the people to the laws."[25] The example
of Lycurgus by itself was insufficient to extort approval of
Lycurgan methods and means.

At this time, during the first nine months of the Convention, the position of Robespierre and Billaud-Varenne was
not greatly different. Both believed virtue was indispensable in a republic; both would regenerate Frenchmen.[26]
Like Saint-Just, a somber flame, austere, industrious, and
frugal,[27] with a character fortified by classical example,
Robespierre would draw men to a republic of political virtue. Billaud-Varenne, going a bit farther, would extirpate
depravity by checking luxury, and check luxury by re-
ducing inequality of wealth. Both agreed that a radical
course was in theory advisable. Robespierre said the time-
serving spirit of Solon must be shunned.[28] Billaud-Varenne
was for abrupt reform.[29] Saint-Just, too, had said: "It
does no good to be feeble." But in practice both would
realize ultimate radical perfection with a circumspect
gradualism. Neither would imitate the radical antiquity

[24] *Œuvres*, I, 353, 380, 419.

[25] *Ibid.*, p. 423.

[26] Billaud-Varenne, *Les éléments du républicanisme* in *A.P.*, LXVII (June 24,
1793), 224, 231–32, 234; for an earlier statement see Billaud-Varenne, *Acéphocratie*, p. 44; Robespierre, *Lettres à ses commettans*, I, No. 1, 6; II, No. 2, 49–51.

[27] Vilate, *Causes secrètes de la Journée du 9 au 10 thermidor*, p. 183; Hamel,
*Robespierre*, I, 19; Saint-Just, *Œuvres*, I, xiii.

[28] Robespierre, *op. cit.*, I, No. 1, 2; I, No. 8, 342; II, No. 1, 23, n. i.

[29] *A.P.*, LXVII (June 24, 1793), 239; for an earlier statement see Billaud
Varenne, *Le peintre politique* (1789), p. 28.

they admired. Equality of wealth, said Billaud, must come, not through an equal division of land, impossible and chimerical, but through laws distributing large inheritances to the poor.[30] This reform, though radical, had the merit of not producing "a sudden and convulsive upheaval," which arouses the opposition of all, renders the efforts of the lawgiver unavailing, and exposes him to the danger of assassination. Witness the sad end of the radicals Lysander and Agis at Sparta, Solon at Athens, and the Gracchi at Rome.[31]

As for Robespierre, his advice was often so discreet and so moderate that Solon might have approved. Until the new laws and moral customs are fixed, conciliate, he said, the religious prejudices of mankind and tolerate the religious, sacred bases of morality. "Do not disdain to recall with what wisdom the greatest legislators of antiquity . . . . humored the weakness or the prejudices of their fellow-citizens."[32] Until, furthermore, we have preserved the people and given them a constitution, let us postpone the establishment of a system of public instruction. To this advice, someone may oppose the example of Sparta. But, though Robespierre himself esteemed Lycurgus and his laws, he asked the objector to reflect. "He will see that he is speaking of a little city whose laws were founded on two principles which are abhorrent to us: poverty and community of goods."[33] The objector, moreover, will see that there liberty and a sound virtue had already been established. We, however, have just emerged from servitude into a period of storm and faction, unsuited to far-reaching educational reform.

30 *A.P.*, LXVII (June 24, 1793), 239, 240, 242, 243, 244.

31 *Ibid.*, p. 239.

32 Robespierre, *op. cit.*, I, No. 8, 342.    33 *Ibid.*, II, No. 2, 57.

I [too, he continues] could parade brilliant descriptions of national festivals, and perhaps produce a moment of illusion by presenting to you the phantom of some Lacedaemonian institutions; . . . . but, before forming a people, it is necessary to preserve it and give it a constitution.[34]

With all three men the power and problems which came to them as sharers in the dictatorship of the Terror altered their plans. Shortly after Billaud-Varenne wrote his *Eléments du républicanisme* in June, 1793, the retreat of French armies, the revolt of the Vendée and the Midi, and the decline of the assignats were compelling legislators to postpone establishment of permanent institutional reform while they built up a provisional Terror government to meet immediate needs. In the winter of 1794, however, even while the factional fight with Hébert and Danton was on, and more especially in the spring, the pressure of immediate necessity began slowly to lessen. All the invading armies were finally checked and then thrown back; the domestic uprisings were localized and sometimes suppressed; and the Terror dictatorship was completely organized. At this time the talk of planning permanent institutions for a permanent republic was revived by Billaud-Varenne, Robespierre, and Saint-Just, partly because they found in the Terror a new means to realize their plan, partly because they found in their plan a means to justify the Terror to themselves and their critic, Desmoulins.

The latter, it may be recalled, had questioned the wisdom of the Terror, made light of its alleged necessity, and had quoted Solon. He had obliquely made enticing allusions to the gay, luxurious, "Athenian" good times his countrymen might be having if only liberty came and the Terror was discontinued. In their reply, Robespierre, Saint-Just, and Billaud-Varenne sought to outbid critics

[34] *Ibid.*, p. 59.

like these by declaring that they too had a plan and that their plan would bring a higher, a more virtuous, felicity to Frenchmen. But such felicity, these three intimated, presupposed a virtuous citizenry and a republic that would endure; hence, regeneration of Frenchmen; hence, vigorous, improving institutions to reform the weak, and the Terror to weed out the incorrigible.[35] Where, however, could they find a congenial example to justify such ruthless radicalism? Not in America, England, Holland, or Italy; but only in antiquity, and perhaps only in Sparta. So Billaud-Varenne cited with praise the example of Lycurgus, the severity and rapidity of his reform, and contrasted it with the weak and futile moderation of Solon.[36] Indeed, the Lycurgan example teaches, he said, that regeneration by the Lycurgan method "can be accomplished more easily and more rapidly than the perversion of an honest heart," and that it would bring "the fairest days of the ancient republics" to compensate for "so many centuries of persecution and of barbarism."[37]

Saint-Just, too, now referred with praise to Lycurgus, whose "pitiless severity" had established his reforms.[38] More than that, Saint-Just now advocated the establishment of institutions to constrain conduct.[39] This was the

[35] *A.P.*, LXXIX (November 18, 1793), 452; *Moniteur*, No. 62 (November 22, 1793), p. 474; No. 97 (December 27, 1793), pp. 51, 52; No. 139 (February 7, 1794), pp. 401–2, 403; No. 159 (February 27, 1794), pp. 566, 568; No. 174 (March 14, 1794), p. 689; No. 212 (April 21, 1794), pp. 263, 264; No. 229 (May 8, 1794), p. 407.

[36] *Moniteur*, No. 212 (April 21, 1794), p. 264; Billaud-Varenne, *Principes régénérateurs du système social* (Paris, Pluviôse, l'an 3), p. 53. Though this latter work was published after the Terror, it probably expresses the views of Billaud-Varenne during the Terror as well.

[37] Billaud-Varenne, *Système social*, pp. 38, 58; see also pp. 5, 30–31, 37, 59–60, 60–61, 109–10, 134–36.

[38] *Moniteur*, No. 159 (February 27, 1794), p. 568.    [39] *Ibid.*, p. 566.

same Saint-Just who only a year before had declared that force should not be used and constraint would not be needed. In addition, he now was ready to solve the problem of regeneration by following the recommendations of Authority, Tradition, and Prestige—by attempting, in other words, the feat of transplanting certain specific classical institutions to France.[40] His power as a member of the Terror dictatorship and his old "Lycurgan" belief in the might of the legislator had apparently induced him to feel free to dare, to plan, and to do.

Had his life not been cut short by the guillotine, in a few days he would have moved before the Convention[41] the organization of a system of public festivals;[42] the setting-up, supposedly after a classical model, of elderly censors to blame, if necessary, the private life of youths and of officials;[43] and, more important, the creation of an educational régime in part modeled after that of Sparta. On the latter point, a comparison of similar, though not always like, passages of Plutarch's *Lives* and Saint-Just's posthumous report will reveal some of the indebtedness of Saint-Just to Sparta and will lay bare, perhaps, a process of his thinking (see p. 160). As in Sparta, furthermore, so in France: reading and writing would be taught, but things military would be stressed. From the ages of ten to sixteen, adolescents would be drilled in all the infantry and cavalry maneuvers; from twenty-one to twenty-five all citizens would enter the national militia. In all this, of course, the Lycurgan ex-

[40] On the problem of regeneration and its solution by institutional reform see Saint-Just, *Fragmens d'institutions républicaines*, pp. 361–62, 374, 379, 381.

[41] Mathiez, *Girondins et Montagnards* (Paris, 1930), p. 163; Saint-Just, *Nachgelassene Schriften und Reden* (Kassel, 1852), p. 221.

[42] Saint-Just, *Fragmens d'institutions républicaines*, pp. 506–8.

[43] *Ibid.*, pp. 408–10.

| PLUTARCH | SAINT-JUST |
|---|---|
| In Sparta the male children were taken from their parents at the age of seven and raised by the country for nine years. | The male children are raised, from ages five to sixteen, by the country. |
| They were enrolled in certain companies. | They are distributed in companies. |
| Of these, he who showed the best conduct and courage was made captain. | The teachers name, each month, the chief from among those who manifested the best conduct. |
| They were lodged together in little bands upon beds made of rushes. | They sleep on straw mats. |
| Their fare was plain and consisted of salads and herbs. | They eat in common, and live only on roots, fruit, vegetables, milk, bread, and water. |
| Children in Sparta, by a habit of long silence, came to give just and sententious answers. | The children are brought up in the love of silence. |
| They taught them to comprehend much matter of thought in few words. | They are formed to laconic speech.[44] |

ample affected the thought of Saint-Just, simply because it aided him to give precise form to the promptings of his own laconism, austerity, and military ardor. As someone has said, "It takes two to make an influence." Where, therefore, the Spartan example did not harmonize with his own tastes and principles, Saint-Just departed from the Spartan ideal. In contrast to the Spartan ideal of leisure for citizens, Saint-Just would have all learn farming and a trade.[45] Though willing to adopt the slightest details of the

[44] *Ibid.*, pp. 395–97; Plutarch, *"Parallel Lives,"* I, 83–85, 91.

[45] Saint-Just, *Fragmens*, pp. 397–98.

Spartan scheme with a reverence almost superstitious, still he would point these details to an end truly modern, would rear these youths in a modern respect for manual labor. For in the labor of all, not in the leisure for the few, had he ever found the sovereign remedy for the economic and social ills afflicting France.

Without direct proof, it may be assumed that Robespierre, the ally, and at times even the collaborator, of Saint-Just, knew of the latter's neo-Greek and neo-Spartan projects for public festivals and education in common; and it may be assumed that these projects had his approval. True, in the winter of 1792–93, Robespierre had indirectly censured in advance any scheme to create an educational system remotely resembling the Spartan; he had then ridiculed those who propose festivals, and had criticized educational reform as untimely. But when times changed, Robespierre changed too. What he once had censured when proposed by others, he now hailed with enthusiasm when proposed by himself. In the summer of 1793, with the Girondist faction out of the way and a constitutional foundation nearly laid, he led the fight for the adoption of Lepeletier's posthumous plan to educate children in communal lodgings away from their parents. In principle Lepeletier's scheme did not greatly differ from Saint-Just's more Spartan project. Since Robespierre was willing to support the first plan, it may be surmised that he was no less willing to adopt the second. In May, 1794, furthermore, he appropriated, while enlarging the work of the Committee of Public Instruction on public festivals, a work which had been set in motion by the speeches of Rabaut de Saint-Etienne and of Chénier, themselves inspired by antiquity. With the energy of the Terror available, and with himself able in part to direct its use (especially since, in the Committee of Public Safety, public instruction was his special province), Robespierre in May, 1794, proceeded to do what he once had ridiculed, proceeded to parade brilliant descriptions of national festivals, and to produce a moment of illusion by presenting the phantom of a classical institution.

> They speak [he said] with enthusiasm of the national festivals of Greece; yet they had as their object hardly more than games in which shone physical force, skill, or, at the very most, the talent of poets and of orators. But Greece was there; one saw . . . . the people who had been victorious over Asia, and whose republican virtues had raised them at times above humanity. One saw the great men who had saved and distinguished the country; fathers pointed out to their sons Miltiades, Aristides, Epaminondas, Timoleon, whose mere presence was a living lesson in magnanimity, in justice, and in patriotism. (*Applause*).[46]

As if it were not enough to equal the Greeks, whose virtues "sometimes raised them above humanity," Robespierre would have the French give to their own assemblies a greater scope and a nobler character. How easy, he thought; for all that was needed was a public festival every tenth day to honor some single civic and social virtue—to honor liberty, equality, love of country, frugality, or the Supreme Being. And how desirable! For a system of national festivals is "the dearest bond of fraternity and the most powerful means of regeneration." It is no wonder that he would institute them immediately, and, linking the festivals to his civil religion inspired by Rousseau, would celebrate the festival of the Supreme Being at once. This latter suggestion was, in fact, immediately carried out by the Convention.

Because Robespierre, Saint-Just, and to a lesser extent Billaud-Varenne appeared eager to make live again the institutions and the *beaux jours* of Greece and of Sparta, conservatives have sometimes assumed that during the Terror the leading Conventionnels were entirely over-

---

[46] *Moniteur*, No. 229 (May 8, 1794), pp. 409-10.

powered by a mad desire to remold French institutions and men after the Spartan model. There have always been those, however, who denied this accusation.[47] Of these, Barère, himself a leading Terrorist, was perhaps the first. The Convention, he said, was not so stupid as to attempt to make Spartans of Parisians.

The Conventionnels [he added] acted according to the necessity of the moment, in order to preserve the territory in its entirety and the nation in its independence. That was the only question in 1793 and 1794. . . . . It was therefore not a question of copying the ancient republics.[48]

It is easy to see why Barère might, in this case, believe what he wrote. Strange weathercock though he was— turning with, yet helping to turn, the winds of revolutionary doctrine—still in all his gyrations he had never been greatly taken with the project of a thoroughgoing imitation of antiquity. Then, too, much that Barère knew supported his view. He was no doubt aware that from August, 1793, up to the winter of 1794, when the Terror government was being built up, interest in antiquity exerted no appreciable influence. The present need to save the country and a sense of the expedient then dictated decisions. During the Terror, therefore, serious interest in antiquity was limited in time—to the winter and spring of 1794. It was also limited in the number of persons influenced; among the leaders, to three—Saint-Just, Robespierre, and Billaud-Varenne. Among these few, its influence was limited in scope. Probably to none of these three did the Lycurgan instance suggest the *method* of reform. Robespierre never seemed enamored of the Lycurgan example. As for the other two, before the Terror both expressed the desire to go slow; while in addition Saint-Just, and doubtless

[47] Besides Barère, see M. A. Baudot, *Notes historiques* (Paris, 1893), p. 127.

[48] *Op. cit.*, I, 102.

Billaud-Varenne, wished to be reasonably gentle. But once the Terror policy, with its ruthlessness, its regimentation, its comparative radicalism, was invented to defend a provisional régime, then both were for applying this policy to the task of permanently regenerating France. It is possible, in view of the antique temper of these men, that the Lycurgan example suggested this application. But it may be more plausibly assumed that the decision to use the Terror policy in establishing their reform was inspired simply by the belief that this policy gave them the power to do rapidly what they had always longed to do, the Lycurgan example serving only to defend and fortify a decision already made.

Of these three, furthermore, only to two—Robespierre and Saint-Just—did antiquity suggest specific *means* to be used, specific institutions to be set up. In the program of these two, moreover, these classic institutions were not the whole but only a part. There is no evidence to show that their famous scheme to confiscate the property of the enemies of the Revolution and to distribute it among needy patriots was the product of imaginations diseased by the vision of Spartan equalitarianism. Saint-Just's speeches indicate other motives. Of the twenty-five pages, furthermore, which outline the civil institutions which Saint-Just (and perhaps Robespierre) planned for France, eighteen bear no mark of classical influence. Yet these eighteen range over a variety of problems involving marriage, guardianship, adoption, the inheritance of property, contracts, funerals, the police, the army, commerce, colonies, and the public domain—problems to whose solution classical experience could have sometimes been applied. The only pages which betray admiration for antiquity deal with schools, festivals, and censors. Saint-Just, and also Robespierre, linked the classical past only with these questions

with which it had already been linked by other Conventionnels. As far as the imitation of specific institutions was
concerned, the thought of these two merely continued the
movement of the preceding year.

It was, however, as an influence on the *goal* of reform
that a certain conception of the classical past became a
power. This conception, cherished by Robespierre and
Saint-Just, was a consummation of a progressive with-
drawal of classical Greek history from portrayal of the
harsher, uglier features of reality. Plutarch initiated the
development when he accentuated the good and slighted
the bad in his historical characters; Montesquieu and
Rousseau, with their stress on the political virtue and the
frugality of the Greeks, and with their talk of the giants of
another age, revived and exaggerated the Plutarchian
tendency; while Robespierre and Saint-Just, ignoring, as
Plutarch, Montesquieu, and Rousseau had never done, the
injustices of the populace and the occasional lapses of their
great men, raised these Greeks "above humanity" and
transformed their flesh-and-blood heroes into flawless, life-
less symbols of the abstract virtues, like characters in a
miracle play. When, in addition, it was observed by Plutarch and the *philosophes* that when virtue decayed the
classical republics declined, everything was ready for these
two logical revolutionaries to reason that, to preserve their
own French republic from a similar fate, they must create
and maintain a similar, superhuman virtue. At first they
merely proposed to revive the classical love of country, of
liberty—of the republic, in brief—a plan that was neither
unreasonable (for if republican institutions do not live in
the hearts of the people, their life is apt to be precarious)
nor impracticable. Under the Terror, this older, more
moderate plan was not entirely forgotten. Now, as before,
in terms borrowed from Montesquieu, himself inspired by

observation of the classical republics, Saint-Just and
Robespierre still discussed the necessity of political virtue
in the French Republic. As Saint-Just said: "Un gouvernement républicain a la vertu pour principe."[49] As
Robespierre explained:

> What is the fundamental principle of a democratic and popular
> government, that is, the essential motive which supports it and makes
> it move? It is virtue: I speak of the political virtue which accom-
> plished so many prodigies in Greece and in Rome, and which ought to
> produce far more astonishing ones in republican France; of that virtue
> which is nothing else than the love of our country and of its laws.
> But since the spirit of the republic . . . . is equality, it follows that
> love of country necessarily embraces the love of equality.[50]

But at the height of the Terror, Robespierre and Saint-
Just went farther. This revival of virtue after the classical
conception, hitherto considered solely as a means to establish a durable republic, now became, in addition, an end in
itself. As Robespierre exclaimed: "We wish an order of
things where every passion that is cruel and vile will be
unknown, where every passion that is beneficent and noble
will be awakened by the laws"—where, in brief, all the ig-
noble passions of ambition, cupidity, and personal pride
will be sublimated in a noble love of country.[51] At the same
time, these two men now assumed that not only the political virtue of the classical past but also its simplicity, its
frugality, and indeed all the virtues that antiquity and
frustrated desire could suggest, should be made to live
again. For, after all, as Robespierre said, "This sublime
sentiment [the love of country] assumes a preference for

[49] Saint-Just, *Fragmens*, p. 381.

[50] *Moniteur*, No. 139 (February 7, 1794), p. 402; for other passages where
Robespierre and also Saint-Just identify their conception of virtue with their
vision of antiquity, see No. 97 (December 27, 1793), p. 52; No. 139 (February 7,
1794), p. 403; No. 174 (March 14, 1794), p. 689; No. 192 (April 1, 1794), p. 97;
No. 229 (May 8, 1794), pp. 404, 407-8, 411.

[51] *Ibid.*, p. 402.

the public interest over every private interest, whence it results that love of country again assumes or produces all the virtues."[52] In a preceding paragraph he enumerated these virtues. There he pictured a millennial future possessed with all the excellences that the virtues of the classical republics and the vices of the *ancien régime* could suggest. In France, he planned to substitute:

. . . . morality for egoism, probity for honor . . . . pride for insolence, greatness of soul for vanity, love of glory for love of money, . . . . the greatness of man for the pettiness of the great; a people which is magnanimous, powerful, and happy for a people which is amiable, frivolous, and wretched—that is, all the virtues and all the miracles of the republic for all the vices and all the absurdities of the monarchy.[53]

In addition to political virtue, Saint-Just would awaken in Frenchmen courage and frugality,[54] both classical virtues, and a love of Arcadian, "antique" simplicity. For Saint-Just, a small-town youth in the big city, was discontented with his agitated, complex existence in Paris. He sighed for the time (so an intimate tells us) when, with a congenial mate, he could retire from the revolutionary turmoil, contemplate nature, and enjoy "the repose of private life in a rustic retreat . . . . far from the poisoned gaze of city-dwellers."[55] And into his Heavenly City of Virtue, he projects not only the vision of antiquity but also this more personal utopia. In replying to Desmoulins, he writes that there are those who arouse the aristocracy by reawakening

. . . . the desire for that happiness which consists of the forgetfulness of others and the enjoyment of the superfluous; . . . . but it is not the happiness of Persepolis which we offer [but that] of Sparta and of Athens; . . . . of virtue; . . . . the happiness which is born of the enjoyment of the necessary without superfluity. . . . . The people make the republic by the simplicity of their manners and morals. . . . . The happiness which we offer is not that of corrupt peoples; . . . . a plow, a field, a thatched hut . . . . a family . . . . —that is happiness.[56]

[52] *Ibid.*  [53] *Ibid.*  [54] Saint-Just, *Fragmens*, p. 361.  [55] Saint-Just, *Œuvres*, I, xiii.
[56] *Moniteur*, No. 174 (March 14, 1794), p. 689.

Desmoulins, too, it may be remembered, had found the state of Athens ideal because there one lived in ease and luxury and enjoyed the superfluities that make life worth while. Saint-Just also seemed to admire ancient Athens, but contrasted its happiness with that of Desmoulins and Persepolis. He seemed to view Athens, therefore, as a place where one lived simply, using only necessities and rejecting superfluities. If this be true, then each framed his conception of Athenian life in accordance with his frustrated desires for what he thought admirable. No wonder both could admire life in the same city.

This would suggest that in the personal evolution which made the creation of a commonwealth of classical virtue first the means and then the end of republican endeavor, the moral character of Saint-Just and of Robespierre was a factor. Conceivably with a different character, they would have adopted, perhaps, that other eighteenth-century conception of antiquity, made familiar by Voltaire and his admirer Desmoulins. These latter viewed with pleasure Athenian good times; ridiculed the simple frugality of Sparta and of early Rome; scoffed at the notion that the life of republics (including the classical) depended on private virtue; and were told by Reason, which, like Nature, speaks a various language, that all republics were founded on some sort of personal appeal—to man's ambition and to his jealousy of the success of others, said Voltaire; to man's desire for self-indulgence, said Desmoulins; in brief, to self-love, to that side of human nature which has ever been one of the constants in history. But this conception harmonized ill with the simple, non-luxury-loving, stoic life of Robespierre and Saint-Just. It told them, if anything, that their inflexible austerity was unnecessary, was unimportant, was indeed a stupidity in a republic. No wonder these two scorned the penetration of Voltaire or the chatter of Desmoulins. Especially when they could find in the works of their own favorites, Montesquieu and Rousseau, a congenial conception of classical history which helped the two Terrorists to believe that virtue such as they practiced and professed was the mainstay of republics, including the classical. Thus it might seem that not antiquity but the character of these two determined that the revival of virtue should become their goal.

Such a theory, however, ignores the fact that before the Convention their characters were themselves affected, partly formed, and largely fortified by the examples of antiquity. Such a theory, moreover, merely explains why a certain conception of antiquity was accepted; it does not deny the influence this conception exerted. It does not deny that in the development whose history we have sketched, antiquity, as mediated by Plutarch, Montesquieu, and Rousseau, played the more active part. It suggested that virtue was necessary in a republic; it defined what sort of virtue was needed; and it assured that such virtue would indeed bring happiness, prodigious valor, *les beaux jours de l'antiquité*. The mind and the character of Saint-Just, and especially of Robespierre, took the more passive part. The two men accepted the suggestion; they welcomed the assurance; and they adopted the definition of virtue, stopping only to fill in its outlines with concrete details inspired by discontent either with the *ancien régime* or with life under the Terror.

Influenced, therefore, by the classical past and by their ethical tastes, themselves strengthened and perhaps partly fashioned by antiquity, Robespierre and Saint-Just now dreamed of making over the moral nature of a people, of creating a commonwealth of virtue. It was one of those ideals for which men die and kill others. For it was largely this extraordinary goal, whose attainment required ex-

traordinary means, that led these two in the spring of 1794
to fight for the prolongation of the Terror policy after it was
somewhat perilous to do so and after the immediate necessity which had occasioned the development of that policy
had passed away.[57]

[57] The fact that a few individuals like Desmoulins confessed a desire for an
"Athenian" republic, while others, like Saint-Just, avowed a preference for
things Spartan has led later writers to describe revolutionary party differences
in classical terminology. Buonarotti, for example, a confederate of the famed
equalitarian Babeuf, spoke of the dissensions in the Convention as quarrels between those who "sighed for the riches, the superfluities, and the magnificence
of Athens" and those "who desired the frugality, the simplicity, and the plain-
ness of the fairest days of Sparta." To the first group belong, he added, the
Girondists and the Indulgents (the party of Danton and Desmoulins); to the
second, the Terrorists. Aulard, though later of a different opinion, also once asserted that "doubtless, the Mountain dreamed of a Spartan or Roman republic;
the Gironde, an Athenian republic." Perhaps Buonarotti and Aulard were merely
using a classical reference to define, in terms easily understood, the party programs.
But if, in addition, they meant that those disparate attitudes toward antiquity
that differentiated Saint-Just from Desmoulins also differentiated parties, then
their view is apparently, but probably only apparently, supported by a few
scattered facts. There were Girondins and Indulgents who praised Athens or
condemned Sparta, sometimes contrasted the two, and developed their views in
detail—for example, Vergniaud, Villette, Baudot, and Condorcet (A.P., LXVI
[May 8, 1793], 331; Chronique de Paris, No. 31 [January 31, 1793], p. 122; Baudot, op. cit., pp. 15, 80, 121-22, 165, 166, 167, 312; H. Monin, "Histoire extraordinaire des papiers Baudot," Annales révolutionnaires, II [1909], 188, 197;
Condorcet, Œuvres, VI, 71-72, 74, 75, 391, 417-18, 423, 427, 456). These in-
stances are in part supported by a cursory analysis of the classical allusions appearing in the debates of the Convention from its opening to June 2, 1793; and
then from June 2 to Thermidor. During the first period, the analysis reveals that
there was a tendency for only members of the more moderate parties, for only the
Girondists, members of the Plain, and the Indulgents-to-be to urge the imitation
of Athenian institutions. (There are two exceptions: two Jacobins—Souhait and
Fabre (Hérault)—requested the imitation of an Athenian institution.) In addition, there was a tendency for only members of the more radical groups, the radical Jacobins, and the Indulgents-to-be, to urge the imitation of Spartan institutions. (There are three exceptions: three Girondists—Rabaut, Lidon, and Ducos—requested the imitation of a Spartan institution.) Or, to state the points
negatively: No member of the Plain and, with three exceptions, no Girondist
openly adhered to the cult of Sparta; with two exceptions no Jacobin adhered to
the cult of Athens. Some of the Indulgents-to-be urged the imitation of both
Athens and Sparta. During the second period, the radical Jacobins took up the
former position of the Indulgents: some of them urged the imitation of both
Athens and Sparta; while some of the Indulgents, now that their party had taken
the place of Girondists as the moderate party in the Convention, seemed to take
over the moderate position in regard to the Grecian republics and praised only
the institutions of Athens.

# CHAPTER XIV

## SOCRATES AND PHOCION

AMONG the revolutionary leaders, nothing was more common than self-esteem; and no type of situation more frequently recurred than that in which their right to this self-esteem was implicitly questioned by others. This happened whenever they or their projects were criticized in the Assembly or the press, and more especially whenever, as members of a conservative or liberal minority, they saw the people turn against them, their projects voted down, and themselves imprisoned or menaced with death. In moments like these of external defeat and popular disapproval, leaders found an inner consciousness of their own worth insufficient consolation and compensation for present disaster. They needed, in addition, the assurance that others too—if not the present, then the future, multitude—posterity, in brief—would some day recognize that a high and noble personality once had passed across the revolutionary scene. For only by this assurance could their frustrated wish for recognition be fulfilled and their craving for vengeance, their desire to get even with life and with their political opponents, be satisfied.

Early in the Revolution, during the Constituent, the reactionary journalist Durosy, member of the most impotent minority of the Revolution, had indicated how other minorities might win this assurance. Comparing a conservative naval commander, Albert de Rioms, with Aristides, he noted that the latter, like the former, "had, as a warrior, deserved the gratitude of his fellow-citizens and, as a just

man, their veneration." The Greek statesman, furthermore, opposed all factions, but the flatterers of the Athenian populace were too much for him; the people with base
ingratitude rewarded his services with ostracism, as
Frenchmen had rewarded Albert with imprisonment. To
Aristides, however, posterity had granted the justice contemporaries had withheld; it could not fail, it was intimated, to do the same by Albert. "*A day will come.* . . . .
This idea alone systains the courage of heroes and consoles
the virtuous."[1]

The journal of Durosy, however, was not much read
outside conservative circles. It was left to Robespierre,
therefore, to refresh in the minds of many the memory of
the persecuted great of antiquity. Speaking, as he often
did, of himself, there crept into his orations a recurring re-
frain of the persecution and of the martyr's death that
were to come, as though he foresaw the fate that was
in fact to be his. With a tinge of quiet melancholy, he
seems to have his consolation ready before his trials
have begun—he is ever noting that the classical benefactors of humanity also suffered and were vindicated. Thus,
in May, 1791, identifying himself by obvious implication
with the Aristides who suffered ostracism, he remarks that,
if incorruptible men (like himself and Aristides)

experience at times a passing persecution, that is for them the seal of
their glory and a signal evidence of their virtue; serenely, they trust to
the approbation of a pure conscience, and to the force of truth which
will soon restore to them the good opinion of their fellow-citizens.[2]

The next year, in January, he predicts that, if war comes,
"the defenders of liberty" (like himself, of course) would
be treated as "seditious spirits." As a result, "they would
drink the hemlock, like Socrates, or expire under the sword

[1] *Gazette de Paris*, June 6, 1790, p. 1; see also August 1, 1790, p. 1.

[2] Aulard, *Jacobins*, II, 406.

of tyranny, like Sydney, or would tear out their entrails, like Cato." In the succeeding fall, Robespierre asks his former friend Pétion to read history, where he will see that, though the benefactors of humanity enjoy the esteem of later ages, they often die as martyrs. Witness Agis, Cato, the second Brutus, Socrates, Sydney.[3] You will understand, Robespierre adds to Pétion, that if you were a hero in June, 1792, it was simply because you are not destined to be that in the future centuries. The inference being, of course, that Robespierre, who was not yet the hero he was to become, would, like the other persecuted benefactors of humanity, enjoy the esteem of posterity. Robespierre at least was so persuaded. For about this time he identified his critics with Cato's attackers and himself with Cato, and observed that "we do not know the names of the vile factionists who threw stones at Cato . . . . ; the eyes of posterity rest only on the sacred image of that great man."[4]

During the Convention, this identification of one's self or one's friends with the persecuted of antiquity became popular. It is easy to see why. To illustrious victims of the guillotine it gave a wanted assurance of posterity's esteem, while it required of them nothing they did not already possess—a smattering of classical history; popular disapproval such as Aristides, for example, had experienced; a sturdy self-esteem sufficient to sustain the comparison of one's self with the classical great; and a conviction that history (in this case, posterity's praise) repeated itself—an acceptance, in other words, less expressed than implied, of the familiar philosophy of history taught in the *collèges*.

The first to employ this method of identification during the Terror were the imprisoned Girondists. Of these, the

---

[3] Robespierre, *Lettres à ses commettans*, I, No. 6, 334; see also I, No. 12, 568.

[4] *A.P.*, LIII (November 5, 1792), 160.

first to be imprisoned (on May, 1793) was Mme Roland.
During the first month or so of her imprisonment, however,
she did not need the consolations the past had to offer. She
knew that Buzot, her lover, platonic or otherwise, was in
safety; she hourly expected the triumph of her Girondin
friends in the provinces; she hoped, as a result, that liberty
and justice for France and for herself would follow, and
that, in any case, if her death preceded her release,

the success of my friends, the triumph of the true republicans, consoled
me for everything in advance; I should have submitted to an unjust
judgment or succumbed before some unforeseen atrocity, with the calm,
the pride, and even the joy of innocence which despises death and
knows that its own will be avenged.[5]

With the rout of the Girondin forces, it soon became apparent, however, that in the immediate future vengeance
by her friends was not to be hers.[6] If she were to be consoled for her death and the failure of her Utopian dreams
for France, it was now all the more necessary, therefore,
that she be assured of vengeance and recognition by posterity. As if to secure this assurance, she turns to the classical past. It is only now that in her *Mémoires* references to
the fate of the martyrs of Athens appear. She now recalls
the "death of Socrates, the exile of Aristides, the condemnation of Phocion." She becomes aware that heaven has
destined her "to be a witness to crimes similar to those of
which they were the victims, and to participate in the
glory of a persecution of the same kind."[7] Viewed thus
"from the perspective of the centuries," to quote Mr. Becker, her death in her mind became "an event of more than
personal or local significance, an event which . . . . might
be . . . . record[ed] in humanity's great book of martyr-

[5] *Mémoires*, I, 281; see also I, 41, 298–99; II, 336, 356, 485, 486.

[6] *Ibid.*, I, 300; II, 61, 63–64, 68, 181.

[7] *Ibid.*, II, 105; see also II, 257–58, 307.

doms.[8] This in itself was a consolation. Then, too, she comes to recognize that posterity, impartial and discriminating, gives everyone his due—to Socrates, who died in prison, as well as to Sulla, who died in bed.[9] She, too, expects an equal justice:

"Roland [she writes] will never die in posterity and I also, I shall have some measure of existence in future generations." Her memoirs she entitled, *An Impartial Appeal to Posterity*, and Bosc, who edited them, tells us that "Citoyenne Roland endeavored to find in the esteem of posterity the means of consoling herself for the injustice of contemporaries, and in future glory compensation for her anticipated death." Posterity was for Madame Roland, as for Diderot, what the other world was for the religious: sustained, like the Christian martyrs of an earlier time, by the hope of immortality, she could mount the scaffold with courage and lift unflinching eyes to the poised and relentless knife.[10]

Like Mme Roland, other victims of the guillotine found consolation and strength in the thought that in suffering a martyr's death they were dying and would, in the future, be rewarded like Phocion and Socrates. This spirit comes out in the prison letters, the prison memoirs, and the projected trial defenses of some of the more illustrious victims, as a few selections (arranged chronologically by day of death) will serve to show:

[Brissot in his prison *Mémoires*:] I judged that my enemies would make me mount the scaffold. The images of Sidney and of Russel presented themselves to my mind; I recalled the fate of Phocion, and, in my misfortune, I congratulated myself on sharing the destiny of these great men. I had the certainty that posterity would avenge my memory.[11]

[8] C. L. Becker, *The Heavenly City of the Eighteenth Century Philosophers*, p. 153. (Quoted with the permission of the author, and of the publisher, the Yale University Press.)

[9] Mme Roland, *op. cit.*, I, 328.

[10] Becker, *op. cit.*, pp. 153–54. (Quoted with the permission of the author, and of the publisher, the Yale University Press.)

[11] *Mémoires*, I, 9; see also p. 10, where he adds that these images of Socrates, Phocion, and Sidney "élèvent l'âme et la soutiennent" in the presence of death; also II, 227.

[Gensonné in a prison memoir:] Socrates and Phocion drank the hemlock; Sidney perished on a scaffold; and the same people who had applauded their death accorded to their memory the justice which, during their lives, they had refused to their virtue.[12]

[Vergniaud in notes for his defense:] I did not flatter. . . . . I sometimes preferred to displease them and to broach a good counsel.

Woe to him who prefers his popularity.
Great men, victims of antiquity.[13]

[Lasource, after his sentence of death was read out, quoted Phocion:] I die when the people have lost their reason; you will perish when they recover it.[14]

[Dufriche-Valazé in his defense:] . . . . Robespierre, you who can figure here only as Anytus and Agnonides did in the famous trials of Socrates and of Phocion.[15]

[Guiter:] Posterity will render to each the justice that is due him. Cato's memory is venerated; that of Caesar is execrated.[16]

[Buzot in his *Mémoires*, speaking of Brissot, Roland, etc.:] You died, like Phocion and Sidney, for the liberty of your country; like them, you will live in the memory of honest men.[17]

[Desmoulins in a prison letter to his wife:] But, console thyself, disconsolate widow! The epitaph of your poor Camille is more glorious; it is that of Brutus and of Cato, the tyrannicides.[18]

[Condorcet in the last days of his life:] For four years I have not had a single idea or a single sentiment which did not have as its object the liberty of my country. I shall perish, like Socrates and Sidney, for having served her.[19]

[12] Chauvot, *Le barreau de Bordeaux de 1775 à 1815*, p. 599.

[13] Vatel, *Vergniaud*, II, 264.

[14] Riouffe, *Mémoires d'un détenu* (Paris, 1847), p. 408,

[15] *A.P.*, LXXV (October 3, 1793), 638–39.

[16] *Ibid.*, pp. 673–74.

[17] *Mémoires*, p. 100, see also p. 16, n. 1, and pp. 43–44, 51, 99.

[18] Claretie, *Camille Desmoulins, Lucile Desmoulins*, p. 314.

[19] *Œuvres*, I, 608.

[Le Bon in two prison letters to his wife:] Read ancient history and see how all the useful men were, one after the other, repaid with ingratitude. This death, if it is my fate, is the most glorious which man can desire. Thus perished, in former times, in the midst of calumny and fury, the warmest defenders of the rights of the people; but posterity avenged them, and still will avenge those who have the courage to imitate them.[20]

[Babeuf in his defense:] Ah! we are not, to be sure, the first whom the masters of the earth have persecuted for somewhat similar motives. Socrates .... Jesus .... Lycurgus .... Agis .... the Gracchi .... Manlius .... Cato .... Barneveldt and Sidney.[21]

What Robespierre and Saint-Just thought during the few hours of detention that preceded their execution is unknown. But that their thinking ran in the same groove as that of their contemporaries is likely. Saint-Just, like Robespierre, had already (months before) turned to the classical martyrs.[22] Both men expected the esteem of posterity.[23] Both men had recently exclaimed (Robespierre only two days before) that, when the enemies of the people triumph, nothing remained but to "drink the hemlock."[24] From these facts and from a knowledge of their contemporaries it may be inferred that the antiquity which had given these two inspiration, counsel, and encouragement while they had hope of success, now gave them consolation when they had none.

[20] E. Le Bon, *Joseph Le Bon* (Paris, 1861), pp. 200–201, 230; see also pp. 272–73, 278, 287.

[21] Advielle, *Histoire de Gracchus Babeuf*, II, 13; see also Buonarotti, *Conspiration pour l'égalité dite de Babeuf*, II, 54, 100–101; for expression of somewhat similar prison sentiments by others, see also: C. F. Beaulieu, *Essais historiques sur les causes et les effets de la Révolution de France* (Paris, 1801–3), V, 478; Barère, *Mémoires*, III, 45; Riouffe, *op. cit.*, p. 415; Vatel, *Charlotte Corday*, I, cxxviii.

[22] *Moniteur*, No. 207 (April 16, 1794), p. 221.

[23] *Ibid.*, p. 221; Saint-Just, *Fragmens*, p. 363.

[24] Baudot, *Notes historiques*, pp. 14, 185; *Moniteur*, No. 174 (March 14, 1794) p. 686; No. 315 (August 2, 1794), p. 367.

# CHAPTER XV

## THE THERMIDORIAN REACTION

WITH the death of the leading Girondists and Jacobins, few devoted admirers of antiquity remained. To be sure, Chénier, Billaud-Varenne, and Babeuf were left, the first to talk of reviving the festivals of antiquity, the second to reiterate his faith in regeneration by the Lycurgan method, and the third to lay the foundation of his agitation for the revival of the equalitarianism of Sparta.[1] But Chénier, after a time, tended to stand alone; while Billaud-Varenne and Babeuf found that, as austere, radical idealists, they were isolated and impotent in a conservative Thermidorian reaction which was licentious and cynical. The disillusioned leaders of this reaction, apparently lacking faith in the worth of virtue or in the power of ideals and of institutions, no longer talked of the indispensability of virtue in a republic or of the necessity of regenerating Frenchmen by festivals, censors, and an educational system. Keying their reform to a less exalted strain, they sought simply to set up a "machine of government." But the commonwealths of antiquity, with their slavery and their direct democracy, had little to contribute, as we have said, to the solution of this purely political problem. No wonder that, in the debate over the constitution of 1795, republican antiquity was invoked more frequently in condemnation than in admiration.[2]

[1] Most of Babeuf's activity, however, comes after the period known as the "Thermidorian reaction."

[2] *Moniteur*, No. 176 (March 16, 1795), pp. 681, 683; No. 233 (May 12, 1795), p. 422; No. 298 (July 16, 1795), p. 224; Nos. 302, 303 (July 20 and 21, 1795), pp.

Not only virtue and idealism but also the more extravagant manifestations of the interest in antiquity were, because of their association with the obnoxious, radical Terror, in disrepute. The fad of the Phrygian cap which had begun in March, 1792, was terminated in March, 1795, when young conservative dandies, *la jeunesse dorée*, used violence on those who continued to wear the red *bonnet*.[3] The usurpation of classical names, once so prominent, was now forbidden by the Convention.[4] And the two oratorical clichés—"I speak unto you *en Brutus*" and "Je jure sur la tête de Brutus"—which, during the Terror, had been received by the Convention with gravity, now were greeted with laughter.[5] The Convention, it is true, still kept in its meeting place the bust of Brutus; the artists, decorators, and playwrights continued to turn to the classical past for subject matter; and the women of Paris began wearing costumes *à la grecque*. But from the standpoint of politics, appearances like these possess no significance; and the political cult of antiquity, which had tended first to discourage and then to stimulate revolutionary spirit and action, now did neither, and came to an end.

---

256, 259; No. 304 (July 22, 1795), p. 270; No. 305 (July 23, 1795), pp. 276, 278; No. 306 (July 24, 1795), p. 282; No. 309 (July 27, 1795), p. 312; No. 312 (July 30, 1795), p. 334; No. 314 (August 1, 1795), p. 349; No. 317 (August 4, 1795), p. 375; No. 330 (August 17, 1795), pp. 482, 483.

[3] Aulard, *Paris pendant la réaction thermidorienne et sous le Directoire* (Paris, 1898–1902), I, 539.

[4] *Moniteur*, No. 336 (August 23, 1794), pp. 557–58; see also *ibid.*, No. 75 (December 5, 1794), p. 657, and No. 134 (February 2, 1795), p. 350.

[5] *Ibid.*, No. 111 (January 10, 1795), p. 165; No. 186 (March 26, 1794), p. 43.

# BIBLIOGRAPHY

In this bibliography only those works used in the actual writing of this book have been included. They have been classified under the following headings:

## I. BIBLIOGRAPHIES

Bezard, J. *Documents et monographies sur l'histoire d'établissements français d'enseignement secondaire qui se trouvent à la Bibliothèque du Musée pédagogique.* Melun: Imprimerie administrative, 1904.

Caron, Pierre. *Bibliographie des travaux publiés de 1866 à 1897 sur l'histoire de France depuis 1789.* Paris: E. Cornély et cie, 1912.

———. *Répertoire bibliographique de l'histoire de France,* Vol I. Paris: A. Picard, 1923.

Caron, Pierre, and Brière, Gaston. *Répertoire méthodique de l'histoire moderne et contemporaine de France.* Vols. I–VI. Paris: Société nouvelle de librairie et d'édition.

Ingold, le Père A.-M.-P. *Essai de bibliographie oratorienne.* Paris: Poussielgue frères, 1880–82.

MAIRE, ALBERT. *Répertoire alphabétique des thèses de doctorat ès lettres des universités françaises, 1810–1900.* Paris: Alphonse Picard et fils, 1903.

MONGLOND, ANDRÉ. *La France révolutionnaire et impériale. Annales de bibliographie méthodique et description des livres illustrés.* Tome I: *Années 1789–1790.* Grenoble: Editions B. Arthaud, successeur de J. Rey, 1930.

OETTINGER, EDOUARD-MARIE. *Bibliographie biographique universelle. Dictionnaire des ouvrages relatifs à l'histoire de la vie publique et privée des personnages célèbres de tous les temps et de toutes les nations, depuis le commencement du monde jusqu'à nos jours.* 2 vols. Bruxelles: J. J. Stienon, 1854.

SILVY, A. *Essai d'une bibliographie historique de l'enseignement secondaire et supérieur en France avant la Révolution.* Paris: Société générale d'éducation et d'enseignement, n.d.

TOURNEUX, MAURICE. *Bibliographie de l'histoire de Paris pendant la Révolution française.* 5 vols. Paris: Imprimerie nouvelle (association ouvrière), 1890–1913.

VALLÉE, LÉON. *Bibliographie des bibliographies.* Paris: Em. Terquem, 1883.

————. *Bibliographie des bibliographies: supplément.* Paris: Em. Terquem, 1887.

## II. PRIMARY SOURCES

### A. UNPRINTED PRIMARY SOURCES

ROLAND DE LA PLATIÈRE, MONSIEUR. *Réflexions sur Plutarque; un discours lu à la séance particulière de l'Académie de Lyon, le 16 janvier 1787.* Bibliothèque nationale, Fonds français, Nouvelles acquisitions, Papiers Roland. No. 6243, fols. 89–90. Copied, revised, and perhaps in part inspired by Mme Roland.

*Livres fournis à Monsieur le Principal de Collège de Louis le Grand pour les prix de l'année 1783 par Crapart.* Archives nationales, M. 155, liasse No. 7.

*Régistre pour servir à écrire les soumissions qui doivent être faites par les correspondants des nouveaux boursiers en exécution de l'article XIII du titre III des lettres patentes du premier juillet dernier. A Paris ce vingt trois septembre, mil sept soixante neuf.* (For the period 1769–78.) Archives nationales. $H^3$ 2516.

Registers of sales of books to pupils of the *collège* of Louis-le-Grand. Archives nationales. $H^3$ 2460 (to pupils of *septième* for 1765–66); $H^3$ 2461 (to pupils of *septième* for 1768–69); $H^3$ 2500 (to pupils of *cinquième* for 1765–68, and to pupils of *quatrième* for 1768–69); $H^3$ 2502 (to pupils of *quatrième* for 1765–68).

*Etat des objects qui composoient le mobilier d'Antoine Joseph Gorsas, dans son domicile.* Archives nationales. F⁷ 4729. No date, but must have been drawn up after law of 17 germinal, An III.

### B. Printed Primary Sources

#### I. GREEK AND ROMAN CLASSICS: ENGLISH TRANSLATIONS

Cicero, Marcus Tullius. *The Orations of Marcus Tullius Cicero Literally Tr. by C. D. Yonge.* ("Bohn's Classical Library.") 4 vols. London: G. Bell & Sons, Ltd., 1921. Used for the *Philippics* and for the last two pleadings of the *Verrines*.

————. *The Speeches, with an English Translation: Pro archia poeta—Post reditum in senatu—Post reditum ad quirites—De doma sua—De haruspicum responsis—Pro Plancio.* By N. H. Watts. ("Loeb Classical Library.") London: William Heinemann; New York: G. P. Putnam's Sons, 1923.

————. *The Speeches, with an English Translation: Pro lege Manilia—Pro Caecina—Pro Cluentio—Pro Rabirio.* By H. Grose Hodge. ("Loeb Classical Library.") London: William Heinemann, Ltd.; New York: G. P. Putnam's Sons, 1927.

————. *The Speeches, with an English Translation: Pro Publio Quinctio—Pro Sexto Roscio Amerino—Pro Quinto Roscio Comodeo—De lege agraria I., I., III.* By John Henry Freese. ("Loeb Classical Library.") London: William Heinemann, Ltd.; New York: G. P. Putnam's Sons, 1930.

————. *The Speeches, with an English Translation: Pro T. Annio Milone—In L. Calpurnium Pisonem—Pro M. Aemilio Scauro—Pro M. Fonteio—Pro C. Rabirio Postumo—Pro M. Marcello—Pro Q. Ligario—Pro rege Deiotaro.* By N. H. Watts. ("Loeb Classical Library.") London: William Heinemann, Ltd.; New York: G. P. Putnam's Sons, 1931.

Livius, Titus. *Livy, with an English Translation by B. O. Foster.* ("Loeb Classical Library.") 5 vols. London: W. Heinemann; New York: G. P. Putnam's Sons, 1919–29.

*Plutarch, "Parallel Lives." The Translation called Dryden's.* Corrected from the Greek and revised by A. H. Clough. 5 vols. Boston: Little, Brown & Co., 1891. Used for chaps. i–ix of this book.

*Plutarch, "Lives of Illustrious Men."* Translated from the Greek by John Dryden and Others. New York: P. F. Collier & Son, 1900. This edition was used for chaps. x–xv of this book.

Sallustius Crispus, C. *Sallust, with an English Translation by J. C. Rolfe.* ("Loeb Classical Library.") London: William Heinemann; New York: G. P. Putnam's Sons, 1921.

TACITUS, CORNELIUS. *Annals of Tacitus; Translated into English, with Notes and Maps.* By ALFRED JOHN CHURCH and WILLIAM JACKSON BRODRIBB. London and New York: Macmillan & Co., 1895.

——. *The Histories, with an English Translation by Clifford H. Moore.* ("Loeb Classical Library.") 2 vols. London: W. Heinemann, Ltd.; New York: G. P. Putnam's Sons, 1925.

### 2. SOURCES CONCERNING THE "COLLÈGES"; ALSO DACIER'S "PLUTARCH"

ADRY, JEAN-FÉLICISSIME. *Le meilleur gouvernement, plaidoyers, ou l'on compare l'état populaire, l'oligarchie et la monarchie composés en 1778 et qui furent prononcés par les écoliers de rhétorique, dans la salle des actes du Collège de Troyes-Pithou, le 18 août, jour de la distribution solennelle des prix.* Paris: A. Delalain, 1816.

——. *Notice sure le Collège de Juilly.* Seconde édition, revue et augmentée. Paris: Auguste Delalain, 1816.

CICÉRON. *Oraisons choisies de Cicéron, traduction revue par M. de Wailly, avec le Latin à côté sur l'édition de M. l'Abbé Lallemant, et avec des notes.* 3 vols. Paris: Chez J. Barbou, 1772.

DUMESNIL, GARDIN. *Préceptes de rhétorique tirés de Quintilien, à l'usage des écoliers.* Paris: Chez Brocas et Humblot, 1762. Also see identical editions, Chez Brocas, 1765, 1779.

*Exercice sur l'histoire de France depuis l'établissement de la monarchie jusqu'à François Ier, et sur l'histoire des animaux domestiques. En forme de dialogue. Par Messieurs les écoliers de quatrième.* Boulogne: De l'imprimerie de François Dolet, n.d. Archives nationales, M. 230, liasse No. 38. To take place May 14, 1783.

*Exercice littéraire, sur l'histoire sainte et sur celle des Egyptiens, des Assyriens, etc. par MM. les écoliers de cinquième.* Mans: De l'Imprimerie de Pivron, 1783. Archives nationales, M. 230, liasse No. 38. At the Collège de Mans.

*Exercices de Messieurs les pensionnaires de l'Académie royale de Juilly, durant le mois d'aoust 1772, pour la distribution générale des prix.* S. l.: De l'Imprimerie de Lottin, l'aîné, 1772. Archives nationales, M. 222, liasse No. 10.

*Exercices publics de MM. les élèves de l'Ecole Roïale-Militaire d'Effiat sous la direction des prêtres de l'Oratoire. Ils commenceront le 30 d'Aoust.* Clermont-Ferrand: Chez Delcros, 1785. Archives nationales, M. 222, liasse No. 7.

HERIVAUX, L.-P. *Consolation à Madame la Dauphine, poème latin, avec la traduction française.* Paris: Chez Barbou, 1766.

——. *Ode latine à Monseigneur le cardinal de la Roche-Aymon, archevêque et duc de Rheims, ... .* Paris: Chez P. G. Simon, 1772.

HERIVAUX, L.-P. *Ode latine à son altesse Monseigneur le Prince Louis de Rohan, coadjuteur de Strasbourg ... avec la traduction française.* Paris: Chez P. G. Simon, 1777.

HEUZET, JEAN. *Selectae e profanis scriptoribus historiae.* Paris: Apud viduam Estienne et filios, 1764.

NEPOS, CORNELIUS. *De vita excellentium imperatorum. Latin et français, traduction nouvelle, avec des notes géographiques et historiques.* Paris: Chez J. Barbou, 1771.

PLUTARQUE. *Les vies des hommes illustres de Plutarque, traduites en français, avec les remarques historiques et critiques, par M. Dacier.* Nouvelle édition, revue et corrigée. 14 vols. Paris: Par la compagnie des libraires, 1762. See also 1778 edition, which also has Dacier's notes, Preface, and letter to the king.

QUINTE-CURCE. *Histoire d'Alexandre le Grand traduite par M. Beauzée.* 2 vols. Paris: Chez Barbou, 1781.

———. *Histoire d'Alexandre le Grand. Traduite par M. Vaugelas; nouvelle édition augmentée des supplémens de Freinshemius: avec des notes historiques, géographiques, et grammaticales.* 2 vols. Paris: Chez J. Barbou, 1764.

ROLLAND D'ERCEVILLE. *Mémoire sur l'administration du collège de Louis-le-Grand, et collèges y réunis, depuis le moment de la réunion, jusqu'au premier janvier 1771.* Paris: Chez P. G. Simon, 1778.

———. *Recueil de plusieurs des ouvrages de Monsieur le président Rolland, imprimé en exécution des délibérations du bureau d'administration du Collège de Louis-le-Grand, des 17 janvier et 18 avril 1782.* Paris: Chez. P. G. Simon et N. H. Nyon, 1783.

ROLLIN, CHARLES. *De la manière d'enseigner et d'étudier les belles lettres, par rapport à l'esprit et au cœur.* Paris: Chez Mme Veuve Dabo, 1823.

SALLUSTE. *Les histoires de Salluste, traduites en français; avec le latin revu et corrigé, des notes critiques et une table géographique par M. Beauzée.* Paris: Chez Barbou, 1770.

———. *Traduction de Salluste, avec la vie de cet historien et des notes critiques par J.-H. Dotteville.* Seconde édition. Paris: Chez A. M. Lottin, l'aîné, 1763.

SOCIÉTÉ DE JÉSUS. *Programme et règlement des études de la Société de Jésus comprenant les modifications faites en 1832 et 1858.* Traduction par H. FERTÉ. Paris: Hachette et cie, 1892.

### 3. WORKS OF THE "PHILOSOPHES"

MABLY, L'ABBÉ DE. *Les entretiens de Phocion.* (*Collection complète des œuvres de l'Abbé de Mably,* Vol. X.) Paris: De l'imprimerie de Ch. Desbriere, l'An III de la République.

––––––. *De la législation, ou principes des loix.* (*Collection complète des œuvres de l'Abbé de Mably*, Vol. IX.) Paris: De l'imprimerie de Ch. Desbriere, l'An III de la République.

MONTESQUIEU. *Considérations sur les causes de la grandeur des Romains et de leur décadence.* Nouvelle édition, revue, corrigée et augmentée par l'auteur. Lausanne: Chez Marc-Michel Bousquet et cie, 1750.

––––––. *Esprit des lois.* Paris: Firmin-Didot et cie, 1893.

ROUSSEAU, J. J. *Considérations sur le gouvernement de Pologne, et sur sa réformation projetté.* (*Collection complète des œuvres de J. J. Rousseau*, Vol. I.) Genève, 1782.

––––––. *Du contrat social.* (*Collection complète des œuvres de J. J. Rousseau*, Vol. I.) Genève, 1782.

––––––. *Discours sur l'économie politique.* (*Collection complète des œuvres de J. J. Rousseau*, Vol. I.) Genève, 1782.

––––––. *Emile.* (*Collection complète des œuvres de J. J. Rousseau*, Vols. IV and V.) Genève, 1782.

VOLTAIRE. *Brutus.* (*Œuvres complètes de Voltaire*, Vol. I.) Kehl: De l'imprimerie de la société littéraire-typographique, 1785.

––––––. *La mort de César.* (*Œuvres complètes de Voltaire*, Vol. II.) Kehl: De l'imprimerie de la société littéraire-typographique, 1785.

#### 4. WORKS OF THE REVOLUTIONARY GENERATION

##### a) BOOKS, LETTERS, AND MEMOIRS

ARNAULT, A. V. *Souvenirs d'un sexagénaire.* 4 vols. Paris: Librairie Duféy, 1833.

BABEUF, FRANÇOIS NOËL, dit GRACCHUS. *Babeuf, ex-administrateur du département de la Somme, et successivement du district de Mondidier, aux comités de salut public, de sûreté générale et des législation de la Convention nationale.* Paris: De l'imprimerie de Prault, cour de la maison de Justice, n.d.

––––––. *Babeuf, tribun du peuple à ses concitoyens.* Paris: De l'imprimerie de Franklin, n.d.

––––––. *Cadastre perpétuel ... avec l'exposé de la méthode d'arpentage de M. Audiffred.* Paris: Chez les auteurs, 1789.

––––––. *Dernière lettre de Gracchus Babeuf, assassiné par la prétendue Haute-Cour de Justice, à sa femme et à ses enfans, à l'approche de la mort.* Paris: De l'imprimerie de l'Ami du peuple (R. F. Lebois), n.d.

––––––. [Under the name of SÉBASTIEN LALANDE.] *L'Eclaireur du Peuple, ou le défenseur de 24 millions d'opprimés.* Paris: De l'imprimerie de l'Eclaireur du Peuple, n.d.

––––––. *A Messieurs du Comité des recherches de l'Assemblée nationale.* Roye, 1790.

––––––. *Du système de dépopulation ou la vie et les crimes de Carrier.* Paris: L'Imprimerie de Franklin, An III.

BARBAROUX. *Mémoires inédits de Pétion et mémoires de Buzot et de Barbaroux précédés d'une introduction par C. A. Dauban.* Paris: Henri Plon, 1866.

BARÈRE DE VIEUZAC, BERTRAND. *Eloge de Jean-Baptiste Furgole, avocat du Parlement de Toulouse.* Toulouse: De l'Imprimerie de Declassan, 1783.

——. *Eloge de Louis XII, Roi de France, surnommé le Père du Peuple. S. l.,* 1782.

——. *Eloges académiques.* Paris: Chez A. A. Renouard, 1806.

——. *Mémoires de B. Barère.* Publiés par MM. HIPPOLYTE CARNOT et M. DAVID (D'ANGERS), précédés d'une Notice historique, PAR H. CARNOT. 4 vols. Paris: Jules Labitte, 1842.

——. *Montesquieu peint d'après ses ouvrages.* Imprimé en Suisse et réimprimé en France, l'an cinquième de la République française.

BARNAVE. *Coup d'œil sur la lettre de M. de Calonne. Dauphiné, 28 mars 1789.*

——. *Esprit des édits, enregistrés militairement au Parlement de Grenoble, le 10 mai 1788. S. l.,* n.d.

——. *Œuvres de Barnave mises en ordre et précédées d'une notice historique sur Barnave par M. Bérenger de la Drome.* 4 vols. Paris: Jules Chapelle et Guiller, 1843.

BAUDOT, MARC-ANTOINE. *Notes historiques sur la Convention nationale, le Directoire, l'Empire et l'exil des votants.* Publié sous les auspices du ministère de l'instruction publique. Paris: Imprimerie D. Jouaust, 1893.

BEAULIEU, C. F. *Essais historiques sur les causes et les effets de la Révolution de France, avec des notes sur quelques événemens et quelques institutions.* 6 vols. Paris: Chez Maradan, 1801–3.

BESNARD, FRANÇOIS-YVES. *Souvenirs d'un nonagénaire; mémoires de François-Yves Besnard, publiés sur le manuscrit autographe par Célestin Port.* 2 vols. Paris: H. Champion; Angers: Lachèse et Dolbeau; le Mans: Pellechat, 1880.

BEUGNOT, COMTE. *Mémoires du Comte Beugnot, ancien ministre (1783–1815). Publiés par le Comte Albert Beugnot, son petit-fils.* Deuxième édition. 2 vols. Paris: E. Dentu, 1868.

BILLAUD-VARENNE, J. N. *L'Acéphocratie ou le gouvernment fédératif, démontré le meilleur de tous, pour un grand Empire, par les principes de la politique et les faits de l'histoire.* Paris, 1791.

——. *Le dernier coup porté aux préjugés et à la superstition.* Londres, 1789.

——. *Despotisme des ministres de France ou exposition des principes et moyens employés par l'aristocratie, pour mettre la France dans les fers.* 3 vols. Amsterdam, et se trouve a Paris: Chez Godefroy, 1789.

————. *Plus de ministres ou point de grâce, avertissement donné aux patriotes françois, et justifié par quelques circonstances de l'affaire de Nancy.* Paris: Chez Denné, 1790.

————. *Principes régénérateurs du systême social.* Paris: De l'imprimerie de R. Vatar, Pluviôse, l'an 3.

BOISSEL, FRANÇOIS. *Le catéchisme du genre humain. S. l.,* 1789.

BONNEVILLE, N. *De l'esprit des religions: ouvrage promis et nécessaire à la confédération universelle des amis de la vérité.* 2 vols. in 1. Paris: A l'imprimerie du Cercle social, 1791.

BOUILLÉ, LE MARQUIS DE, LOUIS-JOSEPH-AMOUR. *Souvenirs et fragments pour servir aux mémoires de ma vie et de mon temps.* Publiés pour la Société d'histoire contemporaine par *P.-L. de Kermaingant.* 3 vols. Paris: Alphonse Picard et fils, 1906.

BRAESCH, F. *Papiers de Chaumette publiés avec une introduction et des notes.* Paris: Au siège de la Société de l'histoire de la Révolution française, 1908.

BRISSOT DE WARVILLE, J.-P. *Bibliothèque philosophique du législateur, du politique, du jurisconsulte; ou choix des meilleurs discours, dissertations, essais, fragmens, composés sur la législation criminelle par les plus célèbres écrivains.* 10 vols. Berlin, et se vend à Paris: Chez Desauges, 1782–85. Contains his "Réflexions sur le code de Pensylvanie (1783)" in Vol. III, pp. 233–58; his "Recherches philosophiques sur le droit de propriété et sur le vol, considérés dans la nature et dans la société (1782)" in Vol. VI, pp. 261–339; and his "De la décadence du barreau françois (1782)" in Vol. VI, pp. 341–409.

————. *Correspondance et papiers précédés d'un avertissement et d'une notice sur sa vie par Cl. Perroud.* Paris: Alphone Picard et fils, 1911.

————. *Correspondance universelle sur ce qui intéresse le bonheur de l'homme et de la société.* Neuchâtel: De l'imprimerie de la Sociéte typographique, 1783.

————. *Un défenseur du peuple à l'Empereur Joseph II sur son réglement concernant l'émigration, ses diverses réformes, etc.* Dublin, 1785.

————. *Dénonciation au public d'un nouveau projet d'agiotage ou lettre à M. le Comte de S\*\*\* sur un nouveau projet de compagnie d'assurance contre les incendies à Paris.* Londres, 1786.

————. *Examen critique des voyages dans l'Amérique septentrionale, de M. le Marquis de Chatellux.* Londres, 1786.

————. *Journal du Licée de Londres ou tableau de l'Etat présent dessciences et des arts en Angleterre.* 2 vols. Paris: Chez Perisse le jeune; London: Au Bureau-Général du Licée, 1784.

————. *Un indépendant à l'ordre des avocats, sur la décadence du barreau en France.* Berlin, 1781. See also 1782 edition under BRISSOT, *Bibliothèque philosophique.*

BRISSOT DE WARVILLE, J.-P. *Lettre à l'Empereur sur l'atrocité des supplices qu'il a substitués comme adoucissement à la peine de mort.* Bruxelles, 1787.

———. *Mémoire sur les noirs de l'Amérique septentrionale lu à l'assemblée de la Société des Amis des Noirs, le 9 février, 1789.* Paris: Au bureau du *Patriote français,* 1789.

———. *Mémoires (1754–1793) publiés avec étude critique et notes par Cl. Perroud.* Paris: Alphonse Picard et fils, n.d.

———. *Les moyens d'adoucir la rigueur des loix pénales en France, sans nuire à la sûreté publique, ou Discours couronnés par l'Académie de Châlons-sur-Marne en 1780.* Châlons-sur-Marne: Chez Seneuze, 1781.

———. *New travels in the United States of America: Including the Commerce of America with Europe; particularly with France and Great Britain.* 2 vols. London, 1794(?).

———. *Observations d'un républicain, sur les différens systêmes d'administration provinciales, particulièrement sur ceux de MM. Turgot et Necker, et sur le bien qu'on peut en espérer dans les gouvernemens monarchiques.* Lausanne, 1788.

———. *Le Philadelphien à Genève, ou lettres d'un Américain sur la dernière révolution de Genève, sa constitution nouvelle, l'émigration en Irland, etc., pouvant servir de tableau politique de Genève jusqu'en 1784.* Dublin, 1783.

———. *Point de banqueroute ou lettre à un créancier de l'Etat, sur l'impossibilité de la banqueroute nationale, et sur les moyens de ramener le crédit et la paix.* Londres, 1787.

———. *Point de Banqueroute ou lettres à un créancier de l'Etat, sur les conséquences de la révocation des deux impôts, relativement à la dette nationale.* Seconde partie. Paris, 1787.

———. *Seconde lettre contre la compagnie d'assurance.* Londres, 1786.

———. *Testament politique de l'Angleterre.* S. l., 1780.

———. *Théorie des loix criminelles.* Berlin, 1781.

———. *De la vérité ou méditations sur les moyens de parvenir à la vérité dans toutes les connaissances humaines.* Neuchâtel: De l'imprimerie de la société typographique, 1782.

BRISSOT DE WARVILLE, J.-P., and CLAVIÈRE. *Lettre à l'auteur du "Mercure" politique.* Par les auteurs du traité intitulé: De la France et des Etats-Unis. Bouillon, 1787.

BRISSOT DE WARVILLE, J.-P.; CONDORCET; and CLAVIÈRE. *Le Moniteur.* S. l., 1788.

BRY, JEAN DE. "Autobiographie," *Annales révolutionnaires,* XI (1919), 69–79, 376–87, 520–34.

BUONAROTTI, PH. *Conspiration pour l'égalité dite de Babeuf, suivie du procès auquel elle donna lieu, et des pièces justificatives, etc.* 2 vols. in 1. Bruxelles: A la librairie romantique, 1828.

Buzot. *Mémoires inédits de Pétion et mémoires de Buzot et de Barbaroux précédés d'une introduction par C. A. Dauban.* Paris: Henri Plon, 1866.

Cazalès. *Discours et opinions de Cazalès précédés d'une notice historique sur sa vie par M. Chare, avocat.* Paris: Chez Kleffer et Moreau, 1821.

Chabot, François. *François Chabot, représentant du peuple à ses concitoyens qui sont les juges de sa vie politique.* Mémoire apologétique publié pour la prèmière fois par Albert Mathiez. Paris: Ernest Leroux, 1914.

———. "Le testament du conventionnel Chabot," *La Révolution française,* XLIV (1903), 461–65.

Condorcet. *Œuvres publiées par A. Condorcet O'Connor et M. F. Arago.* 12 vols. Paris: Firmin Didot frères, 1847–49.

Cournand, l'Abbé Antoine. *De la propriété ou la cause du pauvre, plaidée au tribunal de la raison, de la justice, et de la vérité.* Paris, 1791.

Desmoulins, Camille. *Œuvres de Camille Desmoulins recueillies et publiées d'après les textes originaux augmentées de fragments inédits, de notes et d'un index et précédées d'une étude biographique et littéraire par Jules Claretie.* Paris. Bibliothèque-Charpentier, 1906.

Dumas, Mathieu. *Souvenirs du lieutenant-général Comte Mathieu Dumas, de 1770 à 1836 publiés par son fils.* 3 vols. Paris: Charles Gosselin, 1839.

Dumouchet. *Opinion sur la royautè, sur Louis XVI et sa famille, sur l'établissement d'une République française.* Paris: De l'imprimerie de Vᵛᵉ Herissant, 1792.

Dumont, Etienne. *Souvenirs sur Mirabeau et sur les deux premières assemblées législatives.* Paris: Charles Gosselin, 1832.

France, Anatole. "La bibliothèque de Billaud-Varenne à la Guyane," *Almanach de la Révolution pour 1870 publié par Jules Claretie.* Paris: Librairie centrale, 1869.

Fribourg, André. *Discours de Danton: édition critique.* Paris: Société de l'histoire de la Révolution française, 1910.

Gorguereau, François. *Le duel considéré dans tous les rapports historiques, moraux et consitutionnels, et moyens de l'anéantir radicalement.* Paris: De l'imprimerie d'An.-J. Gorsas, 1791.

Grégoire. *Histoire patriotique des arbres de la liberté précédée d'un essai sur sa vie et ses ouvrages par M. Charles Dugast et d'une introduction par M. A. Havard.* Paris: Adolphe Havard, 1833.

Grégoire, B. H. *Mémoires de Grégoire, précédés d'une notice historique sur l'auteur par M. H. Carnot.* 2 vols. Paris: J. Youet, 1840.

Isnard, Maximin. *Proscription d'Isnard.* Paris: Chez l'auteur, l'an III de la République.

Jullien, Mme Rosalie. *Journal d'une bourgeoise pendant la Révolution, 1791–1793. Publié par son petit-fils Edouard Lockroy.* Deuxième édition. Paris: Calmann Lévy, 1881.

LAVICOMTERIE. LOUIS. *Les crimes des rois de France depuis Clovis jusqu'à Louis Seize.* Paris: Petit, 1791.

LAVICOMTERIE, M. DE. *Du peuple et des rois.* Paris: Chez les marchands de nouveautés, 1790.

LEFEVRE, FRANÇOIS-NOEL. *Ce que doit faire la Convention nationale.* Paris: De l'imprimerie de C. F. Cagnion, 1792.

MALLET DU PAN. *Mémoires et correspondance de Mallet du Pan pour servir à l'histoire de la Révolution française. Recueillis et mis en ordre par A. Sayous.* Paris: Amyot, J. Cherbuliez, 1851.

MALOUET, PIERRE VICTOR. *Mémoires de Malouet, pub. par son petit fils, le baron Malouet.* 2 vols. Paris: Didier et cie, 1868.

MARAT, J. P. *Les chaînes de l'esclavage.* Paris: De l'imprimerie de Marat, l'an premier de la République.

————. *La constitution ou projet de déclaration des droits de l'homme et du citoyen, suivi d'un plan de constitution juste, sage et libre.* Paris: Chez Buisson, 1789.

————. *Découvertes de M. Marat, docteur en médecine et médecin des gardes-du-corps de Monseigneur le Comte Artois, sur le feu, l'electricité et la lumière, constatées par une suite d'expériences nouvelle.* Paris: De l'imprimerie de Clousier, 1779.

————. *Eloge de Montesquieu présenté à l'Académie de Bordeaux le 28 mars 1785 publié avec une introduction par Arthur de Brézety.* Libourne: G. Maleville, 1883.

————. *De l'homme ou des principes et des loix de l'influence de l'âme sur le corps et du corps sur l'âme.* 3 vols. Amsterdam: Chez Marc-Michel Rey, 1775.

————. *Lettre de Marat au Roi, ou l'Ami du Peuple au Père du Peuple.* S. l.: De l'imprimerie de Marat, n.d.

————. *Lettres de l'observateur Bon-Sens à M. de\*\*\* sur la fatale catastrophe des infortunes Pilatre de Rosier et Romain, les Aéronautes et l'Aérostation.* Londres, 1785.

————. *Mémoire sur l'électricité médicale, couronné le 6 août 1783, par l'Académie des sciences, belles-lettres et arts de Rouen.* Paris: De l'imprimerie et L. Jorry, 1784.

————. *Offrande à la patrie, ou discours au Tiers Etat de France. S. l.:* Au temple de la liberté, 1789.

————. *Plan de législation criminelle. S. l.,* n.d.

————. *Supplément de l'offrande à la patrie, ou discours au Tiers-Etat. S. l.:* Au temple de la liberté, 1789.

MARMONTEL, JEAN FRANÇOIS. *Œuvres complètes.* Paris: Chez A. Belin, 1819.

MAURY, CARDINAL. *Correspondance diplomatique et mémoires inédits du Cardinal Maury (1792-1817). Annotés et publiés par Mgr. Ricard.* 2 vols. Lille: Société de Saint-Augustin, Brouver et cie, 1891.

MERCIER, L. S. *Tableau de Paris*. Nouvelle édition corrigée et augmentée. Amsterdam, 1782–88.

MONTLOSIER. *Mémoires du Comte de Montlosier (extraits)*. ("Bibliothèque des mémoires relatifs a l'histoire de France pendant le 18ᵉ siècle." Nouvelle série avec introduction, notices et notes par M. DE LESCURE. Vol. XXXVI.) Paris, Firmin-Didot et cie, 1881.

MOUNIER, J.-J. *Appel au tribunal de l'opinion publique, de rapport de M. Chabroud, et du décret rendu par l'Assemblée nationale le 2 Octobre. Examen du mémoire du Duc d'Orléans, et du plaidoyer du Comte de Mirabeau, et nouveaux éclaircissements sur les crimes du 5 et du 6 Octobre, 1789*. Genève, 1790.

———. *De l'influence attribuée aux philosophes, aux francs-maçons et aux illuminés, sur la Révolution de France*. Paris: Ponthieu, 1822.

———. *Recherches sur les causes qui ont empêché les françois de devenir libres, et sur les moyens qui leur restent pour acquérir la liberté*. 2 vols. Genève, 1792.

PÉTION. *Mémoires inédits de Pétion et mémoires de Buzot et de Barbaroux précédés d'une introduction par C. A. Dauban*. Paris: Henri Plon, 1866.

PROYART, L'ABBÉ. *Œuvres complètes*. 17 vols. Paris: Chez Méquignon, 1819.

RIOUFFE. *Mémoires d'un détenu pour servir à l'histoire de la tyrannie de Robespierre*. ("Bibliothèque des mémoires relatifs à l'histoire de France pendant le 18ᵐᵉ siècle." Avec avant propos et notes par M. Fs. BARRIÈRE. Vol. IX.) Paris: Firmin Didot frères, 1847.

ROBERT. *Avantages de la fuite de Louis XVI, et nécessité d'un nouveau gouvernement*. Paris: Paquet, Rue Jacob et Petit, au Palais Royal, 1791.

ROBERT, F. *Le républicanisme adapté à la France*. Paris, 1790.

ROBESPIERRE, CHARLOTTE. *Mémoires de Charlotte Robespierre sur ses deux frères. (Œuvres de Maximilien Robespierre*. Avec une notice historique, des notes et des commentaires, par LAPONNERAYE; précédées de considérations générales par ARMAND CARREL. II, 353–496.) Paris: Chez l'éditeur, 1840.

ROBESPIERRE, MAXIMILIEN. *Œuvres complètes de Maximilien Robespierre publiées par Victor Barbier et Charles Vellay*. Tome premier: *Œuvres judiciaires, 1782–1789*. Paris: Aux bureaux de la *Revue historique de la Révolution française*, 1910.

———. *Œuvres complètes de Maximilien Robespierre*. Edited by EMILE LESUEUR. Première partie: *Robespierre à Arras*. Tome premier: *Les œuvres littéraires en prose et en vers*. Tome deuxième: *Les œuvres judiciaries (1782–1786)*. Paris: Ernest Leroux, 1912, 1913.

ROLAND DE LA PLATIÈRE, MME MARIE-JEANNE (PHLIPON). *Lettres d'amour de 1777 à 1780*. Publiées par CLAUDE PERROUD. Paris: Alphonse Picard et fils, 1909.

Roland de la Platière, Mme Marie-Jeanne (Phlipon). *Lettres de Madame Roland publiées par Claude Perroud. Nouvelle série: 1767–1780.* 2 vols. Paris: Imprimerie nationale, 1915.

———. *Lettres de Madame Roland publiées par Claude Perroud: 1780–1793.* 2 vols. Paris: Imprimerie nationale, 1902.

———. *Mémoires de Madame Roland écrits durant sa captivité. Nouvelle édition revue et complétée sur les manuscrits autographes et accompagnée de notes et de pièces inédites par M. P. Faugère.* 2 vols. Paris: Hachette et cie, 1864.

———. *Mémoires de Madame Roland. Nouvelle édition critique contenant des fragments inédits et les lettres de la prison publiées par Claude Perroud.* 2 vols. Paris: Plon-Nourrit et cie, 1905.

———. *Œuvres de J. M. Ph. Roland, femme de l'ex-ministre de l'intérieur.* Précédés d'un discours préliminaire par L. A. Champagneux, éditeur. 3 vols. Paris: Chez Bidault, An VIII.

Saint-Just. *Œuvres complètes de Saint-Just avec une introduction et des notes par Charles Vellay.* 2 vols. Paris: Eugène Fasquelle, 1908.

Ségur, M. le Comte de. *Mémoires, souvenirs et anecdotes.* ("Bibliothèque des mémoires relatifs à l'histoire de France pendant le 18ᵉ siècle avec avant-propos et notices." Par M. Fs. Barrière.) Paris: Firmin-Didot et cie, 1890.

Vatel, Charles. *Charlotte de Corday et les Girondins: pièces classées et annotées par M. Charles Vatel.* 3 vols. Paris: Henri Plon, 1864–72.

———. *Vergniaud: manuscrits, lettres et papiers; pièces pour la plupart inédites, classées et annotées par C. Vatel.* Paris: J.-B. Dumoulin, 1873.

Vaublanc, le Comte de. *Souvenirs.* 2 vols. Paris: F. Ponce Lebas et cie, 1838.

Vergniaud. "Lettre et vers de Vergniaud," *Arvhives historiques du département de la Gironde,* XVIII (1878), 552–55.

Vilate. *Causes secrètes de la journée du 9 au 10 thermidor.* ("Collection de mémoires relatifs a la Révolution française.") Paris: Baudouin frères, 1825.

Volney, C. F. *Œuvres complètes.* Paris: Chez Firmin Didot frères, fils et cie., 1860.

*b)* speeches and collections of speeches

Aulard, F.-A. *La Société des Jacobins: Recueil de documents pour l'histoire du Club des Jacobins de Paris.* 5 vols. Paris: Jouast et Noblet; Léopold Cerf et Noblet, 1889, 1891, 1895.

Billaud-Varenne. *Discours de Billaud-Varenne sur notre situation actuelle et quelques mesures à prendre pour assurer le salut public: Prononcé à la Société des Amis de la Constitution, séante aux Jacobins, le 29 juin, 1792.* S. l., n.d.

FRANCE. *Archives parlementaires de 1787 à 1860; recueil complet des débats législatifs et politiques des chambres françaises.* 1. sér.: *1787–1799.* 82 vols. Paris, P. Dupont, 1862–1913. For the debates of the revolutionary assemblies, the *Archives parlementaires* was used until December, 1793; the *Moniteur,* from December, 1793, to October, 1795. In view of the criticism that has been made of the manner in which the editors of the *Archives* in their earlier volumes pieced together their account from newspapers, it may be noted that for the year 1790 their account was checked with the *Moniteur,* and that this checking did not reveal any error in the reporting of classical allusions. Besides, since such allusions usually appear in the written speeches and committee reports, the criticisms that are usually made of the *Archives* do not apply here.

———. Convention nationale, Comité d'instruction publique. *Procès-verbaux du Comité d'instruction publique de la Convention nationale.* Publiés et annotés par M. J. GUILLAUME. 6 vols. Paris: Imprimerie nationale, 1891–1907.

GIREY-DUPRÉ, J. M. *Opinion de J. M. Girey-Dupré, sur la question de savoir quelle sera la conduite de l'Assemblée nationale à l'égard du Roi; prononcée dans la Société des Amis de la Constitution, séante aux Jacobins, le 27 juin 1791.* Imprimée par ordre de la Société. Paris: De l'imprimerie nationale, 1791.

KERSAINT, ARMAND. *Discours de M. Kersaint, prononcé à la séance des Amis de la Constitution, séante aux Jacobins, le dimanche 24 juillet 1791.* Paris: Imp. du *Patriote français,* n.d.

MACHENAUD, F. *Discours sur le parti à prendre envers Louis XVI; prononcé à la Société des Amis de la Constitution, séante aux Jacobins, à Paris, le 30 juin 1791.* S. l., n. d.

RÉAL, P. F. *Opinion de P. F. Réal, sur la question de savoir quel parti il faut prendre dans les circonstances actuelles; prononcée dans la Société des Amis de la Constitution, séante aux Jacobins, le 3 juillet, 1791.* Paris: De l'imprimerie nationale, 1791.

SOULÉS. *Discours de M. Soulés à la tribune de la Société des Amis de la Constitution, sur la grande question de savoir de quelle manière l'Assemblée nationale devrait agir envers le Roi: discours qui fut interrompu par M. Biozat, député de Clermont en Auvergne, sous prétexte que l'opinant parloit contre la constitution.* S. l., n.d.

### c) NEWSPAPERS

*Les actes des apôtres.* (2 novembre 1789—octobre 1791.) Editor: JACQUES PELTIER, aided by a number, including RIVAROL, BERGASSE, SULEAU, LE COMTE DE LANGERON, LE COMTE DE LAURAGUAIS.

*L'ami des patriotes, ou le défenseur de la Révolution.* (27 novembre 1790—novembre 1791.) Editor until September 27, 1791: ADRIEN DUQUESNOY. After that, REGNAULT DE SAINT-JEAN D'ANGÉLY.

*L'ami du peuple ou le publiciste parisien, journal politique, libre, et impartial.* Par une SOCIÉTÉ DE PATRIOTES, et rédigé par M. MARAT. (16 SEPTEMBRE 1789—21 SEPTEMBRE 1792.) See also *Journal de la République française*, and *Le publiciste de la République française.*

*L'ami du roi, des Français, de l'ordre et surtout de la vérité.* Par les continuateurs de FRÉRON. (1er juin—5 novembre, 1790.) To August 26, edited by THOMAS-MARIE ROYOU, MONTJOIE, and CRAPART; after that by CRAPART alone.

*L'ami du roi, des Français, de l'ordre et surtout de la vérité.* Par M. MONTJOYE, fondateur et rédacteur de ce journal, depuis le 1er juin 1790. (1er septembre 1790—10 août 1792.) On November 6, 1790, CRAPART joined with MONTJOIE.

*L'ami du roi, des Français, de l'ordre et surtout de la vérité.* Par les continuateurs de FRÉRON. (1er septembre 1790—4 mai 1792.) Editor: ROYOU.

*Chronique de Paris.* (1er octobre 1791—25 août 1793.) Editors at least until the Convention: AUBIN-LOUIS MILLIN and JEAN-FRANÇOIS NOEL, with CONDORCET to write reports of debates of the Legislative Assembly and at first of the Convention. With Nos. 3–68 of 1793 the title also said: "Rédigée, pour la Convention nationale par J.-A.-N. CONDORCET et J. DELAUNAY; la politique, par J.-P. RABAUT; la littérature et les arts, par A. L. MILLIN"; the Nos. 117–50 of 1793 carry the title: Rédigée par DUCOS et J.-P. RABAUT, députés."

*Courrier de Provence, pour servir de suite aux Lettres du comte de Mirabeau à ses commettans.* (24 juillet, 1789—30 septembre 1791.) Nominal editor: MIRABEAU. Aided by ETIENNE MEJAN, ETIENNE DUMONT, DUROVERAY, CLAVIÈRE, LAMOURETTE, CHAMFORT, and others.

*Le courrier de Versailles à Paris et de Paris à Versailles.* Par M. GORSAS. (5 juillet 1789—1er octobre 1791; 22 septembre 1792—31 mai 1793.) Title repeatedly changed from foregoing to "Le Courrier de Paris dans les provinces, et des provinces à Paris; to Le Courrier de Paris dans les 83 départements; to Le Courrier des LXXXIII départements; to Le Courrier des départements."

*Le défenseur de la constitution par Maximilien Robespierre.* (mai—août or septembre 1792.)

*Gazette de Paris, ouvrage consacré au patriotisme, à l'histoire, à la politique et aux beaux arts.* (1er octobre 1789—10 août 1792.) Editor: B. FARMIAN DU ROZOY.

*Journal de la République française.* Par MARAT. (25 septembre 1792—11 mars 1793.)

*Journal de la société de 1789.* (5 juin—15 septembre 1790.)

*Journal de Paris* (1er janvier 1789—31 juillet 1790.)

*Lettres de Maximilien Robespierre à ses commettants.* (Septembre 1792—mars 1793.)

*Mercure de France.* (1790–92.) Editor: MALLET DU PAN. Title varies; also as *Mercure historique et politique.*

*Le Moniteur.* (1ᵉʳ novembre 1793—5 novembre 1795.) *Réimpression* used.

*Le patriote français, journal libre, impartial et national.* Par une SOCIÉTÉ DE CITOYENS, ET DIRIGÉ par J.-P. BRISSOT DE WARVILLE. (28 juillet 1789—2 juin 1793.)

*Le Point du jour, ou Résultat de ce qui s'est passé la veille à l'Assemblée nationale par M. D\*\*\*.* (17 juin 1789—1ᵉʳ octobre 1791.) Editor: BARÈRE.

*Le Postillon par Calais.* (Février 1790—4 octobre 1791.) The "par Calais" was added to the title only with No. 53. Each number is followed by a separate supplement entitled: "Observations."

*Le Publiciste de la République française, ou Observations aux Français par Marat, l'ami du peuple.* (14 mars—14 juillet 1793.)

*Le Républicain ou le Défenseur du gouvernement représentatif, par une société de républicains.* (Juillet, 1791.) Editors: CONDORCET, THOMAS PAINE, ACHILLE DUCHASTELET.

*Révolutions de France et de Brabant, et des royaumes qui, demandant une assemblée nationale et arborant la cocarde, mériteront une place dans ces fastes de la liberté.* Par CAMILLE DESMOULINS. (28 novembre 1789—12 décembre 1791.)

*Révolutions de France et de Brabant.* Seconde partie: *L'an premier de la République de France.* Ouvrage périodique, par CAMILLE DESMOULINS et MERLIN DE THIONVILLE. (Octobre—décembre 1792.)

*Révolutions de Paris, dédiées à la nation et au district des Petits-Augustins.* Publiées par LE SIEUR PRUDHOMME. (12 juillet 1789—28 février 1794.)

*La Tribune des patriotes ou Journal de la majorité. Ouvrage destiné à servir de suite au No. 86 et dernier des "Révolutions de France et de Brabant."* Par CAMILLE DESMOULINS et FRÉRON. (30 avril—mai 1792.)

*Le Vieux cordelier; journal rédigé par Camille Desmoulins.* (25 novembre 1793—24 février 1794.)

### *d*) PAMPHLETS OF THE REPUBLICAN MOVEMENT

In addition to those mentioned below, the following pamphlets (as listed in Tourneux) were read in connection with the republican movement: Nos. 2266, 2267, 2268, 2270, 2271, 2275, 2276, 2277, 2280, 2281, 2282, 2286, 2290, 2291, 2294, 2298, 3349, 3357, 3359, 3361; and in addition Adrien's *Qu'est-ce qu'un roi* (*s. l.*, n.d.). None of these listed pamphlets, however, revealed any interest in antiquity. It may be observed that two pamphlets (Nos. 2271 and 2290 in Tourneux) are incorrectly placed, both by the Bibliothèque nationale and by Tourneux, with the pamphlets appearing in 1791 immediately after the flight of the king to

Varennes. But No. 2271 was written after June 20, 1792 (see p. 12 of the pamphlet); while No. 2290 was written after June 3, 1792 but before July 14 (see pp. 6 and 7).

Unless otherwise stated, the pamphlets listed below were unsigned and appeared in the summer of 1791.

*Avis aux amis de la constitution.* S. l., n.d. Monarchist. No mention of antiquity. Republic would destroy French national unity and lead to civil war.

*Avis aux Français par un patriote raisonnable.* S. l., n. d. TOURNEUX: No. 2283. Monarchist. No mention of antiquity. France too large for a republic.

*Discours prononcé aux Jacobins, sur la question suivante: Que faut-il faire dans les circonstances actuelles?* S. l., n.d. TOURNEUX: No. 2289. Monarchist. Roman and Greek examples prove republic possible only in a small, moral country.

*Grande visite de Mademoiselle République chez notre mère la France, pour l'engager à chasser de chez elle Madame Royauté et conversation très-intéressante entre elles.* De l'imprimerie de Fiévée, n.d. A pamphlet burlesque which gives Mme République a Greek coiffure, a Roman nose, and a *Par Brutus!* as her favorite oath. No definite conclusion either for monarchy or republic.

*Lettre des deux Brutus au peuple français.* S. l., n.d. The two Bruti conclude that France should have a monarchy; a republic would lead to civil war.

*Lettre d'un homme libre à Louis XVI, premier agent de la Nation française.* S. l., n.d. TOURNEUX: No. 3351. Written in 1792. Republican. French should emulate Romans who tied kings to their cars of triumph.

*Nous ne mordrons point à une grappe empoisonnée.* S. l., n.d. TOURNEUX: No. 3356. Written in 1792. Monarchist. No mention of antiquity. France too large to be a republic.

*Opinion d'un ami de la Constitution sur l'enlèvement du Roi.* S. l., 1791. TOURNEUX: No. 2278. Monarchist. No mention of antiquity. France too large for a republic.

*Réflexions sur la situation critique du Roi, de l'Assemblée nationale, et de la France.* Paris, 1791. TOURNEUX: No. 2297. Monarchist. No mention of antiquity. France too large for a republic.

*Le Roi, traité comme il le mérite.* Paris: De l'imp. de Guilhemat, n.d. TOURNEUX: No. 2269. Monarchist. Liberty at Rome meant that a blind and imbecile multitude, slaves to the ambitious, made laws; elections led to civil troubles.

COUÉ-LANNE. *Adresse aux Français.* Paris: De l'imprimerie de l'ami de l'ordre, n.d. TOURNEUX. No. 2285. Monarchist. No mention of antiquity. France too large for a republic.

DROUET. *Voilà ce qu'il faut faire du roi.* Paris: Chez Guilhemat, n.d. Monarchist. At Rome, a republic had meant bloody anarchy and rule by a despotic senate.

DUCANCEL. *Opinion de M. Ducancel sur la question: Quelles sont les mesures à prendre par l'Assemblée nationale relativement à Louis XVI?* Paris. De l'imprimerie nationale, n.d. Try the king. Liberty brought great characters, Scaevolas and Bruti, to Rome. Will also do so in France.

## III. SECONDARY SOURCES

### A. WORKS ALREADY WRITTEN UPON PHASES OF THE SUBJECT

BADOLLE, MAURICE. *L'Abbé Jean-Jacques Barthélemy (1716–1795) et l'Hellénisme en France dans la seconde moitié du XVIIIᵉ siècle.* Paris: Les presses universitaires de France, n.d. See pp. 341–70, the chapter entitled "Le goût de l'antiquité grecque et les Assemblées révolutionnaires."

BENAZÉ, DE. "Révolutionnaires et classiques," *La Révolution française,* IV (1883), 900–914, 1073–90.

BERTRAND, LOUIS. *La fin du classicisme et le retour à l'antique dans la seconde moitié du XVIIIᵉ siècle et les premières années du XIXᵉ, en France.* Paris: Hachette et cie, 1897.

HAUTECŒUR, L. *Rome et la renaissance de l'antiquité à la fin du XVIIIᵉ siècle.* Paris: Fontemoing et cie, 1912.

RENARD, GEORGES. "Notes sur la littérature thermidorienne," *La Révolution française,* XII (1887), 769–91.

RIOUX DE MAILLOU. "La littérature et la Révolution," *Revue de la Révolution,* XIV (1889), 201–22; XV (1889), 117–37, 377–408.

As the works of Hautecœur and of Bertrand deal only with the artistic and literary side of this latter-day Renaissance, they do not concern us. To the works of the other four, this study owes a quotation from the Comte de Ségur (given by De Benazé), one from Chateaubriand (given by Badolle), and one from Saint-Simon (found in De Maillou). But if this book owes so little to the works in question, it is not entirely their fault, for they do have their points. Badolle, for example, for thirty pages pieces together quotations from revolutionary debates to give a spirited and a faithful picture of the use of classical allusions in the revolutionary assemblies. Rioux de Maillou throws out a suggestive phrase or two concerning the cult for the heroes of antiquity, phrases which might have been developed in this book had the sources permitted a fuller treatment of the interest in classical heroes, as distinguished from the interest in classical institutions.

Renard takes as his thesis the decline of classical influence from the 9th Thermidor to the 18th Brumaire; and though he devotes most of his article to listing facts which disprove this thesis, facts which tend to show that in arts and manners classical influence did not decline, yet he is correct when he observes that in politics at least the desire to imitate "lovely and virtuous antiquity" diminished in force during this period. In this respect, therefore, the conclusions of chapter xv of this book were anticipated, though not suggested, by Renard's article.

De Benazé is interested in drawing analogies between the "esprit classique" which animated Racine, Corneille, and Boileau and the spirit of the revolutionaries, in noting, for example, that both the artists and the revolutionaries created an ideal conception of human nature. Analogies like these may exist, perhaps; but they scarcely concern us, especially since De Benazé fails (save by casual inference) to connect the revolutionary ideal of a virtuous humanity with the vision of the virtue of antiquity. On the whole, the article is haphazard and illogical.

## B. Works on Eighteenth-Century Secondary Education

AUBERTIN, CHARLES. *Recherches historiques sur les anciennes écoles et le collège de Beaune.* Beaune: Imprimerie Arthur Batault, 1882.

BABEAU, ALBERT. *Le théâtre de l'ancien collège de Troyes.* Troyes: Imprimerie et lithographie Dufour-Bouquot, 1881.

BERTHOMÉ, MAXIME. *L'enseignment secondaire dans la Haute-Vienne pendant la Révolution (1789–1804).* Paris et Limoges: Imprimerie Guillemot et de Lamothe, 1913.

CARRÉ, GUSTAVE. *L'enseignement secondaire à Troyes du moyen âge à la Révolution.* Paris: Hachette et cie, 1888.

CAULY, L'ABBÉ E. *Histoire du collège des bons-enfants de l'Université de Reims depuis son origine jusqu'à ses récentes transformations.* Reims: F. Michaud, 1885.

CHAUVIN, A. *Les oratoriens instituteurs à propos de deux ouvrages récents.* Paris: Aux bureaux de l'*Instruction publique*, 1889.

DEFER, L'ABBÉ. "Le petit séminaire de Troyes," *Mémoires de la Société académique d'agriculture, des sciences, arts et belles-lettres du département de l'Aube,* troisième série, XXIX (1892), 253–306.

DUBARLE, EUGÈNE. *Histoire de l'université depuis son origine jusqu'à nos jours.* Paris: J. L. J. Brière, 1829.

FERTÉ, H. *Rollin: sa vie, ses œuvres et l'Université de son temps.* Paris: Hachette et cie, 1902.

FIERVILLE, CH. *Histoire du Collège de Quimper.* Paris: L. Hachette et cie, 1864.

GAULLIEUR, ERNEST. *Histoire du Collège de Guyenne, d'après un grand nombre de documents inédits.* Paris: Fischbacher, 1874.

GERMAIN, A. *La faculté des arts et l'ancien Collège de Montpellier (1242–1789). Etude historique d'après les documents originaux.* Montpellier: Boehm et fils, 1882.

GOFFLOT, L.-V. *Le théâtre au collège du moyen âge à nos jours avec bibliographie et appendices*. Paris: Honoré Champion, 1907.

GRÉARD, OCTAVE. *Éducation et instruction; Enseignement secondaire*. Deuxième édition. 2 vols. Paris: Hachette et cie, 1889.

GUIBERT, LOUIS. *L'instruction primaire en Limousin sous l'ancien régime*. Limoges: Vᵉ H. Ducourtieux, 1888.

———. *Les manuscrits du séminaire de Limoges: notice et catalogue*. Limoges: Vᵉ H. Ducourtieux, 1892.

HAUTELOCQUE, M. G. DE. "L'enseignement secondaire dans le Pas-de-Calais avant 1789," *Mémoires de l'Académie des sciences, lettres et arts d'Arras*, deuxième série, XIV (1883).

INGOLD, A. M. P. "L'Oratoire et la Révolution," *Revue de la Révolution*, I (1883), 281–91, 474–84; II (1883), 46–57, 183–90.

JALOUSTRE, ELIE. "Les anciennes écoles de l'Auvergne," *Mémoires de l'Académie des sciences, belles-lettres et arts de Clermont-Ferrand*, XXIII (1881), 35–560.

LALLEMAND, R. P. PAUL. *Juilly en 1789*. Paris: Imprimerie D. Dumoulin et cie, 1889.

LEROUX, ALFRED. *Inventaire-sommaire des Archives départmentales antérieures à 1790. Haute-Vienne. Archives civiles: Série D: Fonds de l'ancien collége de Limoges*. Limoges: Imprimerie typographique D. Gely, 1882.

LIARD, LOUIS. *L'enseignement supérieur en France: 1789–1889*. 2 vols. Paris: Armand Colin et cie, 1888.

MAÎTRE, LÉON. *L'instruction publique dans les villes et les campagnes du comté Nantais avant 1789*. Nantes: Mᵐᵉ Vᵛᵉ Camille Mellinet, 1882.

MONIN, H. "Le Collège Louis-le-Grand, séminaire de la Révolution," *Revue historique de la Révolution française et de l'Empire*, IV (1913), 503–7.

MOUFFLET, PIERRE-STANISLAS. *Notice sur le Collège de Saintes (1571–1850)*. Avec notes et appendice par M. LOUIS AUDIAT. Saintes: Mme Z. Mortreuil, 1886.

QUERUAU-LAMERIE, E. "L'instruction secondaire pendant la Révolution: le collège et les écoles d'Angers," *Revue de la Révolution*, IX (1887), 127–41.

RATHERY, E. J. B. "Les anciens collèges de Paris," *Journal général de l'instruction publique et des cultes*, Vol. XXIV (1855), Nos. 4, 9, 13, 21, 41, 45, 57, 62, 69.

ROCHEMONTEIX, P. CAMILLE DE. *Un collège de Jésuites aux XVIIᵉ et XVIIIᵉ siècles: le Collège Henri IV de la Flèche*. 4 vols. Le Mans: Leguicheux, 1889.

SCHIMBERG, ANDRÉ. *L'éducation morale dans les collèges de la Compagnie de Jésus en France sous l'ancien régime (XVIᵉ, XVIIᵉ, XVIIIᵉ siècles)*. Paris: Honoré Champion, 1913.

SICARD, L'ABBÉ AUGUSTIN. *L'éducation morale et civique avant et pendant la Révolution (1700–1808)*. Paris: Poussielgue frères, 1884.

———. *Les études classiques avant la Révolution*. Paris: Perrin et cie, 1887.

UZUREAU, F. "L'ancienne Université d'Angers: les dernières 'Rentrées publiques' avant la Révolution," *Revue des Facultés catholiques de l'Ouest*, VIII (1898–99), 364–85.

XAMBEU, F. *Histoire du Collège de Saintes (Charente-Inférieure)*. Saintes: A. Trepeau, 1886.

## C. BIOGRAPHICAL STUDIES

ADVIELLE, VICTOR. *Histoire de Gracchus Babeuf et du Babouvisme d'après de nombreux documents inédits*. 2 vols. Paris: Chez l'auteur, 1884.

ALENGRY, FRANCK. *Condorcet: guide de la Révolution française, théoricien du droit constitutionnel et précurseur de la science sociale*. Paris: V. Giard et Brière, 1903.

ARNAUD, RAOUL. *Le fils de Fréron (1754–1802) d'après des documents inédits*. Paris: Perrin et cie, 1909.

———. *La vie turbulente de Camille Desmoulins*. Paris: Libraire Plon, les petits-fils de Plon et Nourrit, 1928.

AULARD, A. "Une interview de Bertrand Barère en 1840," *La Révolution française*, LXI (1911), 50–57.

BAPST, GERMAIN. "Inventaire des bibliothèques de quatre condamnés," *La Révolution française*, XXI (1891), 532–36.

BARANTE, M. LE BARON DE. "Notice sur la vie et les ouvrages de M. le Comte de Montlosier," *Annales scientifiques, littéraires et industrielles de l'Auvergne publiées par l'Académie des sciences, belles-lettres et arts de Clermont-Ferrand*, XV (1842), 129–58.

BARROU, DE. *Documens historiques et généalogiques sur les familles et les hommes remarquables du Rouergue dans les temps anciens et modernes*. 4 vols. Rodez: Imprimerie de N. Ratery, 1854.

BECKER, CARL. "The Memoirs and the Letters of Madame Roland," *American Historical Review*, XXXIII (1927–28), 784–803.

BLOTTIÈRE, DR. "Courtois et la duchesse de Choiseul, Danton et Marie-Antoinette," *Annales révolutionnaires*, V (1912), 23–36.

BOUGLER, M. *Mouvement provincial en 1789. Biographie des députés de l'Anjou depuis l'Assemblée constituante jusqu'en 1815*. 2 vols. Paris: Didier et cie, 1865.

BRADBY, E. D. *The Life of Barnave*. 2 vols. Oxford: Clarendon Press, 1915.

CAHEN, LÉON. *Condorcet et la Révolution française*. Paris: Félix Alcan, 1904.

CHUQUET, ARTHUR. "La jeunesse de Camille Desmoulins," *Annales révolutionnaires*, I (1908), 1–26.

CLARETIE, JULES. *Camille Desmoulins. Lucile Desmoulins. Etude sur les Dantonistes d'après des documents nouveaux et inédits*. Paris: E. Plon et cie, 1875.

CLEMENCEAU-JACQUEMAIRE, MADELEIN. *Vie de Madame Roland*. 2 vols. Paris: Editions Jules Tallandier, 1929.

DAUBAN, C. A. *Etude sur Madame Roland et son temps suivie des lettres de Madame Roland à Buzot et d'autres documents inédits*. Paris: Henri Plon, 1864.

DAVID DE SAINT-GEORGES, A. *Achille-François de Lascaris d'Urfé, Marquis du Chastellet, lieutenant général des armées de la République, 1759–1794*. Dijon: Imprimerie Darantiere, 1896.

DESTAINVILLE, H. "La jeunesse de Danton," *Annales historiques de la Révolution française*, nouvelle série, V (1928), 424–29.

DESNOIRESTERRES, GUSTAVE. *Etude sur la vie et les ouvrages de Mercier*. Paris: Pagnerre, 1853.

DUBOR, M. G. DE. "Les conventionnels poètes: Robespierre, Fabre d'Eglantine, Camille Desmoulins, Saint-Just, Collot d'Herbois, etc.," *Revue politique et littéraire: Revue bleue*, quatrième série, I (1894), 812–18.

DU BUS, CHARLES. *Stanislas de Clermont-Tonnerre et l'échec de la Révolution monarchique (1757–1792)*. Paris: Félix Alcan, 1931.

ELLERY, ELOISE. *Brissot de Warville: A Study in the History of the French Revolution*. Boston and New York: Houghton Mifflin Co., 1915.

EMBLARD, LÉON. "Notes historiques sur Barnave," *Bulletin de la Société départementale d'archéologie et de statistique de la Drôme*, XXXII (1898), 201–16, 372–87; XXXIII (1899), 92–105, 224–28, 285–96, 380–402.

GALLIER, ANATOLE DE. *Les hommes de la constituante: l'Abbé Grégoire et le schisme constitutionnel*. Paris: Imprimerie F. Levé, 1883.

GOTTSCHALK, LOUIS R. *Jean Paul Marat; a Study in Radicalism*. New York: Greenberg, 1927.

GOUPIL, PAUL. *La propriété selon Brissot de Warville*. Paris: A. Pédone, 1904.

GUADET, JOSEPH. *Les Girondins: leur vie privée, leur vie publique, leur proscription et leur mort*. Paris: Didier et cie, 1861.

HAMEL, ERNEST. "Un épisode de la jeunesse de Saint-Just: six mois chez Mme de Sainte-Colombe," *La Révolution française*, XXXII (1897), 97–120.

——. *Histoire de Robespierre d'après des papiers de famille, les sources originales et des documents entièrement inédits*. Paris: Librarie internationale, 1865.

——. *Histoire de Saint-Just, député à la Convention nationale*. Paris: Poulet-Malassis et De Broise, 1859.

HÉRISSAY, JACQUES. *Un Girondin: François Buzot, député de l'Eure à l'Assemblée constituante et à la Convention, 1760–1794.* Paris: Perrin et cie, 1907.

KERVILER, RENÉ. *Cent ans de représentation bretonne. Galerie de tous les députés envoyés par la Bretagne aux diverses législatures qui sont succédées depuis 1789 jusqu'à nos jours.* Deuxième série: *L'Assemblée législative.* Paris: Emile Perrin, 1891.

KUSCINSKI, AUGUSTE. *Les députés à l'Assemblée législative de 1791. Listes par départements et par ordre alphabétique des députés et des suppléants avec nombreux détails biographiques inédits.* Paris: La société de l'histoire de la Révolution française, 1900.

———. *Dictionnaire des conventionnels.* Paris: La Société de l'histoire de la Révolution française, 1916.

LANZAC DE LABORIE, L. DE. *Jean-Joseph Mounier: sa vie politique et ses écrits.* Paris: E. Plon, Nourrit et cie, 1887.

LAUNAY, ROBERT. *Barère de Vieuzac (L'Anacréon de la guillotine).* Paris: Editions Jules Tallandier, 1929.

LE BON, EMILE. *Joseph Le Bon dans sa vie privée et dans sa carrière politique.* Paris: E. Dentu, 1861.

LENÔTRE, G. *A Gascon Royalist in Revolutionary Paris: the Baron de Batz, 1792–1795.* Translated by MRS. RODOLPH STAWELL. New York: Dodd Mead & Co., 1910.

LÉVI, LOUISE. "Saint-Just était-il un disciple de Robespierre?" *La Révolution française,* LXXII (1919), 387–415.

LINTILHAC, EUGÈNE. "La défense posthume de Vergniaud d'après son manuscrit," *La Révolution française,* LXVIII (1915), 385–414.

MADELIN, LOUIS. *Danton.* Paris: Librairie Hachette, 1914.

———. *Fouché: 1759–1820.* 2 vols. Paris: Plon-Nourrit et cie, 1901.

MAILLOT, M. L'ABBÉ. *Les noms de l'Avallonnais. Le conventionnel Manuel.* Tours: Imprimerie Paul Bousrey, 1894.

MATHIEZ, ALBERT. *Autour de Danton.* Paris: Payot, 1926.

———. *Etudes robespierristes: la corruption parlementaire sous la Terreur.* Paris: Armand Colin, 1917.

———. "Un faux rapport de Saint-Just," *Annales révolutionnaires,* VIII (1915), 599–611.

———. "Lettres de Volney à La Révellière-Lépaux (1795–1798)," *Annales révolutionnaires,* III (1910), 161–94.

———. "Un mot de Danton rapporté par Jean de Bry," *Annales historiques de la Révolution française,* nouvelle série, I (1924), 380.

MERLIN, ROGER. *Merlin de Thionville d'après des documents inédits.* Paris: Félix Alcan, 1927.

MICHEL. "Camille et Lucile Desmoulins. Notes et documents inédits," *Revue des Bibliothèques,* 18e année (1908), pp. 181–204.

MISERMONT, LUCIEN. "Le conventionnel Lebon avant son entrée dans la vie publique d'après ses lettres et plusieurs documents inédits," *Revue des études historiques*, LXXIX (1903), 274–93.

NETON, ALBÉRIC. *Sieyès (1748–1836) d'après des documents inédits avec un portrait d'après David.* Deuxième édition, revue et augmentée. Paris: Perrin et cie, 1901.

NEUVÉGLISE, M. LE BLOND DE. See PROYART.

PARIS, J. A. "La jeunesse de Robespierre (Fragment)," *Mémoires de l'Académie impériale des sciences, lettres et arts d'Arras*, deuxième série, III (1869), 39–72.

PERROUD, C. "Enfance, première jeunesse et débuts politiques de Barbaroux," *La Révolution française*, LXXI (1918), 501–36.

———. "Une lettre de Pétion à Brissot à propos du veto suspensif," *La Révolution française*, LXX (1917), 73–75.

———. "Madame Louvet (Lodoïska)," *La Révolution française*, LX (1911), 216–36.

PROYART, L'ABBÉ. *La vie et les crimes de Robespierre, surnommé le tyran, depuis sa naissance jusqu'à sa mort.* Augsbourg: Chez tous les libraires, 1795.

RABAUD, CAMILLE. *Lasource: député à la Législative et à la Convention d'après ses manuscrits et les documents originaux.* Paris: G. Fischbacher, Centenaire de 1789.

REBOUL, ROBERT. *Un littérateur oublié.* Paris: A. Claudin, 1881.

ROBINET, LE DOCTEUR. *Danton, homme d'état.* Paris: Charavay frères, 1889.

———. *Danton: Mémoire sur sa vie privée.* Troisième édition. Paris: Charavay frères, 1884.

LÉON-SÉCHÉ, M. "Volney," *Revue illustrée des provinces de l'Ouest*, XXII (30 octobre, 1898), 277–312.

VELLAY, CHARLES. "Une brochure faussement attribuée à Robespierre," *Revue historique de la Révolution et de l'Empire*, IV (1913), 508–9.

———. "Camille Desmoulins et Madame Duplessis," *Revue historique de la Révolution française*, I (1910), 236–40.

———. "Lettres inédites de Saint-Just," *Revue historique de la Révolution française*, I (1910), 481.

———. "Le numéro VII du 'Vieux Cordelier,'" *Annales révolutionnaires*, I (1908), 622–40.

YOUNG, CATHARINE. *A Lady Who Loved Herself. The Life of Madame Roland.* New York and London: Alfred A. Knopf, 1930.

## D. OTHERS WORKS

AULARD, A. *Etudes et leçons sur la Révolution française.* Quatrième série. Paris: Félix Alcan, 1904.

AULARD, A. *Histoire politique de la Révolution française: origines et développement de la démocratie et de la république (1789–1804).* Paris: A. Colin, 1901.

———. "Les noms révolutionnaires des communes," *La Révolution française*, LXXIX (1926), 289–314.

———. *Les orateurs de La Révolution: La Législative et la Convention.* Nouvelle édition, revue et corrigée. 2 vols. Paris: Edouard Cornély et cie, 1906–7.

———. *Paris pendant la réaction thermidorienne et sous le directoire. Recueil de documents pour l'histoire de l'esprit public à Paris.* Paris: L. Cerf, 1898–1902.

———. "Le tutoiement pendant la Révolution," *La Révolution française*, XXXIV (1898), 481–89.

BECKER, CARL. *The Declaration of Independence, a Study in the History of Political Ideas.* New York: Harcourt, Brace & Co., 1922.

BECKER, CARL. *The Heavenly City of the Eighteenth-Century Philosophers.* New Haven: Yale University Press, 1932.

BIRÉ, EDMOND. "La Révolution et l'enfance," *Revue de la Révolution*, I (1883), 64–91.

BLUM, ANDRÉ. "Les fêtes républicaines et la tradition révolutionnaire," *La Révolution française*, LXXII (1919), 193–200.

CARCASSONE, E. *Montesquieu et le problème de la constitution française au XVIIIᵉ siècle.* Paris: Les presses universitaires de France, n.d.

CHALLAMEL, AUGUSTIN. *Les clubs contre-révolutionnaires: cercles, comités, sociétés, salons, réunions, cafés, restaurants et librairies.* Paris: Le Cerf, Charles Noblet, Maison Quantin, 1895.

CHAUVOT, HENRI. *Le barreau de Bordeaux de 1775 à 1815.* Paris: Auguste Durand, 1856.

DREYFUS-BRISAC (ed.). *Petits problèmes de bibliographie pédagogique.* Paris, 1892.

ESPINAS, ALFRED. *La philosophie sociale du XVIIIᵉ siècle et la Révolution.* Paris: Félix Alcan, 1898.

FAŸ, BERNARD. *L'Esprit révolutionnaire en France et aux Etats-Unis à la fin du XVIIIᵉ siècle.* Paris: Librairie ancienne Edouard Champion, 1925.

LÉVY, EDOUARD. *Le manuel des prénoms.* Paris: Rousseau et cie, 1922.

LICHTENBERGER, ANDRÉ. *Le socialisme et la Révolution française: étude sur les idées socialistes en France de 1789 à 1796.* Paris: Félix Alcan, 1899.

———. *Le socialisme utopique: études sur quelques précurseurs inconnus du socialisme.* Paris: Félix Alcan, 1898.

MATHIEZ, ALBERT. *The French Revolution.* New York: Alfred A. Knopf, 1928.

———. *Girondins et Montagnards.* Paris: Firmin-Didot et cie, 1930.

―――. *Les origines des cultes révolutionnaires (1789–1792)*. Paris: Société nouvelle de librairie et d'édition, 1904.

―――. "A quelle date parut le premier numéro du *Défenseur de la Constitution?*" *Annales révolutionnaires*, IV (1911), 671.

MICHON, GEORGES. *Essai sur l'histoire du parti Feuillant: Adrien Duport. Correspondance inédite de Barnave en 1792*. Paris: Payot, 1924.

MONIN, H. "Histoire extraordinaire des papiers Baudot et de leur publication," *Annales révolutionnaires*, II (1909), 180–98.

QUÉRARD, J.-M. *La France littéraire*. Paris: Didot frères, 1835.

SAGNAC, PH. "'Encore les 'Archives parlementaires,'" *La Révolution française*, LX (1911), 51–55.

SAINTE-BEUVE, C.-A. *Causeries du lundi*, Vol. VII. Troisième édition. Paris: Garnier frères, n.d.

TAINE, HIPPOLYTE ADOLPHE. *The French Revolution*. Translated by JOHN DURAND. 3 vols. New York: Henry Holt & Co., 1885.

# INDEX

| DATE DUE | | | |
|----------|---|---|---|
| 5/1/06 | | | |
| | | | |
| | | | |
| | | | |
| | | | |
| | | | |
| | | | |
| | | | |
| | | | |
| | | | |
| | | | |
| | | | |
| | | | |
| | | | |